An Other Testament

groundwork
STUDIES IN THEORY AND SCRIPTURE

The Groundwork series places Mormon scripture in dialogue with contemporary theory. By drawing on a broad range of academic disciplines—including philosophy, theology, literary theory, political theory, social theory, economics, and anthropology—Groundwork books test both the richness of scripture as grounds for contemporary thought and the relevance of theory to the task of reading scripture.

Series Editors

Adam S. Miller
Joseph M. Spencer

Other Groundwork *books include:*

Jad Hatem, *Postponing Heaven: The Three Nephites, the Bodhisattva, and the Mahdi*

An Other Testament

On Typology

Second Edition

Joseph M. Spencer

NEAL A. MAXWELL INSTITUTE for RELIGIOUS SCHOLARSHIP

Brigham Young University
Provo, Utah

A Groundwork book

Neal A. Maxwell Institute, Provo, UT 84602 | maxwellinstitute.byu.edu

First edition published 2012 by Salt Press. Second edition 2016.

Printed in the United States of America

ISBN 978-0-8425-2869-6

Cover and book design: Jenny Webb
Cover image: Photograph by Devan Squires, courtesy of the Crandall Historical Printing Museum

Library of Congress Cataloging-in-Publication Data

Names: Spencer, Joseph M., author.
Title: An other testament : on typology / Joseph M. Spencer.
Description: Second edition. | Provo, Utah : Neal A. Maxwell Institute, Brigham Young University, [2016] | ?2016 | Includes bibliographical references and index.
Identifiers: LCCN 2015040897 | ISBN 9780842528696 (print : alk. paper) | ISBN 9780842529471 (epub) | ISBN 9780842529488 (kindle)
Subjects: LCSH: Book of Mormon--Study and teaching. | Typology (Theology) | Typology (Linguistics) | Church of Jesus Christ of Latter-day Saints--Doctrines. | Mormon Church--Doctrines.
Classification: LCC BX8627.A3 S64 2016 | DDC 289.3/22--dc23
LC record available at http://lccn.loc.gov/2015040897

♾ This paper meets the requirements of ANSI/NISO Z39.48-1992 (Permanence of Paper).

Contents

Foreword

This book is a plow—it breaks ground and its furrow is wide and deep. The future of Mormon studies will be shaped by what is planted in its wake.

Spencer's field is the Book of Mormon, and in order to get his plow to bite, he invents, *de novo*, his own genre of scholarship—a humbling, meticulous, polymathic blend of history, philosophy, literary analysis, biblical studies, and, above all, theological speculation. In this book, Spencer invents Mormon theology as a speculative, scriptural discipline.

Both aspects of this description are vital. Spencer's work is disciplined by an unrivaled attention to the structural, thematic, and literary details of the Book of Mormon. His book is a primer on all we have failed to see, and the richness of his reading implicitly chastens us for having failed even to look. His dedication to the letter of scripture is what gives his plow its edge. Spencer never plays games in the often self-congratulatory sandboxes of skeptical criticism or armchair apologetics. Rather, he *reads* the book.

But it's also true that Spencer's reading of the Book of Mormon is no end in itself. He's compelled to do otherwise because the book, on its own account, refuses to be read in such a way. The Book of Mormon is no curio. Spencer takes the Book of Mormon, not as a field to be fenced and occasionally surveyed, but as earth to be tilled. The Book of Mormon is not ripe fruit waiting to be eaten, ready to be canned; it is soil waiting to be planted. Spencer turns a wedge, scatters seeds, and watches to see what ideas take root. Here is Mormon theology enacted as a *speculative* discipline, as a project propelled by a desire to see how our understanding of the whole world might be rewritten and redeemed by the questions the Book of Mormon poses. Reading the Book of Mormon, Spencer claims no special authority and no special insight. He never commands or defends or decides. Rather, he *thinks*.

Taking up Mormon theology as a speculative, scriptural discipline, Spencer wagers an original reading of the Book of Mormon. Crucially, though, Spencer is not betting that *his* reading of the book is the right one, but that the book itself is worth the trouble of trying again and again. You may agree or disagree with some aspects of his reading, but either way he will collect on his wager because you will never read the Book of Mormon the same way again.

—Adam S. Miller

Preface to the Second Edition

The project represented by *An Other Testament* is now a decade old. In 2004, I wrote up the initial exegetical and theological insights that eventually became the first chapter. In 2007, I finally determined a direction for the larger book project and produced a full draft—the best parts of which became the second and third chapters of the book. In 2009, I did a major rewrite of the entire manuscript, scrapping a hundred pages and writing what would become chapters four and five from scratch. In 2011, I suffered through editing the manuscript, and in 2012, when the book was originally published by Salt Press, I felt as if I could finally be free of the project. Only two and a half years later, in 2014, I find that I am still wrestling with this book, seeing to its republication after Salt Press was acquired by the Neal A. Maxwell Institute for Religious Scholarship. Thankfully, I will close a decade of work by adding only a new preface to the text, rather than by undertaking a complete rewriting of the book—tempted though I am by the latter possibility. Rather than attempting to fix what I now see as the flaws of the book, I will say just a few words about where this preliminary study of the Book of Mormon will take my research next.

Two questions have been posed to me most consistently about the book, both related to method. The first I will address only briefly: What is the status of the Book of Mormon's historicity in my work and in Book of Mormon studies going forward? In many ways, I wish I had been clearer about this problem before I finished the book. In it, I *presuppose* the Book of Mormon's historicity, but I do not much *care* about it. The result is that I have faced worries from both those who feel that the historicity of the Book of Mormon must be defended and those who feel that the historicity of the Book of Mormon must be bracketed. On the one hand, some have asked what a theological reading of the Book of Mormon is worth if the *trustworthiness* of the book has not been adequately established. On the other hand, some have asked what a theological reading of the Book of Mormon is worth if its *faith commitments* are not universally shared. In the end, I am far more sympathetic to the second of these worries than I am to the first. To think that the Book of Mormon must establish its historical bona fides before it can be read profitably is, it seems to me, to get things exactly backwards. By my reading, the Book of Mormon both implicitly and explicitly contests modern secular notions of history, such that it does not make much sense to demand that it be defensible in secular historical terms. Hence, if I were writing the book today, I would do everything I could to make it speak to every potential reader. As it is, I worry that it will speak only to the already-believing. Whether I can find a voice in my future writings that will allow them to speak to both audiences remains to be seen.

The second question I have been asked about this book is, I think, more substantive: What makes this book a work of theology? Some readers seem to have been, as they read, waiting for textual interpretation to end and systematic theology to begin. At no point in my work do I leave texts behind in order to begin sketching a systematic exposition of theological truths, and that has made some worry that there is really very little that is theological about this sort of enterprise. I need to establish first that systematic theology is only *one* sort of theology, and—to be a bit frank—it is in my view the *least* interesting sort on offer. What I practice here and elsewhere in my work is *scriptural theology*. What makes it scriptural, obviously, is that it keeps itself close to canonical texts. What makes it theological is that it refuses to be satisfied with either the strictly referential meaning or even the more robust communicative sense of scripture. The scriptural theologian is convinced that the text has not been exhausted until its *relevance to life* has been investigated. And the *good* scriptural theologian is convinced that that investigation is infinite, that the text will never have been exhausted.

The point of *An Other Testament* is really, then, just to ask about one aspect of the life of faith—namely, concerning what it is to read scripture. Ironically, that means that the point is to ask about what it is to do scriptural theology, and I attempted to find answers to that question by undertaking to do scriptural theology—to do, that is, what I did not know how to do. That is a deliberate puzzle. If the Book of Mormon is to teach us how to read and even to teach us specifically how to read the Book of Mormon, then we have to know how to read the Book of Mormon in order to learn from it how to read the Book of Mormon. It is *this* theological puzzle that animates my entire project here.

What is it to read scripture well? How does reading scripture in the way scripture asks to be read help to transform the life of faith? In answering these sorts of questions, one might also stumble on ideas about the nature of God (what or who is God if he gives us scripture as a guide to reading scripture?), or about the nature of grace (what does it mean to receive scripture as an unearned gift, signal of God's love?), or about the nature of faith (what is faith if one is to root it in scripture first, and only then, derivatively, in God?). It is, however, far from my own purposes to begin to assemble thoughts on all these sorts of questions into a systematic account of the divine. Instead, I want only to ask what it is to live believingly, and one major aspect of that sort of life is to read scripture carefully.

There is more that might be said about my method in undertaking scriptural theology. I've since published a more detailed explanation in a book I coedited with James E. Faulconer called *Perspectives on Mormon Theology: Scriptural Theology* (Draper, UT: Greg Kofford Books, 2015), 7–29, but a few particular points deserve discussion here. In hindsight, I regret my use of the word *exegesis* throughout *An Other Testament* to describe the first stage of textual interpretation. It would have been better to speak of *structural analysis*. In the years since I finished the book, I have seen much more clearly how central textual structure is to my theological work on scripture. It is not simply that a few exegetical preliminaries have to be dealt with before one can responsibly interpret a text theologically. It is rather that the key to good theological interpretation is careful attention to textual structures.

This point perhaps deserves a bit of explanation. At any rate, providing some explanation should allow me to clarify what the road leading forward from *An Other Testament* looks like.

I think it is safe to say that life—and especially the life of faith—has a topology. I want to use that word in a technical way. There is a kind of kernel, formally determinate, at the center of religious life that remains constant despite the variety of circumstances in which such a life is lived out. I might clarify this by using the analogy of a game. Take the game of chess, for example. In chess there is a set of determinate rules—for example, how many spaces and in what directions a pawn can move, depending on its position and the position of other pieces on the board. There is also a set of constraints that do not amount to actual rules—for example, the board is only eight squares by eight squares, no more and no less. These rules and these constraints together give the game of chess a kind of texture, for which one comes to get a feel as one plays. That texture is actually formally identifiable. There are formulas and equations that allow it to be identified in certain ways, even if most players of chess never learn them. The topology of the game remains constant, regardless of whether you play with different people using different strategies, and regardless of whether you play a computerized version of chess or whether you play with physical pieces at a park. And that topology is, moreover, irreducible to the rules and the constraints that nonetheless determine it. To change any one rule or any one constraint would inevitably give the game of chess a different texture, would make of it a different game. But the texture is nonetheless not the same thing as the rules or the constraints. Rather, the rules and the constraints make up the structure of the game, a kind of abstract differential network of laws that, taken as a whole, fully determines the topological makeup of the game as it is actually played.

Something much the same could be said for life lived before God. It has a topology, a texture. One has to develop a feel for good or right living. The topology of the life of faith is constant, an invariant kernel at the heart of otherwise fluctuating circumstances, the ebb and flow of history. And the network of rules and constraints that determine that topology—what constitutes, then, the *structure* rather than the *topology* of religious life—is what needs accommodating if one is ever to begin to develop a sense for life. The wager of my work is that it is in *scripture* that the structure of life before God is to be discerned, and I take scriptural theology to be the almost formal work of finding structure in scriptural texts and then sorting out how such structure helps to determine quite fully the topology of religious life.

This needs more clarification, but I first want to head off a certain misinterpretation of what I mean. One *might* take me to be suggesting that the key to living the life of faith is to follow rules and recognize constraints. That, however, would be a mistake. To be a good chess player is not simply to learn the rules and to recognize the constraints of the game. Nor again is it just to memorize a few good strategies or clever moves. Rather, it is to discern, whether in a prereflective or a fully formal way, the topology of the game. It is to come to inhabit the game, as it were, to develop a kind of indescribable awareness of what is potentially operative in the actual particular game one is playing. Similarly, then, it would be a mistake to think that living the life of faith is a matter just of learning a few rules and a few constraints, or perhaps to memorize a few good strategies or clever moves. Obedience to the laws of chastity and consecration are necessary conditions for the life of faith, but it is hardly sufficient. The rules and constraints only help one to develop a sense for what it is to live well. To think otherwise is to make the mistake against which the apostle Paul contended in so many of his writings. The structure of chess only establishes the conditions for the possibility of playing the game; it does not play the game for you, although it does refer in a way to the topological contours of the game that needs to be played. Similarly, the structure of religious life only establishes the conditions for the possibility of living religiously; it does not live life for you, although it does refer in a way to the topological contours of the life that needs to be lived.

What I find in scripture is remarkable attention to the relationship between what I have here called structure and what I have here called topology. Scripture outlines and illustrates the rules and the constraints of the life of faith. It provides its readers with the *structure* of religious life. And it leaves to its readers the difficult work of seeing how that structure fully determines the *topology* of religious life. To be a good—and by "good" I mean something like "theological"—reader of scripture, it is necessary to begin to see the structures put on display in scripture and to develop an ability to see how those structures determine the topology of the life of faith. The place to begin to find such structures, I am convinced, is to look for what are usually called literary structures in scripture, to see where scripture bears within it certain textual structures that determine in a particularly illuminating way the shape of a life lived in God. One might look, for instance, at the complicated structure of Alma 36—its chiastic frame centered on the question of what it is to know God and its alternating instances of the words *thought* and *memory* at its narrative center—and begin to learn something about what it is to be converted. One might look at the detailed structural elements that organize Nephi's contribution to the small plates—its broad fourfold structure, its privileging of certain chapters as "more sacred," its careful deployment of Isaianic writings—and begin to learn something about what it is to read biblical prophecy. One might look at the subtle structural features of Mormon's history from Abinadi to the New World visit of Christ—the departure from and return to the interpretation of Isaiah, the repeated focus on baptism and the Godhead, the telling rival interpretations of certain biblical passages—and begin to learn something about what it is to stand either individually or collectively before God. It is, I think, in structure that scripture does its most crucial work.

If there is a determinate direction my work will go from here, drawing on the best of what I have done in *An Other Testament,* it will be to look more closely only at structure in scripture and to be all the more rigorous about the theological implications of all such structure. Indeed, as I have revisited the Book of Mormon texts I worked over in *An Other Testament,* my largest regret is that I missed so many clearly intentional structures and that I focused on too many flimsy hints at structure in my analyses. Perhaps I might indicate just a couple of more recent insights into structural elements of the Book of Mormon that would have helped me to interpret the text much better. I will provide just one example from Nephi's writings and just one example from Abinadi's sermon. Hopefully they will together suggest that there is much, much more work to do on these texts.

Since completing *An Other Testament*, I have been struck by the incredibly tight structure of First Nephi. Key to seeing this structure is paying close attention to the original chapter breaks in the Book of Mormon, which were dictated by Joseph Smith along with the actual Book of Mormon text. In the original, First Nephi consisted of seven chapters (designated with roman numerals): (I) what is now 1 Nephi 1–5, (II) what is now 1 Nephi 6–9, (III) what is now 1 Nephi 10–14, (IV) what is now 1 Nephi 15, (V) what is now 1 Nephi 16:1–19:21, (VI) what is now 1 Nephi 19:22–21:26, and (VII) what is now 1 Nephi 22. Moreover, in light of a few unmistakable indications in the text (see the subtitle of First Nephi, as well as 1 Nephi 1:16–17; 10:1), it is clear that First Nephi is divided into two halves: the abridgment of Lehi's record (1 Nephi 1–9, the original text's chapter I and II) and the presentation of Nephi's own reign and ministry (1 Nephi 10–22, the original text's chapters III through VII).

The first of these two halves of First Nephi is clearly organized by structural markers that alert the reader to a set of five distinct records: a heavenly book brought to Lehi in a vision (discussed in the opening sequence of the original text's chapter I), the brass plates brought to Lehi from Jerusalem (discussed in the closing sequence of the original text's chapter I), the record Lehi himself produced (discussed in the opening sequence of the original text's chapter II), the record Nephi first produced upon arriving in the New World (discussed in the closing sequence of the original text's chapter II), and the record—the small plates—Nephi eventually produced (distinguished at every point from the other records discussed). Each of the two narratives making up the first half of First Nephi, moreover, tells the story of how a certain set of prophetic resources came to Nephi's attention. The first narrative—that of the original text's chapter I, today 1 Nephi 1–5—tells the story of how the brass plates came into Nephi's possession. The second narrative—that of the original text's chapter II, today 1 Nephi 6–9—tells the story of how Lehi's crucial dream concerning the tree of life came to Nephi's attention. By the time Nephi comes to the "more sacred" part of his record in 2 Nephi 6–30, it becomes fully clear that his intention is to bring these two sorts of prophecy precisely into relation: the writings of Isaiah as contained on the brass plates and the dream of Lehi as substantially expanded in his own apocalyptic experience. The first half of First Nephi is clearly meant just to provide the necessary stories of how these two sources of prophecy came into Nephi's ambit.

The second half of First Nephi has a more complicated but closely related structure. What were originally its first two chapters (chapters III and IV of the original text of First Nephi) and what were originally its last two chapters (chapters VI and VII of the original text of First Nephi) clearly mirror one another. (Sandwiched between them is the narrative that takes his family from the Old to the New World—originally chapter V, today 1 Nephi 16:1–19:21.) In the former, Nephi experiences his own expansive version of Lehi's dream (originally chapter III, today 1 Nephi 10–14) and then explains that dream to his brothers (originally chapter IV, today 1 Nephi 15); in the latter, Nephi reads from the brass plates Isaiah text (originally chapter VI, today 1 Nephi 19:22–21:26) and then explains that text to his brothers (originally chapter VII, today 1 Nephi 22). Here the focal points of the two narratives from the first half of First Nephi are picked up again: the brass plates retrieved in the original chapter I are the focus in the original chapters VI (where they are read) and VII (where they are interpreted), and the dream had by Lehi in the original chapter II is the focus in the original chapters III (where it is experienced by Nephi) and IV (where it is interpreted). In each case, moreover, each of the prophetic resources acquired in the first half of First Nephi is used to secure the interpretation of the other. Nephi claims in 1 Nephi 15:20 that he used the brass plates writings of Isaiah to assist in his interpretation of his father's dream, and he cites in 1 Nephi 22:3 his own visionary experience when he goes about the task of interpreting Isaiah for his brothers. Long before the "more sacred" portion of his record, Nephi is intermingling his apocalyptic expansion of Lehi's dream and the writings of Isaiah found on the brass plates, preparing his readers for what he will be doing in Second Nephi. From the very beginning, remarkably intricate structures set in order Nephi's larger theological intentions and assist the reader in coming to see the significance of Nephi's writings.

I am afraid I have assembled far too much information in the preceding paragraphs for any of it to be terribly useful. I hope nonetheless to have begun to make clear just how intensely and intentionally structured First Nephi is, far more rigorously and securely than much of what I trace in my analyses in *An Other Testament*. This structure needs to be investigated more closely, its implications traced in detail. Its discovery, I think, requires revisions to a number of my earlier claims—concerning Nephi's larger purposes, concerning the division between First and Second Nephi, concerning the placement of 1 Nephi 19:1–6, concerning the development of Nephi's intentions, and so on. For the moment, however, let me leave all of these details in their rough-hewn state and turn to Abinadi.

In work I have undertaken since *An Other Testament* on Abinadi's sermon, I have realized how much more careful Abinadi's handling of Isaiah is than I originally saw. If one tracks Abinadi's quotations of and allusions to Isaiah 53—which, of course, Abinadi quotes in its entirety in Mosiah 14—a clear pattern emerges, with Abinadi following the basic contours of the story told in Isaiah 53 in rather strict order. In the verses leading up to the quotation of Isaiah 53, Abinadi alludes in succession to verses 1 and 2 of Isaiah 53 (see Mosiah 13:33–34), followed by a direct quotation from verse 7 meant to summarize the poem as a whole (see Mosiah 13:35). After quoting Isaiah 53 in its entirety and then following it with his theologically complicated analysis of Christ's roles as father and son, Abinadi alternates allusions to and quotations of Isaiah 53, first summarizing verses 3–6 (see Mosiah 15:5), then quoting verse 7 (see Mosiah 15:6), then summarizing verses 8b–10a (see Mosiah 15:7), and finally quoting directly from verses 11–12 (see Mosiah 15:8–9). This careful and apparently systematic review of the Isaianic poem is clearly meant to set up Abinadi's more detailed analysis of the only two lines of the poem not addressed in the review: the question "Who shall declare his generation?" from verse 8a, and the affirmation that the suffering servant "shall see his seed" from verse 10b.

It seems clear that Abinadi takes "his generation" to refer to the father-son relation operative in Christ's earthly appearance, and it is unmistakably clear that he takes "his seed" to refer to both the prophets who declare that "generation" and the faithful who receive the prophets' declaration. Coupling generation (the intensely difficult weave of father and son in the origins of one who is fully man and fully God) and seed (the joint community of the declaring and the receiving), Abinadi provides a remarkably novel interpretation of Isaiah's poem. Moreover, this careful extraction from Isaiah 53 allows Abinadi to distinguish between two interpretive tasks he feels he has received from Noah's priests. Rather than interpreting all of Isaiah 52:7–10 at once, as requested by the priests, Abinadi takes as his task first to interpret Isaiah

52:7 and then, in a separate gesture, to interpret Isaiah 52:8–10. He clearly takes as his key to the interpretation of just Isaiah 52:7 the Isaianic question concerning the declaration of the Messiah's origins. Those who bring good tidings and publish peace are, precisely, those who declare the theologically difficult generation of Christ. And then he just as clearly takes as his key to the interpretation of Isaiah 52:8–10 the Isaianic affirmation that the Messiah will see his seed. Those who will see eye to eye when the Messiah's generation is declared are the prophets and their faithful followers, those who declare and those who receive the message concerning the Messiah's generation.

These structural details, intricate though they are, make much clearer how attentive and virtuosic Abinadi's interpretation of the Isaianic text really is. Rather than simply taking the textual proximity between Isaiah 52:7–10 and Isaiah 53 as a motivation for interpreting the former in a Christological way, Abinadi is presented in the text as working out a detailed and astoundingly nuanced interpretation of the text of Isaiah 53, extracting from that text two closely related thematic elements, and then using them to interpret distinct parts of Isaiah 52:7–10, but interconnected in a coherent whole. Closer attention to the structural details reveals a kind of theological intensity and interpretive genius that is far too easily missed if structure is set to one side.

Here again I worry that I have assembled far too much information in far too little space to make it accessible and useful. Again, though, I hope I have nonetheless made clear how much more detailed structural work remains to be done on the texts I address in *An Other Testament*. Again, I suspect that closer reading of these passages and closer investigation of the relevant structures would force me to alter some of my earlier claims. I would at the very least need to do away with any hints in my presentation that Abinadi was less than impressive in his handling of Isaiah's writings than his predecessors. I would also, however, need to work over rather heavily my detailed analyses of key passages throughout Abinadi's sermon, especially those in the last part of Mosiah 13, where Abinadi sets up his quotation of Isaiah 53.

There is, I think, a good deal more work to do on the Book of Mormon, as much at the level of the text as at the level of theological study, where I attempt to focus my own efforts. Whether that remarkable volume of scripture will receive its due soon enough I cannot predict. If my own work assists to pave the way to such work, published under my name or another's, I will call what I have done a real success.

Preface to the First Edition

Put simply, this book is about how the Book of Mormon teaches us to read the Book of Mormon. Such simplicity, though, is a bit misleading because my aim here is to see, *in full recognition of its complexity*, how the Book of Mormon teaches us to read the Book of Mormon.

There is, moreover, a very particular kind of complexity that interests me. Hugh Nibley, in books such as *Lehi in the Desert* and *An Approach to the Book of Mormon*, has shown the profoundly complex historical background that is on display in the Book of Mormon. More recently, Grant Hardy's *Understanding the Book of Mormon* has compellingly shown the immense literary complexity of the Book of Mormon. What I am after, though, is neither historical nor literary. I am interested in the Book of Mormon's specifically *theological* complexity.

By theological complexity I do not primarily mean that the *ideas* presented in the Book of Mormon are complex, though sometimes they are. Rather, I mean that it can be difficult to *bring into focus* some of the Book of Mormon's overarching theological claims, given the book's structural complexity.

There are two aspects of the Book of Mormon that render its theology complex. First, aspects of the book's theology may remain obscure if readers are not attentive to how its authors arrange the ideas presented. At times these ideas are woven into the arrangement of carefully built stories; at times they depend on larger textual structures that can be difficult to see. Embedded in these larger structures, many of the Book of Mormon's ideas draw meaning and especially nuance from their context. Second, what the Book of Mormon has to say may be missed if readers are not attentive to the fact that the ideas it presents are woven into a real—and therefore anything but tidy—history. Anyone acquainted with the history of ideas knows how ideas change with time and circumstance.

Theological ideas in the Book of Mormon are no exception. Both of these difficulties are taken into consideration—often in great detail—in this book.

Since my aim is to look at how the Book of Mormon itself teaches us to read the Book of Mormon, I begin with an examination of Alma 36, where one Nephite prophet (Alma) reads another Nephite prophet (Lehi). There, Alma the Younger recounts his conversion experience to his son, Helaman, but he does so, importantly, by weaving his personal story into a reading of 1 Nephi 1. Alma's weaving together of a scriptural text with his own conversion experience exemplifies how the Book of Mormon should be read.

In this same chapter, Alma even names the kind of reading he models: typology. As Alma develops it, typology is a question of how events—singular, unpredictable experiences with the divine—interrupt the natural flow of history and so allow for the past to be understood in new, redemptive ways. Put in Alma's own words, typology is a question of allowing a new thought to rework memory, so that it becomes possible to advance in the knowledge of God.

From Alma's own reading of Nephite scripture, I gather that the Book of Mormon should be read typologically. But it is necessary to put a finer point on typology, and for that it is necessary to look elsewhere in the Book of Mormon. There are explicit discussions of typology at several points in the Book of Mormon, but if one pays attention to the structural and historical complexities mentioned above, it becomes clear that typology is not a uniform concept in Nephite scripture. Rather, the Book of Mormon presents *two* distinct understandings of typology. One of these is worked out at the beginning of the Nephite tradition by Nephi, son of Lehi. The other emerges centuries later in the teachings of Abinadi, the martyred prophet.

The bulk of this book is devoted to examining the textual structures and historical entanglements that contextualize and complicate what Nephi and Abinadi have to say about typology. This interpretive work is made even more interesting by the fact that both Nephi and Abinadi develop their respective notions of typology in dialogue with Isaiah.

For Nephi, Isaiah was a prophet with a message about the house of Israel, for the house of Israel. As a result, Nephi takes Isaiah's writings as a kind of template for making sense of Israel's actual historical experience, wherever and whenever Israel may be. This approach to typology is what Nephi calls "likening" Isaiah's writings. Thus, though the children of Lehi are located in a time and place that are drastically different from the time and place of Isaiah's original prophecy, they can, according to Nephi, still assume that the writings of Isaiah provide a kind of covenant framework for making sense of their own historical experience. Fueled by this understanding of typology, Nephi develops a near obsession with Isaiah and pays close attention even to the theologically significant internal arrangement of materials in the book of Isaiah.

According to Abinadi, on the other hand, Isaiah, along with all other prophets, was focused less on the singular history of Israel than on the event of Christ's mortal ministry. Abinadi thus ignores, for instance, the importance of Isaiah's internal arrangement in order to give a strictly Christological reading of Isaiah's writings, one that sharply diverges from Nephi's way of reading the prophet. For Abinadi, Isaiah's prophecies are primarily about what would happen in the meridian of time. Consequently, all else Isaiah appears to say must be read in light of the coming Christ event and with an eye to the consequences of that event for each believer—even when, on his own terms, Isaiah seems clearly to be focused on eschatological or covenantal history.

Thus both Nephi and Abinadi formulate their respective approaches to typology in the course of reading Isaiah. But, because they understand the task of (Isaiah's) prophecy so distinctively, they arrive at quite different understandings of typology. For both, typology is a question of knowing how to read scripture in a uniquely Christian way, but what is to be read typologically is different for each of them. This seems, in the end, to be a consequence of Nephi's having discovered his understanding of typology *in* the complexly structured writings of Isaiah, while Abinadi apparently brought his understanding of typology *to* the writings of Isaiah. More explicitly, Nephi draws from Isaiah an understanding of the relationship between the Law of Moses and the Messiah that fits Isaiah's heavy emphasis on the Israelite covenant, while Abinadi imposes on Isaiah an understanding of the relationship between the Law and the Messiah that effectively ignores Isaiah's focus on covenantal questions.

Two models, then: one focused principally on connecting Christ to the world historical unfolding of the Israelite covenant, the other focused principally on connecting Christ to the everyday life of the individual believer. But how is one to decide between them—if indeed they are to be decided between? Two clues in the Book of Mormon point the way. First, crucially, during his visit to the Lehites in Third Nephi, Christ himself intervenes, calling for a kind of return (from Abinadi's) to Nephi's approach to scripture. Second and by way of confirmation, a narrative allusion to Exodus 32–34 in the middle of Abinadi's own speech suggests that the Book of Mormon as a whole is meant to elevate Nephi's understanding of typology to a privileged place, though without thereby disparaging Abinadi's understanding.

In light of these indications, I draw conclusions about how the Book of Mormon—according to the Book of Mormon itself—should be read. Granted the privilege given to Nephi's approach to scripture over that of Abinadi, and given Nephi's deep interest in Isaiah's emphasis on the Israelite covenant, the Book of Mormon asks us to privilege readings of it that stress the centrality of Israel and its covenant. If readers of the Book of Mormon are to read the book as the book itself suggests it should be read, they must pay close attention to what the Book of Mormon says—and enacts—regarding the ancient covenant given to Israel. Not only are readers to be converted by the Book of Mormon to the everyday life of a Christian, they are, in full fidelity to what the Book of Mormon accomplishes as an event, also typologically to convert the whole of world history so that it too is rooted in and revolves around the covenant.

Let me conclude this preface with an aside to my friends in (the justifiably secularized field of) Mormon studies, friends who are likely to feel a complex tension in this book. I recognize the real need to produce serious work on the Book of Mormon that can speak as much to non-Mormon interests as to Mormon interests, and I have produced and will continue to produce such work. This book, however, hovers somewhere between such work and what might be called more traditional (if not more conservative) Mormon scholarship. Thus while I here ask a question that is of as much interest to readers of the Book of Mormon who have no Mormon convictions as to believing Latter-day Saints, and while I believe that I ultimately provide an answer to that question that can speak to both kinds of reader, the road I travel in moving from question to answer is paved with commitments that mark my faith commitments. (I therefore consistently assume the historicity of the Book of Mormon throughout the book, occasionally speculating about authorial motives, historical circumstances behind narrated events, and the like.) I want to assure readers who approach the book from a more secular or secularized point of view that I express such commitments, always implicitly, not in order to alienate either the non-Mormon or the academic, but because I mean to speak as much to the average Latter-day Saint as to scholars, whether Mormon or not. By adding this note, I do not mean to apologize for my faith, only to make clear what the present book does and does not attempt to do. And I hope, not without some trepidation, that scholars of Mormonism generally have *something* to learn from a believing Mormon theologian hard at work on scripture.

Acknowledgments

This book owes more to more people than I can express in an acknowledgment. Particular thanks, however, must be expressed to a few individuals without whose help this book would not have been written.

First, of course, my thanks go to my family. My wife, Karen, has been—in addition to my best friend—my constant interlocutor, and many of her ideas found their way into the book. My children deserve thanks for their patience, manifested every time they are told that "Daddy's writing." Next, I express my gratitude to Robert Couch, Adam Miller, and Jenny Webb, each of whom read drafts of the manuscript. Their help has been indispensable, and their friendship is something I treasure. Adam Miller's patience with my own impatience in the process of editing the manuscript is something I especially appreciate. My mother and my wife's parents have provided means and support of various kinds through the years this project was under way. I greatly appreciate their trust and encouragement.

Finally, Jim Faulconer—in whose classroom the seed of this project was planted—must know how much his support and encouragement have meant to me. For all he has done to encourage precisely this kind of work, I dedicate this book to him.

1

Of Conversion

If we want to understand what the Book of Mormon has to say about reading the Book of Mormon, it would help if we could find a place in the Book of Mormon where one Book of Mormon prophet reads another. There are at least several such places, but I would like to focus on one: Alma 36, which has been described as "the most dramatic and influential" conversion story in "all of the Book of Mormon."[1] Why privilege this text over others? Because it provides what I believe to be the most obvious, most detailed, most interesting, and most theologically productive reading of one Book of Mormon text by another.

Latter-day Saints, moreover, are generally familiar with Alma 36. It is among the Book of Mormon's most touching narratives: Alma's conversion story as he tells it to his son Helaman. The chapter also has become famous because of its apparently chiastic structure. Even seminary students know about the massive chiasm that supposedly gives this chapter its shape. But for all the attention—devotional *and* scholarly—that has been given to it, Alma 36 has never been explored in terms of what it has to say about reading scripture.

In this chapter, then, I work in detail through Alma 36, always with an eye to what it has to say about how to read scripture. I begin with an examination of the structure of the text (which is more complicated than has been recognized) and the scriptural sources on which Alma draws. I turn then to a close reading of the first five verses of Alma 36, looking at what Alma has to say there about the role that knowledge or knowing played in his conversion experience. These introductory verses show that there is something paradoxical about conversion, about coming to know what God wants one to know. Alma frames his words to his son in a way that suggests that the actual experience of conversion is meant to clarify and make sense of that paradox.

What is that paradox? It is that in the course of conversion one comes to know what one cannot know. As Alma puts it in words that will be analyzed in detail in this chapter: "If I had not been born of God I should not have known these things; but God has, by the mouth of his holy angel, made these things known unto me, not of any worthiness of myself" (Alma 36:5). One must be born of God to know the things of God, but one must know the things of God to be worthy of being born of God. But how, then, can one be converted? The way that Alma 36 is framed makes clear that Alma's own conversion experience is meant to answer that question, to explain the apparent impossibility of conversion.

Most of the rest of this chapter then focuses on Alma's actual conversion narrative, a narrative that Alma builds on a series of repetitions of two crucial words: "memory" and "thought." On the reading I offer here, it is the complex entanglement of these two terms that is meant to solve the problem of knowledge presented in the chapter's first verses. In effect, conversion is the event in which a genuinely unanticipated thought interrupts the otherwise closed economy of memory, allowing for a thorough reworking—or rewriting—of memory. And, crucially for the rest of the book, it is this complex entanglement that Alma calls "typology."

The present chapter ends when I step back from Alma's text in order to assess the importance of all these findings. This stepping back gives me the space necessary to formulate a few preliminary conclusions about what it means to read the Book of Mormon. But it also forces me to face up to the central importance of typology in reading scripture. And because Alma only gives us something like the bare outline of typology, it is necessary to ask exactly what the Book of Mormon understands by "typology." That question will lead in rather different directions in subsequent chapters.

Exegetical Preliminaries: Structure

Two classic studies pave the way for any analysis of Alma 36: John Welch's famous analysis of chiasmus in the chapter and George Tate's masterful reading of the role of the exodus theme in the Book of Mormon.[2] These two studies alone reveal the depth and complexity of the text. While

Welch's study limits itself to the content of Alma 36 alone, probing its structure, Tate's study ranges through the whole Book of Mormon to bring to light a central Nephite theme, one crucially at work in Alma 36. Within the space opened between these two approaches to Alma's conversion story, I offer my own exegetical approach.

The story recounted in Alma 36:6–25 is simple enough. Alma, son of the high priest, had joined with the sons of King Mosiah to go about secretly "seeking to destroy the church of God." But one day a "holy angel" who spoke "as it were the voice of thunder, and the whole earth did tremble," suddenly confronted them. Singled out and summoned to stand forth, Alma heard the angel's message: "If thou wilt of thyself be destroyed, seek no more to destroy the church of God." Alma at once "fell to the earth" and could not arise "for the space of three days and three nights." He suffered incredible turmoil—"racked with eternal torment" and "harrowed up to the greatest degree"—until he "remembered also to have heard" prophecies (spoken by his father) "concerning the coming of one Jesus Christ, a Son of God, to atone for the sins of the world." Placing his desperate trust in this one memory, Alma "cried within [his] heart: O Jesus, thou Son of God, have mercy on me, who am in the gall of bitterness, and am encircled about by the everlasting chains of death." Immediately, his "pains"—before "so exquisite and so bitter"—were replaced by "joy" both "exquisite and sweet." Alma then found he could rise, and he began "from that time" to teach the gospel to enable others also to "taste of the exceeding joy" he had experienced.

The story itself is simple enough, but the context of its telling in Alma 36 is complex. Alma relates the experience specifically to his son Helaman and only as part of the larger ceremonial event of passing the Nephite records and relics from father to son.[3] Consequently, questions thoroughly concerned with the passing of the records structurally frame the actual narrative of conversion. In the five verses (36:1–5) preceding as well as in the five verses (36:26–30) following the conversion narrative proper (36:6–25), Alma intertwines his conversion story with the ceremonial event (which spills over into Alma 37 as well). Importantly, the theme that connects Alma's narrativizing of his conversion experience to the ceremony is *knowledge*. Alma 36 is first and foremost about what Alma believes his son must, as keeper of the records, come to know—as well as how he must come to know it.

It is possible, in light of these comments, to make a first, broad structural point about Alma 36: the text appears to be structured as a chiastically framed narrative.

A Verses 1–5 (concerns derived from the ceremonial context)
  B Verses 6–25 (the conversion narrative proper)
A′ Verses 26–30 (concerns derived from the ceremonial context)

On closer analysis, this chiastic framing is more intricate than it first appears. Borrowing details from Welch's already-mentioned study, it is possible to see how tightly woven the chiastic framing of the conversion narrative proper is:

A
My son give ear to my words (v. 1)
 Keep my commandments and ye shall prosper in the land (v. 1)
  Do as I have done (v. 2)
   Remember the captivity of our fathers (v. 2)
    They were in bondage (v. 2)
     He surely did deliver them (v. 2)
      Trust in God (v. 3)
       Supported in trials, troubles, and afflictions (v. 3)
        Lifted up at the last day (v. 3)
         I know this not of myself but of God (v. 4)
          Born of God (v. 5)

B ← Alma's conversion narrative (vv. 6–25)

A′
          Born of God (v. 26)
         Therefore my knowledge is of God (v. 26)
       Supported under trials, troubles, and afflictions (v. 26)
      Trust in him (v. 27)
     He will deliver me (v. 27)
        And raise me up at the last day (v. 28)
    As God brought our fathers out of bondage and captivity (vv. 28–29)
   Retain a remembrance of their captivity (v. 29)
  Know as I do know (v. 30)
 Keep the commandments and ye shall prosper in the land (v. 30)
This is according to his word (v. 30)

Leaving theological analysis of this structure for later, what can be said of the internal structure of the central conversion narrative? Here too Welch provides a chiastic structure, but his case for a chiasm in verses 6–25 is less convincing. Despite some repetition of words and phrases—enough, at any rate, to allow for a rough chiastic reading—whole swaths of the narrative are unaccounted for. (In one place, for example, four verses from one half of the chiasm are taken together as a rough parallel to a single phrase from the other half!)[4] It thus seems best not to force a chiasm onto the *whole* of Alma 36, but rather just to take verses 1–5 and 26–30 as a tightly structured chiastic *framing* that sets off the distinctly structured central conversion narrative of verses 6–25.

Allowing the narrative's *own* structure to emerge by refusing to impose on it the chiastic structure of its frame, one must look to the recurrence of two words in particular. The core of Alma's conversion story—beginning with verse 13 and concluding with verse 22—is punctuated by the consistent repetition of (various forms of) the words "memory" and "thought":

A Yea, I did *remember* all my sins and iniquities (v. 13)
B The very *thought* of coming into the presence of my God (v. 14)
B Oh, *thought* I, that I could be banished and become extinct (v. 15)
A I was harrowed up by the *memory* of my many sins (v. 17)
A I *remembered* also to have heard my father prophesy (v. 17)
B Now, as my mind caught hold upon this *thought* (v. 18)
B And now, behold, when I *thought* this (v. 19)
A I could *remember* my pains no more (v. 19)
A I was harrowed up by the *memory* of my sins no more (v. 19)
B Yea, *methought* I saw . . . God (v. 22)

There is, here, a rather strict pattern of alternating pairs (AB, BA, AB, BA, AB). At the same time, though, the pattern imposes itself on the narrative with a rather erratic rhythm. Breaking with the almost sterile systematicity of the chiastic frame in verses 1–5 and 26–30, the structure of verses 13–22 allows the climax of Alma's conversion story to travel through the scattered points of its trajectory in fits and starts, at times moving with a kind of measured step (as in verses 13–14), at times racing like mad (as in verse 19), and at times stopping dead still (as in verses 20–22). This erratic rhythm is visually arresting when each punctuating moment of the narrative is marked in the text:

Yea, I did

remember

all my sins and iniquities, for which I was tormented with the pains of hell; yea, I saw that I had rebelled against my God, and that I had not kept his holy commandments. Yea, and I had murdered many of his children, or rather led them away unto destruction; yea, and in fine so great had been my iniquities, that the very

thought

of coming into the presence of my God did rack my soul with inexpressible horror. Oh,

thought

I, that I could be banished and become extinct both soul and body, that I might not be brought to stand in the presence of my God, to be judged of my deeds. And now, for three days and for three nights was I racked, even with the pains of a damned soul. And it came to pass that as I was thus racked with torment, while I was harrowed up by the

memory

of my many sins, behold, I

remembered

also to have heard my father prophesy unto the people concerning the coming of one Jesus Christ, a Son of God, to atone for the sins of the world. Now, as my mind caught hold upon this

thought,

I cried within my heart: O Jesus, thou Son of God, have mercy on me, who am in the gall of bitterness, and am encircled about by the everlasting chains of death. And now, behold, when I

thought

this, I could

remember

my pains no more; yea, I was harrowed up by the

memory

of my sins no more. And oh, what joy, and what marvelous light I did behold; yea, my soul was filled with joy as exceeding as was my pain!

> Yea, I say unto you, my son, that there could be nothing so exquisite and so bitter as were my pains. Yea, and again I say unto you, my son, that on the other hand, there can be nothing so exquisite and sweet as was my joy. Yea,
>
> *methought*
>
> I saw, even as our father Lehi saw, God sitting upon his throne, surrounded with numberless concourses of angels, in the attitude of singing and praising their God; yea, and my soul did long to be there. (Alma 36:13–22)

Of course, in the end, the alternating pairs of the narrative's central structure are to be found only within a limited part of the conversion narrative. The terms "thought" and "memory" appear only within verses 13–22, leaving verses 6–12 and 23–25 unaccounted for. However, a brief glance at the content of the narrative makes clear that there is an important distinction in terms of narrative *content* between verses 13–22 and verses 6–12 and 23–25: the material omitted from the pattern of alternating pairs recounts Alma's *external* experiences in the overarching conversion narrative of verses 6–25 (encountering the angel in verses 6–12; preaching repentance in verses 23–25), while the material structured by the pattern recounts Alma's *internal* experiences (three days of torment in verses 13–22).

The whole of Alma 36, then, might for the moment be divided as follows:

A (vv. 1–5) • Chiastic Framing: Tightly Structured
  B_1 (vv. 6–12) • External Narrative: Structureless
    B_2 (vv. 13–22) • Internal Narrative: Erratically Structured
  B_1' (vv. 23–25) • External Narrative: Structureless
A' (vv. 26–30) • Chiastic Framing: Tightly Structured

This way of understanding the broad structure of the chapter foregrounds the uniqueness of verses 13–22. The structureless narrative stretches of verses 6–12 and 23–25 separate the erratically structured narrative-within-a-narrative of verses 13–22 from the tightly structured chiastic framing of verses 1–5 and 26–30. In the end, the closest theological attention is due to the thought/memory entanglement of the narrative-within-a-narrative of verses 13–22. But an eye must also be kept on how both the chiastic framing and the structureless external parts of the larger narrative help determine the meaning of the narrative-within-a-narrative.

Exegetical Preliminaries: Sources

So much, for the moment, for structure. What textual sources lie behind Alma 36? Without pretending to undertake an exhaustive investigation of possible textual echoes, I will explore the relationship between this chapter and possible textual sources that may have influenced the construction of Alma's narrative.

A first possible source, of course, is the one pointed out by George Tate in the article already mentioned. After discussing the presence of the exodus theme in Alma's conversion story as reported in Mosiah 27, Tate says of Alma 36:27–29 specifically that there "Alma summarizes the whole direction—individual and communal—of the [pre-Third Nephi] portion of the book [of Mormon]."[5] Alma does this, Tate explains, by explicitly comparing his conversion experience with the deliverance of his ancestors "out of Egypt" and "into the promised land" (Alma 36:28). Importantly, though, Alma draws not on the *texts* of Exodus, but on the *tradition* of the exodus—a tradition present in the Nephite consciousness long before Alma. But even if Tate therefore fails to provide a direct textual source for Alma's narrative, he does highlight the author's awareness of and entanglement with larger Book of Mormon concerns. And it is precisely an entanglement with other Book of Mormon authors that is at work in the second possible textual source to be discussed: 1 Nephi 1.

Because, as I hope to show, 1 Nephi 1 is immensely important for the literary structure of Alma 36, it is worth summarizing. There, Nephi reports two visions had by his father Lehi before the family left Jerusalem immediately prior to the Babylonian conquest. First, while away from home, Lehi sees a pillar of fire descend onto a rock before him. Second, after he returns home, the Spirit sweeps Lehi away to see, in the open heavens, God enthroned and thronged by angels. One of the angels comes to stand before Lehi and presents him with a book, in which Lehi reads of the destruction of Jerusalem.[6] After mingling his praise with the angelic chorus, Lehi goes forth among the Jews as a commissioned prophet to warn them of the impending destruction.

The sequence of events associated with Lehi's first vision from 1 Nephi 1:5–7 is strikingly parallel to that of Alma's encounter with the angel described in Alma 36:6–12. Just as Lehi "went forth," Alma and the sons of Mosiah "went about"; and just as Lehi was halted by "a pillar of fire" that came and "dwelt upon a rock before him," the rebellious Alma and his friends were stopped short by a "holy angel" who caused "the whole earth" to "tremble." As Lehi "saw and heard much" and hence "did quake and tremble exceedingly," Alma heard "as it were the voice of thunder" and "was struck with . . . great fear and amazement." And, finally, just as Lehi "returned to his own house at Jerusalem" and "cast himself upon his bed, being overcome," Alma "fell to the earth" without power to move either his "mouth" or his "limbs."

If this series of parallels suggests, as with the exodus, only a similarity of *events* (because no undeniable textual tie appears in the foregoing), the *textual* connection emerges explicitly a few verses later when Alma goes on to offer a full-blown quotation of 1 Nephi 1:8—in fact, the longest word-for-word quotation of one Book of Mormon author by another. There can be no doubt that the source is 1 Nephi 1:8, since Alma attributes his quotation: "Yea, methought I saw, *even as our father Lehi saw,* God . . ." (Alma 36:22).[7] On the grounds of this quotation especially, one might argue for an intentional point-by-point correspondence between the two texts. Alma's encounter with the angel, along with its visionary aftermath, is *supposed* to be an echo of Lehi's two visions in 1 Nephi 1.

1 Nephi 1

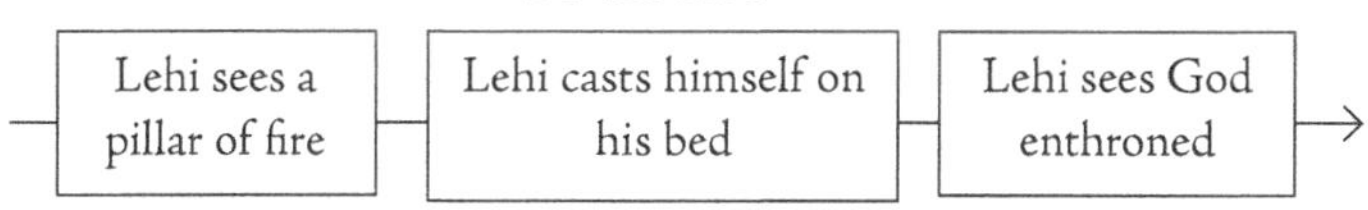

Alma 36

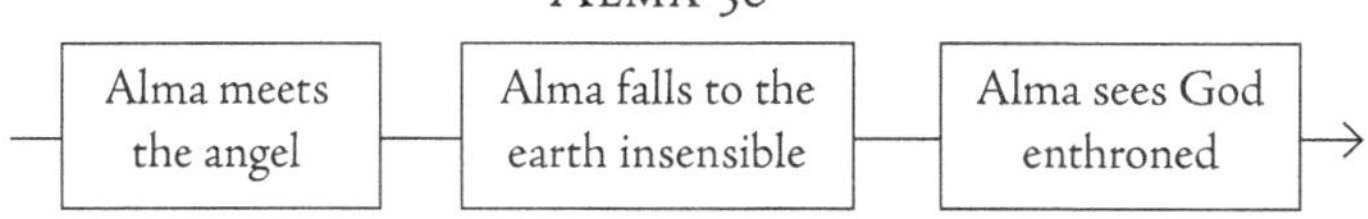

Interestingly, Alma's conversion narrative in Alma 36 follows the First Nephi text only up through 1 Nephi 1:8, to the beginning of Lehi's second vision. If one looks, however, beyond Alma 36 to include Alma 37 as well, it is possible to see further echoes from 1 Nephi 1 in the larger ceremonial setting of Alma's passing of the records to Helaman. In Alma 37, though, the appropriation of the First Nephi text changes significantly. While in the conversion narrative of Alma 36, Alma seems to be enacting what in 1 Nephi 1 is *the role of Lehi*—it is he who casts himself down before being carried away in a heavenly vision—in Alma 37, Alma takes up instead what in 1 Nephi 1 is *the role of the angel holding the book*, while Alma's son Helaman assumes the role of Lehi. Thus, while allusions to First Nephi carry over from Alma 36 to Alma 37, they only do so through a peculiar switching of dramatic roles: Helaman assumes the place of his father, and Alma assumes the place of the angel.

Alma 36	Alma 37
Alma plays the role of Lehi	Helaman plays the role of Lehi; Alma plays the role of the angel

1 Nephi 1:4–8	1 Nephi 1:9–12
Lehi sees a pillar of fire, casts himself on his bed, and then sees God enthroned	Lehi is visted by an angelic messenger with a book, come from God's presence

That Helaman takes Alma's place and Alma takes the angel's place in the transition from Alma 36 to Alma 37 is not surprising. Alma 36–37 records, precisely, the occasion of a crucial succession ritual. But if the switching of roles is unsurprising, Alma's creativity in handling the First Nephi text is impressive. By introducing a twist into the story from 1 Nephi 1 as he transitions from his conversion narrative (Alma 36) to the larger concerns of the ceremonial occasion (Alma 37), Alma marks the complex relationship between, on the one hand, the conversion narrative (Alma 36:6–25) and the epistemological questions it raises (Alma 36:1–5, 26–30) and, on the other hand, the ritual passing of the Nephite records and relics to a new generation (Alma 37). The twist at once differentiates and profoundly intertwines the two chapters that record Alma's words to Helaman. On the one hand, Alma 36 is the story of Alma's identification with Lehi, marked by Alma's concern about his own past conversion experience, while Alma 37 is the story of Helaman's identification with Lehi, marked by Alma's concern that his son take responsibility for the records. On the other hand, both chapters are woven into a creative reenactment of a single scriptural text, namely, 1 Nephi 1. Or again: on the one hand, the text presents Alma and Helaman as two distinct individuals (father and son) who stage a highly ceremonial event; and on the other hand, the text presents a single identity shared by two actors who play the same lead role (Lehi).

Though this last exegetical point is subtle and complex, its implications for the interpretation of the text are crucial. Alma's handling of 1 Nephi 1, distributing the reenactment of its lead role (Lehi) between two distinct actors (Alma and Helaman), implicitly highlights the thematic importance of the chiastic framing of the conversion narrative. It is only within the conversion narrative proper (Alma 36:6–25) that Alma himself plays the role of Lehi in the reenactment of 1 Nephi 1, but the chiastic framing of that narrative (Alma 36:1–5, 26–30) sets off the reenactment as a narratological investigation of the question of *knowledge*—as much of *what* Helaman must come to know as of *how* he must come to know it. It thus becomes clear what role Alma 36 plays in its larger ceremonial setting. Because the Nephite records come to Helaman as if from an angel, it is important that Helaman recognize (1) that encounters with angels are bound up with a philosophical or theological problem of knowledge, and (2) that this problem is only to be addressed narratologically, through the reenactment of a scriptural text. Moreover, as Helaman comes to learn through Alma's careful retelling of his conversion story, the problem of knowledge comes to its solution only through an investigation of thought and memory.

Alma's Epistemology: An Impossible Knowledge

The above exegesis has worked its way to the following points: Alma 36 (1) presents some of Alma's words to his son Helaman on the ceremonial occasion of passing the Nephite records and relics from one generation to another; (2) frames its central conversion narrative with a tightly woven, contextualizing chiastic frame focused primarily on a question of knowledge; (3) distinguishes between an "external" portion of the conversion narrative, unstructured as such, and an "internal" narrative-within-a-narrative, built on a pattern of alternating pairs of the words "thought" and "memory"; and (4) sets forth its conversion narrative as a reenactment of 1 Nephi 1:5–8 (as Alma 37 sets itself forth as a reenactment of 1 Nephi 1:9–12). Compressed into a single statement, these several exegetical points might be put as follows: Alma 36:1–5, 26–30 presents a *question*—specifically, of *knowledge*—to which Alma 36:6–25 serves as an *answer*—specifically, by saying something about *thought and memory.* Theological interpretation of Alma 36 amounts, essentially, to a theological exposition of this compact formula.

Verses 1–3 of Alma 36, through a threefold injunction repeated chiastically in verses 27–30, make clear what Alma expected Helaman to come to know. It nicely divides into three elements: (1) "inasmuch as ye shall keep the commandments of God ye shall prosper in the land" (Alma 36:1); (2) only "the God of Abraham, and the God of Isaac, and the God of Jacob" could have overcome "the captivity of our fathers" (Alma 36:2); (3) "whosoever shall put their trust in God shall be supported in their trials, and their troubles, and their afflictions" (Alma 36:3).[8] The task of coming to know these things seems straightforward and appropriate to the event. But Alma goes on in verses 4–5 to suggest that it is *impossible* for Helaman to fulfill the task. Because verses 1–3 present Alma's invitation to Helaman to come to know certain things and verses 4–5 present Alma's assertion that it is impossible for Helaman to do so, verses 1–5 taken together appear to present an invitation to Helaman *to do the impossible.*

Verse 5 bears the heaviest burden of outlining the impossibility of the epistemological task. First, Alma there states bluntly that he could never *himself* have received the knowledge in question while unworthy: "if I had not been born of God I should not have known these things." Second, however, Alma explains that he *did* receive this knowledge while he was yet unworthy: "but God has, by the mouth of his holy angel, made these things known unto me, *not of any worthiness of myself.*" (The connection between worthiness and being "born of God" is quite direct in Hebrew idiom, where the Hebrew phrase "son of," *ben,* is an expression meaning "worthy of.")[9] Alma, it seems, could not himself have come to know what he wants Helaman to learn if he had not been born of God, but, since to be born of God is to come to know these things, he could not be born of God unless he first came to know them. In effect, according to Alma, to know the things of God, one must already know them. But this, of course, is *impossible.*[10]

Alma presents this problem, not in the abstract, atemporal terms of formal logic, but in the concrete, historical terms of a past experience—in fact, of his *own* past experience. Alma gestures for the first time toward his conversion story precisely as he outlines the impossibility of Helaman's epistemological task in verse 5. Thus, in a single assertion Alma both (1) establishes the impossibility of Helaman's task and (2) states that he has himself successfully accomplished the same task. That Alma makes both of these moves in a single assertion is crucial. Because he points out that he came to know what he could not know *only* as he points out the impossibility of what actually occurred, Alma makes clear his intention to let Helaman know that *the impossible can happen.* But Alma's complicated gesture not only announces that the impossible has happened (and therefore can happen again); it also suggests that the conversion narrative proper—of Alma 36:6–25—explains how the impossible happens. Alma thus relieves Helaman of some of the burden of the impossible. Though Helaman, it seems, will have *existentially* to pass through the impossible as his father did, the burden of *explaining* such a passage falls squarely on Alma as the teller of the conversion narrative.

One must not, though, move too quickly from verses 1–5 to the conversion narrative of verses 6–25. Verses 4 and 5 do more than point away from themselves to the story that follows them. They also provide important resources for understanding the stakes of both the difficulty posed by verse 5 and the solution worked out in verses 6–25. Detailed attention must be given to the employment, in verses 4–5, of the word "know" (in its various forms).

Alma's Epistemology: Clarifications and Complications

The word "know" first appears in verse 4: "And I would not that ye think that I know of myself." Alma only approaches the question of knowledge with a warning, driven by a concern that the nature of knowing may be misunderstood. More specifically, he makes clear that there are different kinds of knowing—one of which is "knowing of oneself"—and he wants Helaman to know which kind of knowing verses 1–3 do *not* indicate. Admittedly, the phrase "knowing of oneself" is ambiguous enough to cause some difficulty of interpretation. But Alma recognizes this ambiguity, since he immediately adds a clarification: "not of the temporal but of the spiritual." Knowing of oneself is equivalent to temporal knowing and is thus distinguishable from spiritual knowing (the kind of knowing Alma experienced in conversion). But what do "temporal" and "spiritual" mean? And how do they qualify two distinct kinds of knowing?

As with the phrase "knowing of oneself," the terms "temporal" and "spiritual" are of little immediate theological help. The words are used too loosely in everyday religious discourse to determine with any rigor how temporal knowing would differ from spiritual knowing.[11] Moreover, a survey of how the terms are used elsewhere in the Book of Mormon helps little. Usage in

Nephite scripture seems generally to be just as loose as in modern religious discourse. However, there may be reason to focus on how the two terms are utilized in one cross-reference in particular: Alma 37:43. Not only does this passage report more of Alma's words from the ceremonial occasion already under consideration, but it also mimics Alma 36:4 rhetorically. Both passages begin with a warning against misunderstanding, and in each case what worries Alma is the possibility that the temporal and the spiritual might be confused.

Alma 37:43 reads as follows: "And now, my son, I would that ye should understand that these things are not without a shadow; for as our fathers were slothful to give heed to this compass (now these things were temporal) they did not prosper; even so it is with things which are spiritual."[12] First, one notes that this passage employs the terms "temporal" and "spiritual" more complexly than does Alma 36:4. In 36:4, Alma seems content merely to distinguish the spiritual from the temporal; but in 37:43, he more audaciously brings these two terms into relation to one another. Both in 37:43 and, two verses later, in 37:45, Alma provides metaphors to clarify this relation. In 37:43 the temporal and the spiritual are bound together by the term "shadow," in 37:45 by the term "type." Whatever can be said, then, about the meanings of "temporal" and "spiritual" for Alma, it seems clear that they cannot be understood thoroughly without some understanding of the notion of *typology*.

Further help comes from 37:43, since this verse allows one to get a clear sense of what Alma means by "temporal." There the word has reference to the *historical* (specifically, to the historical events surrounding the journey of Alma's ancestors to the New World), and so it seems justifiable to say that, for Alma, the temporal *is* the historical. But, as Alma's emphasis on typology makes clear, such a statement calls for qualification. For Alma, the temporal is the *merely* historical, one might even say the *secularly* historical.[13] That is, inasmuch as history divorces itself from the spiritual it becomes, for Alma, merely temporal. But what is the spiritual? The most obvious interpretation would be to take the term to refer to the typological, in the sense that a "spiritual reading" of scripture was once understood always to be a typological one. Inasmuch as the temporal is, for Alma, the merely historical, the spiritual is the typological.

It would therefore be a mistake to take Alma's terms "temporal" and "spiritual" to designate two ontological realms, one material or physical realm and the other immaterial. Rather, it appears that these terms designate for Alma two subjective or existential positions, two ways one might relate to the past. To relate to history temporally is to regard the past event as fixed, an irretrievable fact, while to relate to history spiritually is to see the past event as always still relevant, as if its meaning, implications, or live consequences are not exhausted by the passing of the event into the past.

What, then, to come back to Alma 36:4, would temporal *knowing* be? As a knowing limited by the constraints of the temporal, it would seem to be a knowing unable to draw creatively on the infinite resources of the past. Limited to a finite history, temporal knowing traps the individual within the prison of an irreparable private history. It is thus that temporal knowing is, in Alma's terms, only a knowing *of oneself.* Everything the temporal knower knows begins from or is ultimately rooted in her- or himself. This reading is confirmed when Alma goes on, still in verse 4, to equate temporal knowing not only with knowing of oneself, but also with knowing "of the carnal mind." The temporal knower, knowing only of him- or herself, is strictly limited to the capacities of the mind as it is trapped within and oriented by the (mortal, lustful) flesh.

Over against temporal knowing is Alma's spiritual knowing, a knowing that is not bounded by the closure of history. Spiritual knowing recognizes a reserve of ongoing potential in the history that the temporal knower regards as irretrievably past. To know spiritually would be to know that the implications of an event are infinite, and so that the work of faithfully drawing a genuinely revelatory event's consequences is an infinite task. It is thus that spiritual knowing, as Alma also says, is a knowing "of God"—a knowing that grows out of the unpredictable events that mark God's graceful interventions in history.

For purposes of further discussion, I will assign to the two kinds of knowing outlined in Alma 36:4 the names "historical" (Alma's temporal knowing) and "evental" (Alma's spiritual knowing).[14] Whatever else will have to be said about Alma's accomplishing the impossible in conversion, it can already be said (1) that the impossibility identified by Alma is ultimately rooted in historical closure, and (2) that the happening of the impossible is in turn rooted in the infinite openness of the event.

So much for verse 4. The other two instances of the word "know" are to be found in verse 5. I will make only two brief remarks about them at this point.

The first remark concerns the initial appearance of the word in verse 5, which comes in Alma's already-cited claim that had he not been "born of God," he "should not have *known*" what he came to know. What deserves attention here is the curious fact that Alma attaches spiritual knowing to *birth*, specifically to *being born of God*.[15] The full significance of this knotting together of knowledge and birth will have to be explored further along. For the moment, it is enough to note that spiritual knowing is *familial* as well as *evental*.

The second remark, unsurprisingly, deals with the second appearance of the word "know" in verse 5. This appearance is found in the statement, also already discussed above, that God, despite Alma's unworthiness, "made these things *known* unto" him. What deserves attention here is Alma's grammatical construction, a construction that allows him to break what philosophers call "the epistemological circle."[16] By exchanging the "*I* know" of verse 4 and the "*I* should not have known" of the first part of verse 5 for the "*God made* these things *known unto me*" of the last part of verse 5, Alma shifts himself from the position of the verb's *subject* (nominative case) to that of the verb's *indirect object* (dative case). Again, full analysis of this point will have to come later. For the moment, it is sufficient to recognize that spiritual knowing is knowing received as a gift, in grace—that there is nothing Alma must or even *can* do on his own or of himself. Spiritual knowing is not only *familial* and *evental*, it is also *nonsubjective*.

Thought and Memory: Toward Solipsism

Having dealt with the question of knowledge in verses 1–5 (and, by extension, in verses 26–30), I turn next to the conversion narrative of verses 6–25. To come quite prepared to the narrative-within-a-narrative and its double question of memory and thought, however, it is necessary to begin with the essentially structureless, "external" narrative of verses 6–12 (and, by extension, of verses 23–25).

Alma 36:6–12 traces the trajectory of Alma's retreat from the everyday way of being in the world (his conscious, if subversive, daily activities) to his desperate attempt at complete withdrawal into himself. This retreat is accomplished in a series of isolatable steps:

1. Alma is fully at home in the world, going about with his friends to fulfill his (wicked) desires (36:6).

2. Suddenly, Alma's world is violently shattered when "God sen[ds] his holy angel" to speak with "the voice of thunder" and to cause "the whole earth [to] tremble" (36:6–7).

3. Responding to the rupture of this event that thus de-worlds him, Alma can no longer stand, and he falls to the earth (36:7).

4. Despite his inability to stand, Alma is commanded to arise to "beh[o]ld" the angel (36:8).

5. Adding to the visual shock of the experience, the angel delivers a verbal message concerning destruction: "If thou wilt of thyself be destroyed, seek no more to destroy the church of God" (36:9).

6. In response to this verbal doubling of the visual, Alma attempts to abandon the world completely, rendering him incapable of opening his mouth, using his limbs, or even hearing (36:10–11).

7. Finally, Alma finds himself in "eternal torment" (36:12).

This seven-step attempt at flight into solipsism brings Alma to the border of the narrative-within-a-narrative of verses 13–22, where thought and memory work out their complex relationship.

What might be said of this attempted flight into solipsism? First, it comes to Alma as a natural, instinctual response to the angel. Alma does not deliberate about his flight. Rather, the moment the angel appears, his retreat begins and he immediately falls to the earth. The flight is instinctual, then, but it is *also* interrupted. Alma indeed falls immediately to the earth, but the angel does not allow Alma, in his first attempt at flight, to retreat completely into solipsism, summoning him personally and commanding him to arise. Alma only returns to his flight into solipsism *after* he has arisen in response to the angel's summons and received part of the angel's message. It is the angel's task to *interrupt* Alma's instinctual flight into himself.[17]

Curiously, though, the angel's summons seems both to interrupt and to recommence Alma's flight. The angel interrupts Alma long enough to warn him of the possibility of destruction: "If thou wilt of thyself be destroyed, seek no more to destroy the church of God" (Alma 36:9). But in verse 11, Alma suggests that his return to retreat was spurred by precisely this warning: "when I heard the words—If thou wilt be destroyed of thyself, seek no more to destroy the church of God—I was struck with such great fear and amazement lest perhaps I should be destroyed, that I fell to the earth and I did hear no more." The angel's actual message to Alma serves as both interruption and impetus for Alma's retreat. Thus the angel does not ultimately deny Alma the option of attempting a retreat into solipsism, but he does force him to assume full responsibility for his retreat, to recognize the reality of the threat of destruction.

In the end, then, the angelic message serves primarily to *de-naturalize* or *de-instinctualize* Alma's flight. Inasmuch as Alma's retreat before the angel can be said to be a consequence of the "natural man"—of what Saint Paul as much as Sigmund Freud might call the "death instinct"—the angel's interruption was an attempt to force Alma to see the naturalness of his natural retreat into solipsism, to see that his desire to destroy *the church* veiled a deeper (but unconscious) desire to destroy *himself*. This, at any rate, seems the meaning of the angel's words: "If thou *wilt of thyself be destroyed*, seek no more to destroy the church of God."[18] Thus, finally recognizing that he had long been choosing *real* death, Alma found the angel giving him an opportunity to experience a symbolic death (sealed lips, immobile limbs, closed ears) for "three days" (36:10)—during which Alma could decide to be born again, beyond (symbolic) death. Here, Alma quickly discovered—as the dead inevitably do—that his only companions in death were his own thoughts and memories.

Thought and Memory: The Experience of Torment

Verse 12, as it hands him over to the narrative-within-a-narrative, presents Alma as "racked" or pulled violently in opposed directions. As verses 13–14, the first two verses of that narrative-within-a-narrative, make clear, it is the tension between thought and memory that racks Alma. Verse 13 speaks of memory: "I did *remember* all my sins and iniquities." Thus from the beginning of the narrative sequence, Alma's "memory" consists of his sins, his iniquities, everything he had been doing. Verse 14 in turn speaks of thought: "the very *thought* of coming into the presence of my God." If memory is, from the beginning of the narrative-within-a-narrative, a question of *Alma's* actions, thought is a question instead of *God's* actions—namely, the imminent judgment (and therefore destruction) described by the angel. As Alma passes from the world of everyday engagement into solipsistic retreat, he finds himself being pulled to pieces by the tension between himself in the figure of the sinner (memory) and God in the figure of the Judge (thought).

This basic tension and starting point for Alma's conversion experience clarifies the significance of the angel's interruption. Though Alma naturally tries to flee into solipsism, he cannot complete his flight because of what the angel (as the messenger of God) *gives him to think*. That is, though he allows Alma, after a brief word, to return to his retreat into himself, the angel nonetheless leaves him with an indelible scar, an irrepressible trace in the form of a *thought* that refuses to allow Alma's *memories* to form themselves into an impregnable fortress. Alma's tortuous mental state is therefore a direct consequence of this cognitive remainder, of an unshakable thought that, Alma confesses, "did rack [his] soul with inexpressible horror" (36:14). In Freudian terms, the primal scene of Alma's encounter with the angel comes back again and again during Alma's three-day nightmare to haunt him. Forced to face up to what he wants to forget, Alma finds that—if he wishes to regain his sanity—he must work all the way through his violently neurotic relationship to God.

Taking a clue from verse 4, one might initially approach this tension between memory and thought in terms of the tension between history and event. Alma's memory—his private history of sin—is ruptured by a thought deriving from an event (the angelic encounter), the occurrence of which Alma cannot deny. Alma's suffering thus appears to be rooted in his refusal to allow that event to call his history *fully* into question. Rather than taking the event as an impetus to rewrite his history, as a call to repent, Alma at first attempts to fold the event into his own irreparable history. In other words, rather than allowing the event to transform his unfortunate temporality into something spiritual, Alma avoids the spiritual at all costs—even at the cost of "historicizing" the event. Alma's flight thus marks his reversion from the eminently spiritual event of meeting an angel to his own merely temporal history. Thus, before his *con*version, verses 6–25 trace Alma's *re*version to history and his *a*version to the event.

These two movements—*re*version and *con*version—map onto 1 Nephi 1 in an interesting way. Lehi's *first* vision (1 Nephi 1:5–7) parallels Alma's evental encounter with the angel, which he subsequently attempts to repress in his *re*version by falling to the earth in a curious enactment of Lehi's casting

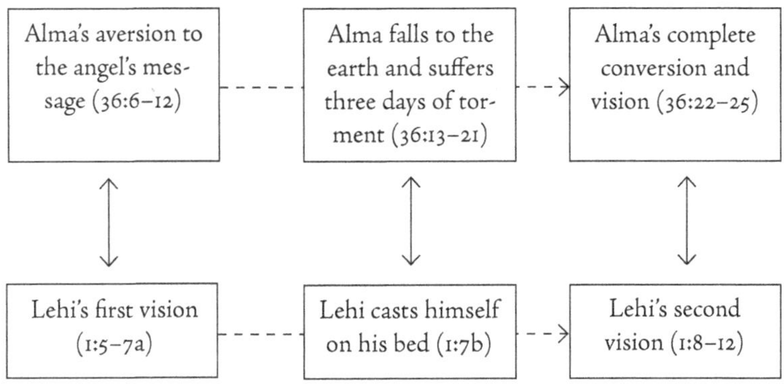

himself on his bed. But Lehi's *second* vision (the thronged throne of God) corresponds to Alma's eventual *con*version, his coming to see the world spiritually as he is reborn. The shift from *re*version to *con*version in Alma 36—worked out between verse 13 and verse 22—thus positions itself, in the reenactment of 1 Nephi 1, uncomfortably *between* Lehi's two visions. That is, the narrative-within-a-narrative of Alma 36:13–22 amounts to a staging of Lehi's short, tormented sleep between visions, a nap from which Lehi awakens in order to witness his vision of the open heavens. The entire drama of thought and memory in Alma 36 is thus, as it were, played out in the space between Lehi's two visions.

As already noted, an erratically distributed pattern of alternating pairs (of the central terms "memory" and "thought") undergirds the narrative of Alma's three days of torment. In the end, this pattern can be understood in two ways. First, the pattern might mark the narrative's exploration of how each iteration of one of the terms recasts the meaning of the other in a dialectical unfolding of the narrative (thus: memory determining thought's significance, then that thought redetermining memory's significance, and then *that* redetermined memory redetermining thought's significance yet again, etc.). Second, the pattern might be understood to trace a series of reversals of the significance of the coupled terms "memory" and "thought" taken together ("memory and thought" always being followed by "thought and memory" and vice versa). These two approaches might be diagrammed as follows:

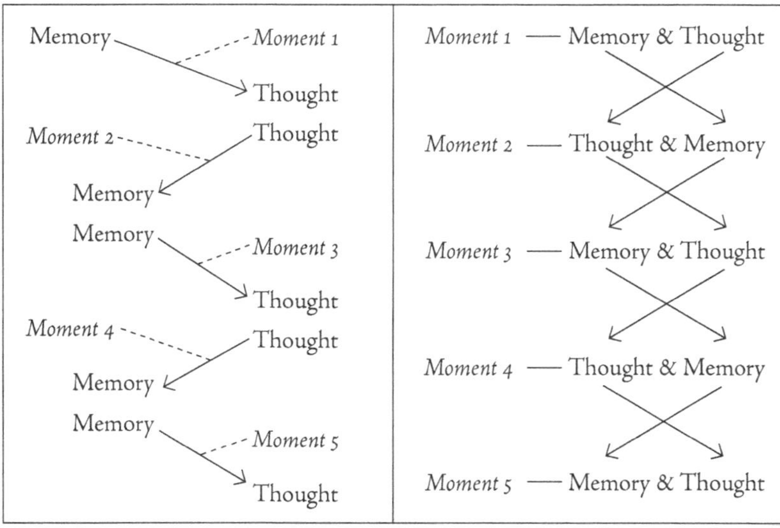

Neither of these approaches, I believe, should be privileged. The best strategy may be to allow both approaches to intermingle. In the analysis that follows, I will take verses 13–22 as a dialectic dissectible into five consistently self-reversing moments (second approach), but I will also look at those reversals locally in each case in terms of the way the text traces the effects of memory on thought or of thought on memory (first approach). Each moment will be considered in turn.

Conversion: Moment by Moment

I have already analyzed the first moment (verses 13–14) in outline. When the dialectic begins, memory (consisting entirely of what Alma remembers of his own sinful past) and thought (the idea of a future judgment) interlock in a harrowing tension. Moreover, thought first takes its bearings from memory. The horror associated with the thought of judgment derives immediately from Alma's taking his miserable memories to be irreparable and fundamental. As Alma himself puts it in the text: "I did *remember* all my sins and *iniquities*, . . . [and] *so great had been my iniquities*, that the very *thought* of coming into the presence of my God did rack my soul with *inexpressible horror*" (Alma 36:13–14).

In the second moment (verses 15–17a) of the dialectic, Alma radicalizes his response to the thought of verse 14. Not only is the idea of judgment inexpressibly horrible; it drives Alma to desire (impossible) annihilation: "Oh, *thought* I, that I could be banished and become extinct both soul and body, that I might not be brought to stand in the presence of my God, to be judged of my deeds" (36:15). What in verses 6–12 was an implicit "death instinct" here becomes a full-blown "annihilation instinct." Willing to obliterate the very possibility of being, Alma wishes that his flight into *pure* solipsism—that is, into absolute nothingness—were actually completable. But Alma thus gives himself to pure fantasy and finds himself tormented by an inevitable lack of satisfaction: "And now, for three days and for three nights was I racked, even with the pains of a damned soul" (36:16).

Nonetheless, this radicalization leads in the same moment to the first hint of a change in Alma's memory. The second moment of the dialectic oddly ends in the middle of a sentence (the remainder of the sentence marks the third moment): "And it came to pass that as I was thus racked with torment, while I was harrowed up by the *memory* of my many sins . . ." The suspended, anticipatory nature of this second mention of memory shows that already—with the radicalized response to the thought of judgment—Alma's memory *begins* to crack. After so much torment, his memory finally opens onto something, as yet unnamed, besides his sin—onto something besides himself.

In the third moment (verses 17b–18) of the dialectic, the tiny crack in Alma's memory splits wide open: "And it came to pass that as I was thus racked with torment, while I was harrowed up by the memory of my many sins [*end of second moment*], behold [*beginning of third moment*], I *remembered* also to have heard my father prophesy unto the people concerning the coming of one Jesus Christ, a Son of God, to atone for the sins of the world" (36:17). Before this point in the narrative, Alma remembered only a fixed historical past, his already-committed sins. But as this memory of his father's prophecy comes suddenly into his consciousness, Alma grapples, for the first time, with the memory of an event that outstrips the merely historical: his father prophesied, *back then,* of something *still to come,* of something still future at the time of Alma's torment. Thus in the third moment, Alma comes up against something historical whose significance cannot be definitively temporalized. Stumbling on this memory, Alma discovers the consistency of his memory—made up, before, only of his own sinful actions—effectively shattered, and he comes face to face with the possibility that, in the course of his own private history, *an event occurred.*

With the consistency of his memory questioned, Alma alters his response to the thought introduced by the angel: "Now, as my mind caught hold upon this *thought*, I cried within my heart: O Jesus, thou Son of God, have mercy on me, who am in the gall of bitterness, and am encircled about by the everlasting chains of death" (36:18). With this move, though his thought remains oriented to the future, Alma for a moment does not regard the future as threatening. Abandoning his desire for annihilation, he rivets his newfound hope to a future defined by the coming of Christ, to a future characterized less by fiery judgment than by the revelation of grace. Giving names to both the past event of his father's prophecy and to the future event of Christ's advent ("my mind caught hold upon this thought"), Alma abandons the historical for the evental.

But if the third moment of the dialectic is evental, it is also both *nonsubjective* and *familial.* First, the singular memory on which Alma places his hope outstrips Alma's subjectively constituted memory, since the event happened in the first place and comes to mind in the second place regardless of—or even against—Alma's subjective desires. Second, the event Alma suddenly remembers is doubly a question of family. Not only does the memory feature Alma's father as the prophet announcing the future, but it offers the prophecy of Christ only by labeling him "a son of God." Thus, precisely as anticipated in verses 4–5, an evental, non-subjective, and ultimately familial knowing paves the way toward full conversion.

The fourth and shortest moment (verse 19a) of the dialectic then follows: "And now, behold, when I *thought* this, I could *remember* my pains no more" (36:19). Here, for the first time, the narrative brings thought and memory into syntactical proximity (only three words separate them). This signals that the crucial third moment of the dialectic has released the original tension between thought and memory. And this release of tension derives from the fact that only in the third moment has Alma been able to give *both* his thought *and* his memory to *one and the same thing,* namely, the prophecy of Christ. Moreover, by putting the work of both remembering and thinking to the single task of being faithful to the prophetic event, Alma, for the brief duration of the fourth moment, exchanges the (inerasable) memory of sin for the (now-erased) memory of pain.

Finally, then, comes the fifth and last moment (verses 19b–22) of Alma's conversion experience. Here, Alma's memory—which, for a moment, had been a question of (forgetting) his history of *pain*—becomes again a question of (remembering) his history of *sin*. But that history, now oriented to and restructured by the grace of the prophetic event, is no longer a source of torment: "yea, I was harrowed up by the *memory* of my sins no more" (36:19). Moreover, as the agony of the memory disappears, Alma's relationship to his past becomes an occasion for joy:

> And oh, what joy, and what marvelous light I did behold; yea, my soul was filled with joy as exceeding as was my pain! Yea, I say unto you, my son, that there could be nothing so exquisite and so bitter as were my pains. Yea, and again I say unto you, my son, that on the other hand, there can be nothing so exquisite and sweet as was my joy. (36:20–21)

Still more, Alma goes on immediately to reveal that the final moment of conversion consists in a reenvisioning of the thought of judgment. Thus, in the climactic final verse of this narrative-within-a-narrative, Alma witnesses the heavenly court preparing their judgment, but he now expresses his desire to join the angelic throng: "Yea, me*thought* I saw, even as our father Lehi saw, God sitting upon his throne, surrounded with numberless concourses of angels, in the attitude of singing and praising their God; yea, and my soul did long to be there" (36:22).

Rewriting History

The preceding discussion of Alma 36:13–22 focuses primarily on the turning point of moment three. It must not be missed, however, that the last moment of the dialectic marks a full return to the first moment. The definitions of "memory" and "thought" change moment-to-moment in the course of the narrative-within-a-narrative, but these definitions come full circle in verses 19–22. Thus, while memory (1) first comprises an internally consistent collection of remembered sins, it (2) proceeds through a fracturing of sorts so as (3) to come to include an essentially inconsistent memory of a prophetic event; and whereas, as a result of this splitting open, Alma's memory (4) ceases even to be memory of sins (becoming instead only a dispelled memory of pain), Alma's remembered history (5) becomes again, at last, solely the memory of sin.

Similarly, thought, (1) defined first as the idea of an imminent judgment, (2) passes through a radicalized desire for complete annihilation only (3) to become the thought of Jesus Christ's coming into the world; but, whereas

Alma's thought (4) stays fixed on the prophesied Jesus for a moment, it (5) definitively returns, in the end, to its original definition as the thought of the day of judgment.

This movement of return, however, does not imply that Alma has, in the end, gotten nowhere. Rather, it indicates precisely that he has experienced conversion or *con-versio*, literally (in Latin), *a complete cycle*. Conversion appears here to be less a complete changing out of the elements making up a situation than a reordering of those elements among themselves—a reordering accomplished through a supplementation of the original situation. Conversion is, in other words, the process of allowing the new to reorient the old without replacing it. Thus, at the beginning of Alma's three-day passage, the newly introduced thought clashed violently with his memory, but by the end the two terms came to complement each other perfectly. In effect, the addition (or reremembering) of something that had been excluded (the prophetic event) allows polar opposites (thought and memory) to be reconciled. Alma is left, in the end, with the same past history of sin and the same idea of future judgment, but the conversion process has, by way of typology, brought him to see the relationship between that history and that idea in a novel way. This novel point of view, it seems, is Alma's spiritual knowing.

In light of this understanding, it is possible to clarify the impossibility of the task outlined in verses 4–5. Spiritual knowing is only impossible *from the temporal point of view*. Wherever the passage of time—the creation of history—is taken merely as the irreversible process of transforming the undetermined future into the foreclosed past, genuine change (conversion) becomes impossible. But where past history can be ruptured by new or unexplored events, all things remain possible—even and especially conversion. Thus, what made knowing the things of God impossible at the beginning was Alma's belief that his history could never be *gracefully* reconciled with a final judgment. Before conversion, Alma believed that history and judgment could only be reconciled through *punishment*. But when Alma stumbled, almost haphazardly, on an event he could not have anticipated and the occurrence of which he did not earn, he found himself joyfully able to reconcile history and judgment through a typological reinterpretation of his own past. Conversion is thus rendered possible only by the unanticipated and unearned—that is, *only by grace*.

Reading Lehi, Reading the Book of Mormon

The great majority of the discussion to this point has centered only on what Alma 36 has to teach us about conversion. But it must not be forgotten that this whole investigation into Alma 36 began with a different question, namely, that of reading. Alma 36 is as much a reading of a text—specifically, of 1 Nephi 1—as a relating of a narrative. How does Alma 36 function as a model for reading the Book of Mormon?

Poignantly, Alma 36 offers a reenactment of, not just any text, but a text that *itself* concerns reading: 1 Nephi 1 recounts the story of Lehi's reception and reading of the heavenly book. It thus appears that Alma 36 is doubly evental. Not only does Alma tell a story in which history is reconciled with a revelatory event, he also relates that story—as a fragment of history—to *another* revelatory event, namely, that of 1 Nephi 1. While the prophetic event remembered within the narrative spiritualizes Alma's past history of sin, the visionary event reenacted in Alma's telling of the narrative spiritualizes Alma's past history of conversion. The interweaving of Alma's conversion experience with 1 Nephi 1—in which 1 Nephi 1 is taken *as evental*—keeps that very conversion experience from itself hardening into an irretrievable past.

But there is something different about this second evental aspect of Alma 36. Rather than simply a past event, it is here an evental *text* that recodes history. If Alma's return to the event of his father's prophecy can be called typological in a broad sense, his return to the event of 1 Nephi 1 can be called typological in a narrower, ultimately more appropriate sense: he is dealing with texts and interpretation. Moreover, the act of interweaving a scriptural text with a historical experience allows both to breathe life into each other. The scriptural text, on the one hand, comes to life and reveals its latent universality. The historical experience, on the other hand, refuses to ossify into a mere historical fact and reveals its relationship to authoritative scripture. If the typological moment *within* Alma's conversion narrative marks a graceful reenvisioning of an otherwise tormented memory, the typological moment *of* Alma's telling his conversion narrative marks a graceful resurrection of scriptural events in the present, an "eventalization" (and therefore de-historicization) of one's life. Alma's instantaneous and once-in-a-lifetime gift of spiritual renewal during his three days of torment opens onto the constant, lifelong work of spiritually resurrecting scriptural texts—of living through and giving life to the scriptures.

Thus, though some kind of conversion experience precedes every genuine reading of scripture, one lesson of Alma 36 is that conversion has to realize itself again and again, *and precisely in the act of reading*. There are two distinct notions of conversion here: (1) conversion as the inaugural, graceful, de-historicization of an individual's past history of sin; and (2) conversion as the unending work of de-historicizing the whole of world history through typological engagement with scripture. But the very fact that Alma refuses to disentangle these two notions of conversion—the very fact that he weaves them into a single typological narrative—suggests that they cannot be cleanly separated. If the first kind of conversion does not give way to the second, or if the second is not predicated on the first, conversion has not actually taken place. In the end it might be said that the *second* kind of conversion is the "more important" of the two. Where the second kind of conversion lapses, one's experience of the first kind of conversion hardens into a past, historical fact—a fact that can only be de-historicized and revivified through a return to the typological reading of scripture. In the end, scripture reading—serious, typological reading of scripture—*is* conversion.

It is perhaps this that is most deeply meant when Latter-day Saints speak—quite commonly—of the Book of Mormon as the "missionary tool for conversion."[19] It does not mean that scriptural texts are means to an end, but ends in themselves—or perhaps *means without end*.[20] It is a tool of conversion indeed, but the work of conversion is not therefore *outside* or *beyond* the task of reading the book; conversion is, rather, *the work of reading the book itself*, of reading the book in a certain way—on its own terms or in the way it itself prescribes. The Book of Mormon thus comes, as every graceful thing does, announcing only itself. It asks its reader nothing more than to read it, nothing more than to be converted *in* reading it. The Book of Mormon comes into one's hands, in a word, *with the force of an event*.

This implies, moreover, that *every* reader of the Book of Mormon lives out—like Alma and Helaman—a reenactment of Lehi's visionary experiences. One is without warning and while about one's own business unexpectedly confronted by a messenger who proffers a book and bids one to read. Whether the messenger is a friend, a parent, or two missionaries from halfway around the world, the experience is the same. The Book of Mormon comes as an unanticipated, unearned *gift*, a dispensation one has the freedom to reject, but that comes with a very real demand (something Alexander Campbell ironically made clear in 1831: "I would ask them how they knew that it was

God's voice which they heard—but they would tell me to ask God in faith. *That is, I must believe it first, and then ask God if it be true!!*").[21] But if one accepts the gift as a gift—as a grace—one is already converted as one begins to read it, precisely in that one begins to read it. The reader inevitably finds the book startling, a surprising *event* that rewrites all of history by orienting it to the day of judgment when one will be judged out of the things written in the very book being read.

Importantly, this idea—namely, that the Book of Mormon is evental—has been argued before, and by a non-Mormon. Jan Shipps, in her study *Mormonism: The Story of a New Religious Tradition*, describes "the profound historylessness of early Mormonism," effected precisely by the appearance of the Book of Mormon.[22] At some length, she analyzes that rupture in history, brought about for the believer: "Since [the Book of Mormon] was at one and the same time prophecy (a book that said it was an ancient record prophesying that a book would come forth) and (as the book that had come forth) fulfillment of that prophecy, the coming forth of the Book of Mormon effected a break in the very fabric of history."[23] Latter-day Saints are thus, according to Shipps, "suspended between an unusable past and an uncertain future," giving themselves to a "replication" (an evental resurrection) that amounted to an "experiential 'living through' of sacred *events* in a new age."[24] Mormons are, for Shipps, a thoroughly typological people.

I believe this analysis clarifies the problem of the Book of Mormon's historicity. On my argument, the Book of Mormon must be regarded as neither historical nor unhistorical, but as *non-historical*. This is not to suggest that the events it records did not happen. On the contrary, it is to claim that it must be subtracted from the dichotomy of the historical/unhistorical because the faithful reader testifies that the *events*—rather than the *history*—recorded in the book not only took place, but are of infinite, typological importance. Any enclosure of the Book of Mormon within a totalized world history amounts to a denial of the book's unique claim on the attention of the whole world.[25] In the end, then, to take the Book of Mormon as *either* historical *or* unhistorical may be to miss the nature of the book entirely. Both positions in the debate about Book of Mormon historicity—whether critical or apologetic—are founded on a common, backwards belief. The historicity *of the Book of Mormon* is not in question. Rather, as Alma makes clear, it is the Book of Mormon that calls the historicity *of the individual* into question.

Granted the above, what then can be said about the methodology of a typological reading? What does typological reading look like in practice? Instead of mining Alma 36 further for preliminary answers to this question, I would like to turn elsewhere in the Book of Mormon, and for two reasons. First, while Alma 36 does a beautiful job of intertwining the problems of conversion with the complexities of reading, it has little to say explicitly about methods or models of typology. Other Book of Mormon texts, however, are explicit and detailed on this point. Second, there are arguably *two* models of typological interpretation to be found in the Book of Mormon—models of typology that prove to be echoes of the two models of conversion outlined in Alma 36.

Notes

1. Jeffrey R. Holland, *Christ and the New Covenant* (Salt Lake City: Deseret Book, 1997), 108.

2. John W. Welch, "A Masterpiece: Alma 36," in John L. Sorenson and Melvin J. Thorne, eds., *Rediscovering the Book of Mormon* (Salt Lake City: Deseret Book and FARMS, 1991), 114–131; George S. Tate, "The Typology of the Exodus Pattern in the Book of Mormon," in Neal A. Lambert, ed., *Literature of Belief: Sacred Scripture and Religious Experience* (Provo, UT: Brigham Young University Religious Studies Center, 1981), 245–260.

3. Note that there is a second account of the passing of the records and relics from Alma to Helaman in the Book of Mormon, to be found at Alma 45:2–19.

4. See a more detailed critique of Welch's chiastic reading of verses 6–25 in Earl M. Wunderli, "Critique of Alma 36 as an Extended Chiasm," *Dialogue: A Journal of Mormon Thought* 38.4 (Winter 2005): 103–106. See also the discussion in Brant A. Gardner, *Second Witness: Analytical and Contextual Commentary on the Book of Mormon*, 6 vols. (Salt Lake City: Greg Kofford Books, 2007), 4:497; as well as in Grant Hardy, *Understanding the Book of Mormon: A Reader's Guide* (New York: Oxford University Press, 2010), 137–142, 303–304.

5. Tate, "Typology of the Exodus Pattern in the Book of Mormon," 254.

6. The similarities between Lehi's second vision and the vision of John in Revelation 4–5 are unmistakable.

7. All emphases in scriptural texts are my own throughout this book.

8. These three elements of knowledge might be connected with the records and relics themselves: the brass plates (which contained the commandments to be obeyed),

the sword of Laban (retrieved in a deliverance only God could have performed), and the Liahona (the physical sign that God supports those who trust him).

9. See, for instance, Deuteronomy 25:2, where "if the wicked man be worthy to be beaten" translates what in Hebrew literally says "if the wicked one is a son of the beating." See also 1 Samuel 26:16.

10. I draw the theme of "the impossible" more or less directly from John Caputo's readings of Jacques Derrida. See especially John D. Caputo, ed., *Deconstruction in a Nutshell: A Conversation with Jacques Derrida* (New York: Fordham University Press, 1997); and John D. Caputo, *The Prayers and Tears of Jacques Derrida: Religion without Religion* (Bloomington: Indiana University Press, 1997). Obviously, however, because I see Alma as suggesting that the impossible can happen, I part ways with Caputo/ Derrida.

11. Brant Gardner provides what is perhaps the usual interpretation of Alma's words: "To Alma . . . 'know[ing] of myself' seems equivalent to 'know[ing] by thinking it out.' . . . His ways of knowing are not personal, temporal, or intellectual but spiritual and 'of God.' I would rephrase this statement, in moderately modernized language, as: 'I would not want you to think that I know these things by study or temporal learning; rather, I know them by spiritual learning from the mind and teaching of God.'" Gardner, *Second Witness,* 4:498. That more philosophical rigor is called for here seems clear to me.

12. The compass mentioned is the Liahona.

13. Both "temporal" and "secular" come from etymological roots meaning "to cut" or "to cut off."

14. So far, I have used the word "event" in a non-philosophical way. Hereafter, however, I will use it in a more strictly philosophical sense. Though I hope the way I use the term is relatively straightforward, it is worth mentioning its philosophical genealogy: the theme of the "event" is a staple in twentieth- and twenty-first-century philosophy, something inaugurated by Martin Heidegger, but more recently exposited in various ways by Michel Foucault, Jacques Derrida, Jean-Luc Marion, Gilles Deleuze, and Alain Badiou among European philosophers, and by David Lewis, W. V. O. Quine, Donald Davidson, and Jaegwon Kim among Anglo-American philosophers. If any particular philosophy of the event informs my interpretation, it is unquestionably that of Alain Badiou. See especially Alain Badiou, *Being and Event,* trans. Oliver Feltham (New York: Continuum, 2006); Alain Badiou, *Logics of Worlds: Being and Event II,* trans. Alberto Toscano (New York: Continuum, 2009); and Alain Badiou, *Saint Paul: The Foundation of Universalism,* trans. Ray Brassier (Stanford: Stanford University Press, 2003).

15. The echo, in the phrase "being born of God," of verse 4's "knowing of God" should not be missed.

16. The epistemological circle was first articulated by Plato in the *Meno,* 80e: "Do you realize what a debater's argument you are bringing up," Socrates asks Meno, "that a man cannot search either for what he knows or for what he does not know? He cannot search for what he knows—since he knows it there is no need to

search—nor for what he does not know, for he does not know what to look for." The translation here is G. M. A. Grube's, to be found in John M. Cooper, ed., *Plato: Complete Works* (Indianapolis: Hackett, 1997), 880.

17. Awkwardly, at least one commentary denies that it is the actual visit of the angel that is at the root of Alma's ultimate change: "When we read Alma's declaration that he had been 'born of God,' it is imperative that we understand that his new birth was not occasioned by the manifestation of an angel but rather through his suffering for his sins and his willing acceptance of Christ." Joseph F. McConkie and Robert L. Millet, *Doctrinal Commentary on the Book of Mormon*, 4 vols. (Salt Lake City: Bookcraft, 1987–1992), 3:263–264. There is little to recommend this interpretation of Alma 36.

18. The echo here of "knowing *of oneself*" in verse 4 should not be overlooked.

19. See especially Terryl L. Givens, *By the Hand of Mormon: The American Scripture That Launched a World Religion* (New York: Oxford University Press, 2002), 62–88. FARMS's 1996 *Comprehensive Annotated Book of Mormon Bibliography* lists over two hundred books and articles that discuss the Book of Mormon as an instrument for proselytizing efforts. Donald W. Parry, Jeanette W. Miller, and Sandra A. Thorne, eds., *A Comprehensive Annotated Book of Mormon Bibliography* (Provo, UT: FARMS, 1996), 618, 629. The actual phrase "missionary tool for conversion" comes from a more recent article by Joseph B. Wirthlin, "The Book of Mormon: The Heart of Missionary Proselyting," *Ensign* (September 2002): 13–17.

20. I draw the concept of "means without end" from the work of Giorgio Agamben, though I believe I use it with a somewhat distinct nuance. See Giorgio Agamben, *Means without End: Notes on Politics*, trans. Vincenzo Binetti and Cesare Casarino (Minneapolis: University of Minnesota Press, 2000).

21. Alexander Campbell, "Delusions," *Millennial Harbinger* 2 (7 February 1831): 94, emphasis in original. This same point is made in Moroni's famous "promise" at the end of the Book of Mormon: one is to ask if these things are *not* true, thus beginning from the assumption that they *are* true. (Ironically, Moroni's "promise" is generally reversed so as to render it more comfortable and less paradoxical. Missionaries usually invite their investigators to pray to know if the Book of Mormon *is* true, thus beginning with the assumption that the book is *not* true. Brant Gardner presents an interpretation somewhat similar to but ultimately distinct from my own: "[Moroni] phrases our responsibility in an interesting 'negative' formulation. He doesn't ask that we pray to see if they are true but rather to ask if they are *not* true. Why this unusual request? Moroni is testifying to something that he knows is true. This truth is so obvious that the only reason for asking is if his future reader does not yet know the truth. For Moroni, the only person who would ask would be one who did not yet know it was true." See Gardner, *Second Witness*, 6:408.)

22. Jan Shipps, *Mormonism: The Story of a New Religious Tradition* (Urbana: University of Illinois Press, 1985), 51–52.

23. Ibid., 52.

24. Ibid., emphasis added.

25. On this point, I recommend both Richard Bushman's interpretation of the Book of Mormon as calling for a reworking of all of world history and Adam Miller's philosophical analysis of the Book of Mormon's essential anachronicity. See Richard Lyman Bushman, "The Book of Mormon in Early Mormon History," in Richard Lyman Bushman, *Believing History: Latter-day Saint Essays*, ed. Reid L. Neilson and Jed Woodworth (New York: Columbia University Press, 2004), 74; and Adam S. Miller, "Messianic History: Walter Benjamin and the Book of Mormon," in James M. McLaughlan and Loyd Ericson, eds., *Discourses in Mormon Theology: Philosophical and Theological Possibilities* (Salt Lake City: Greg Kofford Books, 2007), 227–243.

2

Typology for Nephi: Exegesis

ALMA 36 MAKES CLEAR that to read the Book of Mormon as the Book of Mormon suggests it should be read is to read it typologically. But Alma 36 sketches only a basic—though theologically rich—outline of typology: to read typologically is to read in such a way that history is effectively rewritten in light of a graceful event. It is necessary now to say what it means in more "practical" terms to read typologically. And there are two distinct models of typological interpretation in the Book of Mormon, one propounded by Nephi, the other by Abinadi. In the present chapter and the one that follows it, I will focus entirely on Nephi.

Two passages—the only passages in Nephi's writings that deal directly with typology—will be the focus of this analysis: 2 Nephi 11:4 and 2 Nephi 25:24–27. Importantly, these two texts are situated at either end of the "Isaiah chapters" that play such a dominant role in Second Nephi. This structural positioning of Nephi's two discussions of typology is not accidental. Consequently, a good deal of exegetical exposition of Nephi's larger project must precede any attempt to address directly the meaning of Nephi's two passages on typology. Postponing analysis of Nephi's explicit takes on typology until the next chapter, I focus the work of the present chapter on the preliminary work of exegesis. The aim of this chapter, then, is to clarify the overarching structure of Nephi's record, always with an eye to the place of Isaiah's writings in that structure.

The exegetical work undertaken in the present chapter follows a simple plan. The first section establishes the fourfold theological structure of Nephi's record. The record begins with (1) an account of the creation of the Lehite people (1 Nephi 1–18) and is followed by (2) an account of their fall or division into Nephites and Lamanites, with the latter group being cut off from the presence of the Lord (1 Nephi 19–2 Nephi 5). A string of texts then deals with (3) reconciliation, a theme structurally privileged in Nephi's record as "the more sacred things," and focuses on the eschatological reconciliation of the Lamanites with God (2 Nephi 6–30), followed by (4) a brief epilogue centered principally on baptism (2 Nephi 31–33).

Having established the basic structure, I then look in more detail at each of the four divisions of Nephi's record, giving the most attention to the "more sacred things" of 2 Nephi 6–30, investigating the focus on Isaiah that is clearly on display in those structurally privileged chapters. Finally, I take this focus on Isaiah as a clue and look in more detail at the complex role played by Isaiah in Nephi's larger record. The picture produced in the course of this investigation is one in which Nephi's record is built on complex, detailed readings of Isaiah, distributed in intentional ways between the two books that make up Nephi's contribution to the small plates.

The Basic Structure of Nephi's Record

In a neglected but vital study of First and Second Nephi, Frederick Axelgard points to the importance of 1 Nephi 19:1–6 for understanding the "overarching framework in Nephi's writing."[1] In these verses, after distinguishing the small and the large plates, Nephi says: "And an account of my making these [the small] plates shall be given hereafter" (1 Nephi 19:5). With this sentence, Nephi points to a later moment in his record, found in the last verses of 2 Nephi 5, where he describes the actual physical production of the small plates. This is important because Nephi goes on in 1 Nephi 19 to explain that only "*then*"—that is, *after* the account of the actual physical production of the small plates at the end of 2 Nephi 5—would he "proceed according to that which [he had] spoken," namely, to fulfill the "commandment that the ministry and the prophecies, the more plain and precious parts of them, should be written upon these [small] plates" (1 Nephi 19:5, 3). Nephi thus identifies for his readers a basic structural division in his record, one he apparently imposed on it consciously and of which he wanted his readers to be aware. Nephi's record divides into two major parts: (1) the twenty-seven chapters stretching from 1 Nephi 1 to 2 Nephi 5, leading up to the account of the physical production of the small

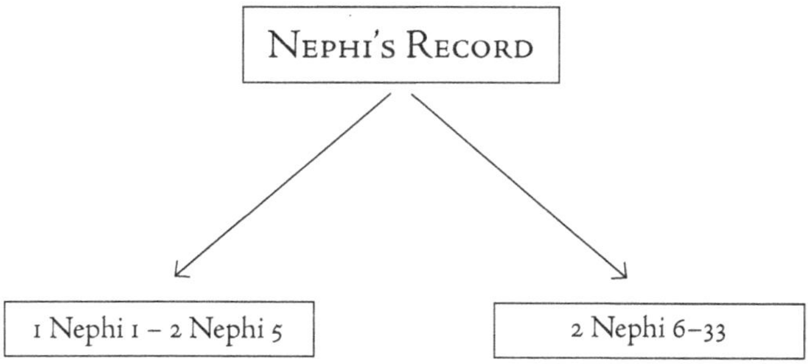

plates; and (2) the twenty-eight chapters stretching from 2 Nephi 6 to 2 Nephi 33, following the account of the physical production of the small plates.

Axelgard further argues that the opening section of Nephi's record can be subdivided into a first stretch of eighteen chapters (chapters 1–18 of First Nephi) and a second stretch of nine chapters (1 Nephi 19 through 2 Nephi 5). As a whole, then, Axelgard understands Nephi's record to bear a three-

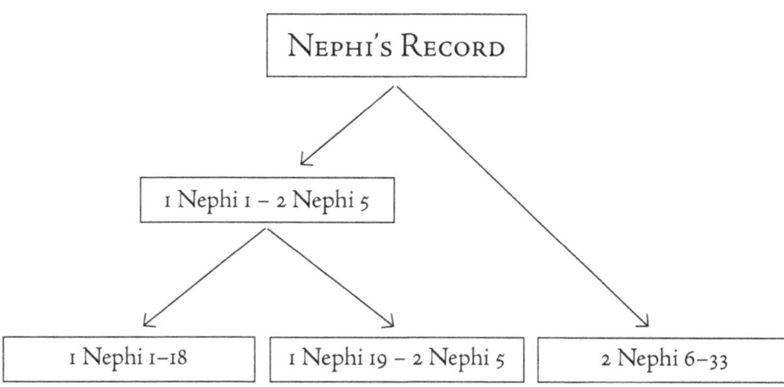

fold, essentially progressive structure, (1) "Nephi's family history" (1 Nephi 1–18) giving way to (2) a series of chapters "focuse[d] on spiritual matters with an intensity that suggests a transitional lead-in" (1 Nephi 19 – 2 Nephi 5) to (3) his "final, completely spiritual-prophetic segments" (2 Nephi 6–33).[2] Going further than Axelgard, it is possible to assert that the second larger division of Nephi's writings (2 Nephi 6–33) should, like the first division, be subdivided—something indicated in the last verse of 2 Nephi 30: "And now, my beloved brethren, I make an end of my sayings." With this straightforward statement, Nephi effectively breaks his second major division into a stretch of twenty-five chapters (2 Nephi 6–30) and a (rather short) stretch of three chapters (2 Nephi 31–33).

Because Nephi only begins to "fulfill the commandment" concerning the small plates with 2 Nephi 6, the break between 2 Nephi 6–30 and 2 Nephi 31–33 turns out to be important: it allows one to identify 2 Nephi 6–30 as the core of Nephi's record. These twenty-five chapters are what Nephi calls, in 1 Nephi 19:5, the "more sacred things" of his record. These structural divisions order Nephi's record as a four-part progression, from (1) the journey to the New World (1 Nephi 1–18) through (2) a series of theological sermons (1 Nephi 19 – 2 Nephi 5) to (3) the culminating, commanded heart of Nephi's record (2 Nephi 6–30) and (4) a brief conclusion (2 Nephi 31–33).

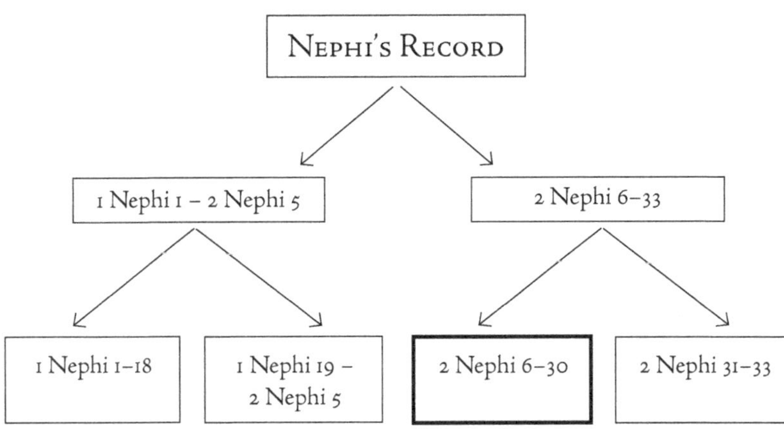

Keeping the More Sacred Things

What is most surprising about 1 Nephi 19:1–6, on the reading I have offered, is that Nephi there privileges 2 Nephi 6–30 as being somehow *more* sacred than the rest of his record—in fact as the only *mandated* part of Nephi's writings.

This claim calls for a more careful look at the indicated passage (with italics added for emphasis and bracketed phrases for clarification):

> And it came to pass that the Lord commanded me, wherefore I did make plates of ore [the large plates] that I might engraven upon them the [historical] record of my people. And upon the plates which I made [the large plates] I did engraven [1] the record of my father, and also [2] our journeyings in the wilderness, and [3] the prophecies of my father; and also [4] many of mine own prophecies have I engraven upon them. And I knew not at the time when I made *them* [the large plates] that I should be commanded of the Lord to make *these plates* [the small plates]; wherefore, the record of my father, and the genealogy of his fathers, and the more part of all our proceedings in the wilderness are engraven upon those first plates of which I have spoken [the large plates]; wherefore, the things which transpired before I [physically] made these plates [the small plates] are, of a truth, more particularly made mention upon the first plates [the large plates]. And *after* I had [eventually] made *these* plates [the small plates] by way of commandment, I, Nephi, received *a commandment that the ministry and the prophecies, the more plain and precious parts of them, should be written upon these plates* [the small plates]; *and that the things which were written should be kept for the instruction of my people*, who should possess the land, *and also for other wise purposes, which purposes are known unto the Lord*. Wherefore, I, Nephi, did make a record upon the other plates [the large plates], which gives an account, or which gives a greater account of the wars and contentions and destructions of my people. And this have I done, and commanded my people what they should do after I was gone [concerning the large plates]; *and* that *these* plates [the small plates] should be handed down from one generation to another, or from one prophet to another, until further commandments of the Lord. And *an account* of my [physically] making *these* plates [the small plates] shall be given hereafter [in, as it turns out, the last verses of 2 Nephi 5]; and *then* [beginning with the first verse of 2 Nephi 6], behold, I [will] proceed according to that which I have spoken [namely, to fulfill the "commandment that the ministry and the prophecies . . . should be written upon these plates"]; and this I do that *the more sacred things* may be kept for the knowledge of my people. *Nevertheless*, I do not write *anything* upon plates [large or small] save it be that I think it be *sacred*. And now, if I do err, even did they err of old; not that I would excuse myself because of other men, but because of the weakness which is in me, according to the flesh, I would excuse myself.

Several remarks are called for. First, these verses sharply distinguish the large plates from the small plates of Nephi—the former being primarily *historical*, the latter primarily *spiritual*, a record of "the ministry and the prophecies." Of course, as Nephi explains, he will only turn directly to spiritual matters beginning with 2 Nephi 6 (and, as already pointed out, ending with 2 Nephi 30). The obvious question to be asked is: Why would Nephi postpone the "more sacred things" of his record until so late (several chapters into his *second* book)? Indeed, why would Nephi write anything *but* "more sacred things" in his record? Nephi answers: "this I do," he says, "that the more sacred things may be kept for the knowledge of my people." This explanation must be read as what it obviously is: *an apology*. Nephi recognizes that what he says he is doing is odd and so he begins in verse 5 to defend his decision.[3]

In addition to the justification just quoted, to which I will return, Nephi offers an important point of clarification: "I do not write *anything* upon plates [whatever in his record that does not qualify as the "more sacred things"] save it be that I think it be sacred." Here, it seems clear, Nephi claims that his record does not mingle the "more sacred things" of 2 Nephi 6–30 with merely *secular* materials; instead, the record frames the *more* sacred by the *less-but-nonetheless* sacred. Curiously, Nephi further explains that in framing the more sacred with the less sacred, he is following important scriptural precedent: "And now, if I do err, even did they err of old." These details help to clarify Nephi's initial justification. Whatever he means when he speaks of keeping the more sacred things for the knowledge of his people, he suggests that this can only be done by employing the apparently common scriptural strategy of framing the more sacred by the less sacred. Two questions, then, need to be addressed. First, what does it mean to keep the more sacred things for the knowledge of the people? And second, how does framing the more sacred with the less sacred accomplish that?

Taking up the first question, one should note that verse 5 (the claim that the more sacred things must be "kept for the knowledge of [the] people") echoes verse 3, where Nephi says: "the things which were written [on the small plates] should be kept for the instruction of my people, who should possess the land." The obvious parallel with "instruction" clarifies what Nephi has in mind with the word "knowledge," though no one will be surprised that Nephi's record is associated with (religious) instruction. But closer reading complicates things. Nephi does *not* claim in either verse that his intention, in framing the more sacred with the less sacred, was to ensure that the record would be *used* for instruction/knowledge. Rather, Nephi's task and concern was to ensure that the record would be *kept* for instruction/knowledge. It thus appears that Nephi's decision to structure his record as he did was rooted in his—and, apparently, the Lord's—concern that the small plates might come into disrepute, or even simply be ignored. In short, the most straightforward reading of 1 Nephi 19:1–6 suggests that Nephi had reason to believe that *the very presence* of the less sacred material in his record (1 Nephi 1 – 2 Nephi 5 and 2 Nephi 31–33) *would guarantee* that the more sacred things (2 Nephi 6–30) would continue to be read indefinitely.

The strength of this reading has already been borne out by the work of Noel Reynolds. In a study meant to disclose the political significance of the small plates, Reynolds explains:

> Every people needs to know that its laws and rulers are legitimate and authoritative. This is why stories of national origins and city foundings are so important to human societies throughout the world. Such stories provide explanations of the legitimate origins of their laws and their rulers. . . . When Nephi undertook late in his life to write a[n] account of the founding events of the Lehite colony, it appears that he wanted to provide his descendants with a document that would serve this [legitimizing] function. His small plates systematically defend the Nephite tradition concerning origins and refute the competing account advanced by the Lamanites. . . . Thus, the writings of Nephi can be read in part as a political tract or a "lineage history," written to document the legitimacy of Nephi's rule and religious teachings.[4]

Drawing on Reynolds's understanding of the "political small plates," one might argue that Nephi hoped the less sacred material in his record, the majority of which would be ideologically important for the Nephites, would ensure that the more sacred things would not be dismissed.

Of course, one might object that such an obviously ideological contextualization of the record's more sacred things would effectively desacralize them, or at least politicize them. But Reynolds's more recent work provides the resources needed to respond to this objection. While still holding that "the need to justify and legitimate the Nephite political regime [in the small plates] was both clear and pressing,"[5] Reynolds has recently "reconsidered" Nephite kingship through an analysis of what he calls "the uncoronation of Nephi" in 1 Nephi 17.[6] In essence, he convincingly argues that Nephi understood his role as "ruler" to be more religious than political, modeled on the prophetic leadership of Moses rather than on the political leadership of the Israelite monarchy. (Laman and Lemuel were, according to this argument, fixated on the monarchical model.) As Reynolds puts it: "It was a contest between the claims of inherited royal right and divine prophetic calling, a contest that necessarily put religious claims at the center of the dispute."[7]

Thus, while the small plates were arguably designed to serve a legitimizing function, even this legitimization was, for Nephi, sacred—though perhaps *less* sacred than the *more* sacred things of 2 Nephi 6–30. At any rate, there seems to be good evidence that the legitimizing narratives of 1 Nephi 1 – 2 Nephi 5 were inserted into the record to guarantee that the more sacred, instructional materials of 2 Nephi 6–30 would remain in the Nephite consciousness.

A Change of Plans

The case for the above interpretation is strong. But a question—not quite an objection—should at this point be raised: Why does Nephi bury his explanation of all this in the (relatively obscure) nineteenth chapter of First Nephi? Why are his structural intentions not, for instance, laid out in the very first verses of 1 Nephi 1, or at least of 2 Nephi 1? Why would Nephi not make it clearer that the purpose of his record was to ensure that his readers took most seriously the more sacred things contained in 2 Nephi 6–30? Would he not want readers of his record to hurry their way to the privileged but postponed portion that comes only after the legitimizing narratives? In short, why is Nephi's table of contents to be found only in 1 Nephi 19?

One way of making sense of this would be to explore the possibility—heretofore unexplored in Book of Mormon scholarship—that the character of Nephi's project changed dramatically after he finished writing 1 Nephi 1–18. Evidence for such a change can be culled from the italicized inscription that serves as First Nephi's heading—an inscription that was part of the original record. The inscription ends with "or, in other words, I Nephi wrote this record." If one assumes that Nephi wrote the inscription *before* he wrote his record, it might be taken as an outline of what Nephi originally planned to write. And, curiously, the inscription sketchily describes only what is now 1 Nephi 1–18. It might be, then, that Nephi eventually took his record in a different direction than he had intended.

Moreover, if this speculation is of any worth, Nephi's change in direction began precisely with the first verses of 1 Nephi 19. If Nephi indeed first intended only to write what is now 1 Nephi 1–18, and if he therefore wrote these chapters before deciding to alter the scope of his record, it would seem that he had no choice but to spell out at the beginning of what is now 1 Nephi 19 the *new* projected structure of his record. On this reading, Nephi's concern in 1 Nephi 19:5–6 that his readers might miss the overarching intentions of his record would have been motivated by the discontinuity of his record resulting from his change of plans. Having decided to restructure his record, Nephi would have to provide an explanation that would gather into the project he *now* saw himself writing what he had *already* written.

This approach is interesting, and it unquestionably provides answers to a few questions (regarding the nature of the inscription that introduces First Nephi as much as the odd placement of Nephi's discussion of textual structure). But is it necessary? Perhaps not, but—at least for the moment—it seems preferable to the only obvious alternative approach, namely, to assume that Nephi meant actually to hide the more sacred portion of his record by obscurely burying his structural explanation. Whatever the strengths of this alternate account,[8] it seems to be at odds with Nephi's consistently professed plainness.

Scriptural Precedent

At this point, it is worth returning to Nephi's claim that he was only following scriptural precedent in framing the more sacred portion of his record with less sacred material. But if Nephi is following rather than blazing a trail, what scriptural precedents can be identified and how does Nephi follow them? Presumably, given that 1 Nephi 19 not only *explains* that Nephi frames the more sacred with the less sacred but *outlines* the larger fourfold structure employed in that framing, Nephi's precedents use the same fourfold structure. In order, then, to look for such precedents, it is necessary to probe into the significance—even the theological significance—of Nephi's fourfold structure. That Nephi bothers to point out the structure suggests its importance, but what can be said about that significance?

The basic theological pattern at work is relatively straightforward: (1) 1 Nephi 1–18 recounts the founding of the Lehite colony in the New World; (2) 1 Nephi 19 – 2 Nephi 5 relates the breaking up of this colony into two rival factions, one of which is cut off from the presence of the Lord; (3) 2 Nephi

6–30 consists of prophecies and sermons focused on the eventual return of that cut-off faction to the Lord's favor; and (4) 2 Nephi 31–33 offers summary reflections on baptism as a crossing of a limit.

> Part 1: Foundation (1 Nephi 1–18)
> Part 2: Division (1 Nephi 19 – 2 Nephi 5)
> Part 3: Redemption (2 Nephi 6–30)
> Part 4: Conclusion (2 Nephi 31–33)

Without much imagination, this basic structure might be recast as a pattern familiar from its consistent employment in Nephite missionary efforts:

> Part 1: Creation (1 Nephi 1–18)
> Part 2: Fall (1 Nephi 19 – 2 Nephi 5)
> Part 3: Atonement (2 Nephi 6–30)
> Part 4: Veil (2 Nephi 31–33)

Nephi's fourfold structure effectively reproduces what the Book of Mormon elsewhere calls the "plan of redemption." Moreover, it reproduces what Nephi takes to be the basic pattern of his own life, as he summarizes it in the famous first verse of First Nephi:

> I, Nephi,
> [Part 1:] having been born of goodly parents . . . ; and
> [Part 2:] having seen many afflictions in the course of my days, nevertheless
> [Part 3:] having been highly favored of the Lord in all my days; yea,
> [Part 4:] having had a great knowledge of the goodness and the mysteries of God,
> *therefore* I make a record of my proceedings in my days.

Through a fourfold repetition, in this verse, of the word "having," Nephi sets forth his life as falling into the above cosmic pattern:

> Creation: born of goodly parents
> Fall: many afflictions
> Atonement: highly favored of the Lord
> Veil: a great knowledge of . . . the mysteries of God,

Importantly, when Nephi says, at the end of the verse, "*therefore* I make a record of my proceedings in my days," it appears he is drawing an explicit connection between the record he is about to produce and the fourfold pattern of his own life—as if the fourfold pattern of 1 Nephi 1:1 were to be taken as a kind of guide for the structure of Nephi's entire record.[9]

Now, if these reflections are not amiss, Nephi's claim in 1 Nephi 19:6 suggests that he borrowed the fourfold pattern of creation, fall, atonement, and veil from earlier scriptural texts with which he was familiar—presumably from the brass plates. A more detailed look at the pattern in Nephi's record makes clear, I think, what scriptural texts Nephi took as his precedents.

Creation, Fall, Atonement, Veil

I have identified the first part of Nephi's pattern with creation. Broadly, the identification seems obvious. 1 Nephi 1–18 tells the story of coming to a new world and creating a new civilization. But such a broad characterization hardly serves as evidence that Nephi *intended* the first part of his record to be a creation story. However, several details from 1 Nephi 18—from the last verses of this first structural subdivision of Nephi's text—offer evidence of a conscious thematization on Nephi's part. Setting 1 Nephi 18:21–25 side by side with Genesis 1, this becomes apparent:

1 Nephi 18	Genesis 1
And it came to pass after they had loosed me, behold, I took the compass, and it did work whither I desired it. And it came to pass that I prayed unto the Lord; and after I had prayed the winds did cease, and the storm did cease, and there was a great calm. And it came to pass that I, Nephi, did guide the ship, that we sailed again towards the promised land. (vv. 21–22)	And the earth was without form, and void; and darkness was upon the face of the deep. And the Spirit of God moved upon the face of the waters. And God said, Let there be light: and there was light. (vv. 2–3)

1 Nephi 18	Genesis 1
And it came to pass that after we had sailed for the space of many days we did arrive at the promised land; and we went forth upon the land, and did pitch our tents; and we did call it the promised land. (v. 23)	And God said, Let the waters under the heaven be gathered together unto one place, and let the dry land appear: and it was so. And God called the dry land Earth; and the gathering together of the waters called he Seas. (vv. 9–10)
And it came to pass that we did begin to till the earth, and we began to plant seeds; yea, we did put all our seeds into the earth, which we had brought from the land of Jerusalem. And it came to pass that they did grow exceedingly; wherefore, we were blessed in abundance. (v. 24)	And God said, Let the earth bring forth grass, the herb yielding seed, and the fruit tree yielding fruit after his kind, whose seed is in itself, upon the earth: and it was so. And the earth brought forth grass, and herb yielding seed after his kind, and the tree yielding fruit, whose seed was in itself, after his kind. . . . (vv. 11–12)
And it came to pass that we did find upon the land of promise, as we journeyed in the wilderness, that there were beasts in the forests of every kind, both the cow and the ox, and the ass and the horse, and the goat and the wild goat, and all manner of wild animals, which were for the use of men. (v. 25)	And God said, Let the earth bring forth the living creature after his kind, cattle, and creeping thing, and beast of the earth after his kind: and it was so. And God made the beast of the earth after his kind, and cattle after their kind, and every thing that creepeth upon the earth after his kind. . . . And God said, Let us make man in our image, after our likeness: and let them have dominion over the fish of the sea, and over the fowl of the air, and over the cattle, and over all the earth, and over every creeping thing that creepeth upon the earth. (vv. 24–26)

These parallels, I believe, make clear that Nephi was making conscious allusions to the basic pattern of the creation story as recorded in Genesis.

The second part of Nephi's text seems to make similar allusions to the biblical narratives surrounding the fall of Adam and Eve. Most striking, perhaps, is the fact that 1 Nephi 19 – 2 Nephi 5 culminates in the announcement that the Lamanites have been—much like Adam and Eve—"cut off from the presence of the Lord" (2 Nephi 5:20).[10] Moreover, that these same chapters recount the death of Lehi (an obvious Adam figure), as well as the murderous rivalry of Lehi's sons (echoes of Cain and Abel), seems significant. Certainly, there is reason to look for a conscious connection between 2 Nephi 5:21 and Genesis 4:15, linking the "cursing" of the Lamanites to the mark set on Cain and his children. But in addition to narrative allusions, these same chapters record several discussions of, precisely, the fall—most notably Lehi's discourse on Eden and its loss in 2 Nephi 2. That Nephi intended to connect 1 Nephi 19 – 2 Nephi 5 with the biblical fall seems clear.

Importantly, on Nephi's telling, both this creation and the fall are rooted in a specific covenant. The foundation of the Lehite colony is laid as early as 1 Nephi 2:19–24 when Nephi, having his first revelatory experience with God, learns that prosperity in the land of promise is predicated on the Lehites' obedience to the commandments. This "Lehitic covenant" thus grounds *both* the creation of the Lehites (they are only led to the promised land as they keep the commandments) *and* their fall (their division into rival camps comes in fulfillment of the covenantal word that the Lamanites, once definitively rebellious, would be cut off from God's presence).

As a result of this heavy covenantal focus in 1 Nephi 1 – 2 Nephi 5, it is not surprising to discover that the atonement portion of Nephi's record is equally covenantal. Indeed, 2 Nephi 6–30 is through and through a question of explaining how the Lehitic covenant—a part of which includes the eventual return of the Lamanites to God's favor—will be fulfilled. It must thus be recognized that the word "atonement" here takes on a sense somewhat distinct from its everyday usage in Mormonism. By atonement, I indicate not *personal* or *individual* salvation but a reconciliation and covenant redemption worked out for *an entire people or community*. On this understanding of atonement, 2 Nephi 6–30 is about nothing but atonement, though it has relatively little—indeed, almost nothing—to say about the events surrounding the death and resurrection of Jesus Christ.

More will have to be said about the atonement portion of Nephi's record and its relationship to the Genesis narrative. First, though, it is necessary to say a few words about 2 Nephi 31–33, the veil portion of Nephi's text.

Nephi, the Veil, and the Temple

The last three chapters of Second Nephi are saturated with the theme of the veil. After a few introductory words, Nephi speaks of baptism as "the gate by which ye should enter" (2 Nephi 31:17), associating passage through that gate with passage through the veil of the Old Testament temple—something indicated when he describes those who pass through the gate as able to "speak with the tongue of angels, and shout praises to the Holy One of Israel" (31:13). The holy of holies in the Old Testament temple was, according to ancient Israelite belief, the dwelling place, precisely, of the angels. Nephi goes on to express concern that his readers have misunderstood him and offers an explanation in terms that confirm that the veil of the temple is what he has in mind: "after I have spoken these words, if ye cannot understand them it will be because ye ask not, neither do ye knock; wherefore, ye are not brought into the light, but must perish in the dark" (32:4). Nephi then promises that those who *do* knock at the veil will be able to part it, and Christ "shall manifest himself unto [such] in the flesh" (32:7). Finally, mourning that he "cannot say more" (32:7), Nephi explains that he is not allowed to describe what lies beyond the veil—though he does say that "what [he] seal[s] on earth, shall be brought against [his readers] at the judgment bar" (33:15).

The theme of the veil thus emerges in 2 Nephi 31–33. That baptism is a veil through which the reader is to pass at the end of his record suggests that the whole of Nephi's fourfold pattern might be connected with the *temple*, or with what might be called "temple theology." In this regard, it is significant that Hugh Nibley, in connection with 1 Nephi 1:1, says:

> But you were always obliged at the end of the initiation (the mysteries) to write down on a tablet, and deposit the tablet there [at the temple], what your experiences had been. At the end of the mysteries, you were required to record this before you could leave the cave, or the temple or whatever it was. You would leave a record of your experiences in the mysteries—whatever visions it was you had. So Nephi said an interesting thing here, "Yea, having had a great knowledge of the goodness and the mysteries of God, therefore I make a record of my proceedings in my days," of what I've been through. Having been through the mysteries of God, I'm under obligation to preserve that knowledge.[11]

Nibley's comments here perhaps confirm that the whole creation, fall, atonement, and veil pattern in Nephi's record should be connected to the temple. It is certainly interesting, at any rate, that Nephi produces the small plates immediately after—if not in connection with—his "build[ing] a temple . . . after the manner of the temple of Solomon" (2 Nephi 5:16). However, in order to explore this possibility more rigorously, I will draw on the research of two students of the Hebrew Bible: Jon Levenson and Margaret Barker.

Levenson, in his book, *Creation and the Persistence of Evil,* argues that creation in the Hebrew Bible is associated with a "dialectical theology" that was at work in the liturgy of the First Temple (Solomon's temple). As the best embodiment of the tension that underlies the dialectic, he compares two Abrahamic narratives from Genesis: the story of Abraham's bartering with the Lord over the citizens of Sodom and Gomorrah (Genesis 18) and the story of the commanded-but-never-completed sacrifice of Isaac (Genesis 22). As Levenson explains:

> *By itself* the theology of Genesis 18 would soon lead to a religion in which God's will had ceased to be a reality. . . . Left to *its* own, Genesis 22, on the other hand, would lead to a religion of fanaticism, in which God would be so incomprehensible that even the praise of him as wise or just would be meaningless. . . . Together, however, the two perspectives delimit a theology in which human judgment neither replaces the inscrutable God who commands nor becomes superfluous within the life lived in faithfulness to him.[12]

This, Levenson argues, is the theology behind the temple: "YHWH in this theology is a deity who can still be aroused, who can still respond to the anguished cry of his cultic [that is, temple] community to effect together a new victory."[13]

Levenson, interestingly, goes on to point to the architecture of the temple as a physical embodiment of this dialectical theology. In the two-room temple, the heavens and the earth are brought together and yet separated by the partition of the veil. But, according to Levenson, this is only accomplished through the displacement to a location *outside* the temple of the brass laver (supported on the back of twelve oxen), a displacement to be understood as a microcosmic representation of the Lord's ancient and yet ever-renewed victory over the waters conquered at the creation. As Levenson explains: "It would make sense for the Temple,

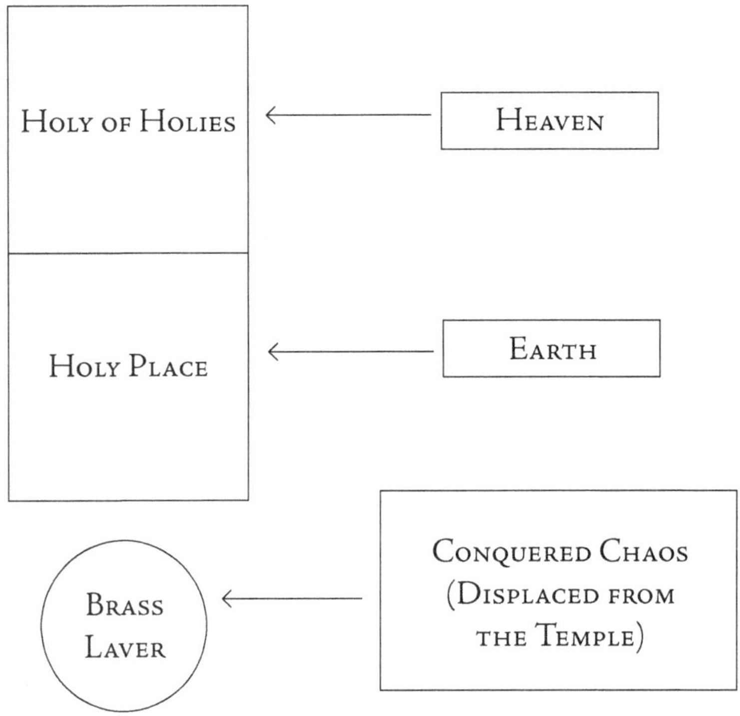

which bears witness to both enthronement and creation, to have featured a metallic representation of the vanquished adversary [the tamed waters of chaos; see Isaiah 51:9–10; 2 Nephi 8:9–10], now reduced to no more than an item of decoration in the precincts of his victor's royal palace."[14] Levenson thus sees in Israelite temple theology an expression of the need to respond to the undeniable reality of evil, of what Nephi calls "affliction." In Levenson's words, this theology "avoids the cheery optimism of those who crow that 'God's in his heaven — / All's right with the world,'" even as it refuses to "allow for an unqualified acceptance of the pessimism that attributes to innocent suffering the immovability of fate."[15] Indeed, Levenson could well have been commenting on the first verse of First Nephi when he wrote: "Present experience . . . is seen [in this theology] as a mysterious interruption in the divine life, an interruption that the supplications of the worshiping community may yet bring to an end."[16] And all of this, it will be remembered, is rooted, according to Levenson, in commitment to the Abrahamic covenant.

While Levenson's work on temple theology expresses the spirit of Nephi's fourfold pattern, Margaret Barker's work expresses both the spirit and the letter of Nephi's pattern.[17] In a book simply entitled *Temple Theology*, Barker has assembled a definitive introduction to what she divides into a fourfold pattern: creation, (broken) covenant, atonement, and (divine) wisdom.[18] The correspondence between what Margaret Barker describes as temple theology and the pattern Nephi uses to structure his record is striking.[19] This correspondence—suggesting that Nephi's record might have been written in association with the newly constructed Nephite temple—needs, however, still to be turned back to the task of interpreting Nephi's record.

How does the recognition that Nephi's text may be tied to the temple clarify the meaning of especially its creation, fall, and atonement portions? Such an approach to Nephi's record may shed light on both 1 Nephi 1–18 and 1 Nephi 19 – 2 Nephi 5, and it has already been shown how it clarifies 2 Nephi 31–33. I want here, though, only to spell out in more detail how this approach clarifies and opens up 2 Nephi 6–30—especially by rooting it (like 1 Nephi 1–18 and 1 Nephi 19 – 2 Nephi 5) in Genesis.

Atonement and Temple

According to a consistent Book of Mormon pattern, Nephi connects the theme of atonement to the appearance of divinely appointed messengers. Examples of this pattern in the Book of Mormon are not difficult to find. King Benjamin, for instance, after reviewing the creation and its fall but before speaking of passing through the veil to be "sealed" to Jesus Christ, introduces the atonement to his hearers through the words of an angel. Later, both Alma the Younger (in Alma 12:22–34) and Mormon (in Moroni 7:20–33) formulated full-blown angelologies along the same lines, making the arrival of divine messengers the crux of atonement in Nephite thought. For Nephi, standing at the beginning of this tradition, the messengers who bring tidings of redemption are less otherworldly than for Alma or Mormon, but they are no less divinely appointed for that reason: Jacob, Isaiah, and Nephi himself. Still more significantly, these messengers come—in 2 Nephi 6–30—as a threesome, as what Jeffrey R. Holland has called the three "sentinels at the gate of the book [of Mormon]," positioned authoritatively to "admit [the reader] into the scriptural presence of the Lord."[20]

That the appearance of three divinely appointed messengers is associated with the temple has been discussed by Hugh Nibley, who quotes a Mandean text thus:

> I'm sending three, God says to them, giving them instructions. He said to the pure Sent One, his Son, "Go call Adam and Eve and all their posterity and teach them concerning everything about the Kingdom of Light and the Worlds of Light. Be friendly with Adam and keep him company, you and the two angels which will be with you. Warn them against Satan; also, teach them chastity."[21]

But the theme of the three messengers is not only to be found in obscure noncanonical texts; it can be found right in the Old Testament—for example in Genesis 18, mentioned above in the discussion of Levenson. There one finds Abraham sitting "in the tent door in the heat of the day" when, "lo, three men stood by him" (Genesis 18:1–2). The visitors share with Abraham and Sarah the promise of Isaac, thus confirming the Abrahamic covenant that will eventually redeem the fallen creation. The overcoming of the fall is thus set in motion in both Nephi and Genesis by the message of three divine messengers.

The parallel is even stronger between Nephi and the Joseph Smith Translation of Genesis 18. There, Abraham's visitors are identified as three "angels which were holy men and were sent forth after the order of God," and they state that their task is to let Abraham know the decisions of the divine council so that, "remembering the things which had been told him," Abraham can himself join the council to converse with God.[22] In short, there is at least reason to suggest that, with his three messengers, Nephi continues his series of allusions to Genesis. After the creation (Genesis 1, 8–9) and the fall (Genesis 2–3, 9–11) comes a redemption/atonement (Genesis 11–25, the Abraham story) in which three messengers sent from God restore fallen humanity to the presence of God and his angels by teaching them how to pass through the veil.

Incidentally, this theme of messengers being sent to provide instruction about how to pass through the veil appears also in the work of Barker and Levenson. Though neither of these scholars focuses on the *three* messengers, they do both discuss the idea that Israelite temple rites were intended to allow human beings to become, in Levenson's words, "the functional equivalent of the pantheon [the council of the gods]."[23] Again: "[Israelite] cosmogony"—that is, the creation of the world—"is not fully grasped until it has been related to the [temple] and to the rites that took place there *and were thought to allow human participation in the divine ordering of the world.*"[24] In short, the temple is where human beings are inducted into the divine council. This idea appears in Joseph Smith's rendering of Genesis 18, but what of Nephi's writings?

The theme appears as early as 1 Nephi 1, in a story marginally explored in chapter 1. As I pointed out there, the small plates open with Lehi's first visions. Overcome by a first, fiery vision in which he "saw and heard much" (1:6), Lehi went home to lie down. But he was snatched from his rest and "carried away in a vision" where he saw—as Alma would later see—"God sitting upon his throne, surrounded with numberless concourses of angels in the attitude of singing and praising their God" (1:8). The vision is appropriate, since Nephi assigns it to "the commencement" of the first year of a new king's rule (1:4), apparently then at the time of coronation, which would have taken place during the Feast of Tabernacles. Barker points out the connection between the angelic chorus and this feast: "The biblical texts show that the song of the angels accompanied the establishing of the creation, and so the renewal of the creation in the New Year rituals of Tabernacles was accompanied by, or perhaps enabled by, the song of the angels."[25] Lehi at first sees this whole scene from a distance, but one of the angelic figures brings him a book, and then, it seems, inducts him into the chorus of angels around the throne. Such is implied by his responsive words of praise: "Great and marvelous are thy works, O Lord God Almighty! *Thy throne* is high in the heavens, and thy power, and goodness, and mercy are over all the inhabitants of the earth; and, because thou art merciful, thou wilt not suffer *those who come unto thee* that they shall perish!" (1:14).

Nephi's record opens by displaying what *can* happen to the righteous and Lehi's induction into the heavenly council serves as a model. Significantly, when Nephi comes to the end of his record, he returns to the theme of angelicization and the divine council. Curiously, no commentator has yet recognized what Nephi must have intended as an obvious connection between 2 Nephi 31:13 and 1 Nephi 1:8. The two passages should be set side by side:

1 Nephi 1:8	2 Nephi 31:13
And being thus overcome with the Spirit, he was carried away in a vision, even that he saw the heavens open, and he thought he saw God sitting upon his throne, surrounded with *numberless concourses of angels in the attitude of singing and praising their God.*	I know that if ye shall follow the Son . . . , repenting of your sins, witnessing unto the Father that ye are willing to take upon you the name of Christ by baptism—yea, by following your Lord and your Savior down into the water, according to his word, behold, then shall ye receive the Holy Ghost; yea, then cometh the baptism of fire and of the Holy Ghost; and *then can ye speak with the tongue of angels, and shout praises unto the Holy One of Israel.*

The unfortunate consequence of this connection's going unrecognized is that 2 Nephi 31:13 has been a consistent source of frustration for Latter-day Saint scholars, who typically—if they at all address the phrase italicized above—suggest either that Nephi has reference to a rather banally defined "gift of tongues" or that Nephi simply uses a fancy phrase to say that the Holy Ghost allows one to speak with power.[26] But the reference is at once simpler and richer than these approaches. In light of the above interpretation of 1 Nephi 1, Nephi offers in 2 Nephi 31 a promise that the obedient can, as Lehi had done, *join the angelic council* to sing and shout praises.[27]

Not only, then, do divine messengers appear in Nephi's record; they appear there, as in the Israelite temple tradition, precisely in order to induct the recipients of their tidings into the presence of God. But before leaving this theme, it should be noted that angelicization appears in one other crucial place in Nephi's text—in a place that calls for detailed discussion.

The Structure of 2 Nephi 6–30

I have already established how the structure of Nephi's record privileges the more sacred atonement material of 2 Nephi 6–30. What, though, of the structure within the structure, the structure of those core twenty-five chapters? Just as with the identification of the theme of the three messengers, it is already possible to recognize a basic structure:

Jacob's words (2 Nephi 6–10)
Isaiah's words (2 Nephi 11–24)
Nephi's words (2 Nephi 25–30)

Looking more closely, however, it seems best to give pride of place to the central "Isaiah chapters," since *both* Nephi's *and* Jacob's contributions to 2 Nephi 6–30 amount to little more than commentaries on Isaiah's writings. In his message, Jacob quotes and comments on Isaiah 50–51 (and a few verses from Isaiah 49), while in his message, Nephi quotes and comments on Isaiah 29 (in addition to offering his reflections on the "Isaiah chapters" more generally). In what is thus a beautifully Trinitarian gesture (*three* messengers, *one* messenger), Nephi offers the atonement portion of his record as being principally about what *Isaiah* has to say about redemption.

One might, then, chiastically rearrange the basic triple structure of 2 Nephi 6–30:

Jacob's words *about Isaiah* (2 Nephi 6–10)
    Isaiah's words *themselves* (2 Nephi 11–24)
Nephi's words *about Isaiah* (2 Nephi 25–30)

As it turns out, this chiastic structure is confirmed by an important parallel between passages at the end of Jacob's contribution and at the beginning of Nephi's contribution: 2 Nephi 10:24 ("after ye are reconciled unto God, ... it is only in and through the grace of God that ye are saved") and 2 Nephi 25:23 ("we labor diligently ... to persuade our children ... to be reconciled to God; for we know that it is by grace that we are saved, after all we can do"). Each of these passages, to which I will return in the next chapter, is crucially coupled *with one of Nephi's two direct discussions of typology* (2 Nephi 11:4–7 and 2 Nephi 25:24–29). Obviously, this will prove to be of some importance.

Nephi thus twice privileges the "Isaiah chapters." Not only are they among the more sacred things of 2 Nephi 6–30, but they form the obviously privileged centerpiece of those more sacred things. Indeed, one might suggest that all of Nephi's careful structural work was intended first and foremost to ensure that his readers would give their most sustained and dedicated study to the "Isaiah chapters." There is, then, an unavoidable irony about the way Isaiah is usually handled by Book of Mormon readers—that is, as a barrier.

But what of the structure of Nephi's Isaiah selection itself? 2 Nephi 12–24 (Isaiah 2–14) consists of five separable oracles:

Oracle against Judah (2 Nephi 12–14=Isaiah 2–4)
Oracle against Israel (2 Nephi 15=Isaiah 5)

Isaiah's call to prophesy (2 Nephi 16=Isaiah 6)
Oracle against Assyria (2 Nephi 17–22= Isaiah 7–12)
Oracle against Babylon (2 Nephi 23–24= Isaiah 13–14)[28]

Just this listing of the distinct Isaianic oracles already betrays a minimal structure: two oracles precede and two follow the central call narrative of Isaiah 6. But from Nephi's historical position (after the Northern Kingdom's fall but still in the thick of the Southern Kingdom's fall), he likely saw these five oracles as having a more intricate and historically relevant structure. Because Assyria had conquered Israel (the Northern Kingdom) and Babylon was about to conquer Judah (the Southern Kingdom), Nephi might have seen a complex chiastic structure here, distributing the destruction-and-then-restoration of the covenant people across two series of events:

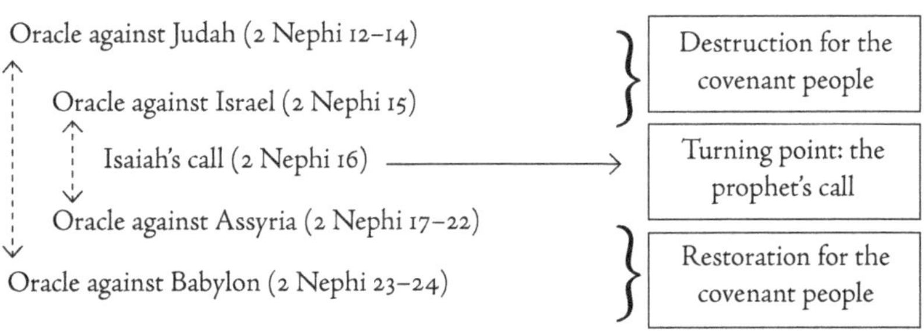

Nephi's subsequent summary of covenantal history seems to confirm this structure:

> And as one generation hath been destroyed among the Jews because of iniquity, even so have they been destroyed from generation to generation according to their iniquities [2 Nephi 12–15=Isaiah 2–5]; and never hath any of them been destroyed save it were foretold them by the prophets of the Lord [2 Nephi 16=Isaiah 6].... And notwithstanding they have been carried away they shall return again, and possess the land of Jerusalem; wherefore they shall be restored again to the land of their inheritance [2 Nephi 17–24=Isaiah 7–14]. (2 Nephi 25:9–11)

This structural reading places at the center (Isaiah 6) of the center (the Isaiah chapters) of the center (atonement) of Nephi's record the account of a vision whose original occasion, according to Marvin Sweeney, "must be identified with the Day of Atonement,"[29] and whose contextual aim, according to Brevard Childs, is to mark "a turning point in God's history."[30] This atonement-focused turning point, structurally privileged several times over by Nephi, recounts—in addition to 1 Nephi 1 and 2 Nephi 31—still another exemplary experience of angelicization, namely, that of Isaiah.

Isaiah 6 (i.e., 2 Nephi 16) begins with the prophet standing—for whatever official or unofficial reason—in the Jerusalem temple.[31] Overwhelmed by the unanticipated appearance of Jehovah, Isaiah bewails what he takes to be his own imminent destruction: "Wo is unto me! for I am undone; because I am a man of unclean lips; and I dwell in the midst of a people of unclean lips; for mine eyes have seen the King, the Lord of Hosts" (Isaiah 6:5; 2 Nephi 16:5). Concerned specifically about his *lips*—the Hebrew word can be translated "language," as it is, for example, in the tower of Babel story in Genesis 11—Isaiah takes himself to be out of place among the seraphic throngs who shout their praise of "Holy, holy, holy!" to "the Lord of hosts" (Isaiah 6:3; 2 Nephi 16:3). Responding to Isaiah's fright, one of the seraphs presses to his lips (to *his language*) "a live coal" (Isaiah 6:6; 2 Nephi 16:6), presumably taken from the altar of incense (the only burning altar within the temple building and significantly symbolic of a kind of truer order of perpetual prayer offered up constantly before the temple's veil). Thus "purg[ing]" Isaiah's "sin" (Isaiah 6:7; 2 Nephi 16:7), the seraph with his white stone inducts Isaiah into the divine council (see D&C 130:10–11), as becomes clear when Isaiah immediately finds he has the means—the language—to speak to God, offering himself for an angelic task: "Here am I; send me" (Isaiah 6:8; 2 Nephi 16:8).

Isaiah's account, situated at the most crucial point in Nephi's entire record, is strongly reminiscent of both 1 Nephi 1 and 2 Nephi 31:

	1 Nephi 1	2 Nephi 31	Isaiah 6
First Vision	there came a pillar of fire and dwelt upon a rock before him (v. 5)	I would that ye should remember . . . that prophet which the Lord showed unto me, that should baptize the Lamb of God (v. 4)	I saw also the Lord sitting upon a throne, high and lifted up (v. 1)

	1 Nephi 1	2 Nephi 31	Isaiah 6
Over-whelmed	he did quake and tremble exceedingly (v. 6); he cast himself upon his bed, being overcome with the Spirit and the things which he had seen (v. 7)	if the Lamb of God, he being holy, should have need to be baptized by water, to fulfil all righteousness, O then, how much more need have we, being unholy, to be baptized, yea, even by water! (v. 5)	Then said I: Wo is unto me! for I am undone; because I am a man of unclean lips; and I dwell in the midst of a people of unclean lips; for mine eyes have seen the King, the Lord of Hosts (v. 5)
Ministered To	the first came and stood before my father (v. 11)	the voice of the Son came unto me, saying: He that is baptized in my name, to him will the Father give the Holy Ghost, like unto me (v. 12)	Then flew one of the seraphim unto me (v. 6)
Mediating Element	the first came . . . and gave unto him a book (v. 11)	then shall ye receive the Holy Ghost; yea, then cometh the baptism of fire and of the Holy Ghost (v. 13)	a live coal in his hand, which he had taken with the tongs from off the altar (v. 6)
Angelic Tongue (Induction)	he was filled with the Spirit of the Lord (v. 12); when my father had read and seen many great and marvelous things, he did exclaim many things unto the Lord . . . after this manner was the language of my father in the praising of his God (vv. 14–15)	and then can ye speak with the tongue of angels, and shout praises unto the Holy One of Israel (v. 13)	he laid it upon my mouth, and said: Lo, this has touched thy lips; and thine iniquity is taken away, and thy sin purged. . . . Then I said: Here am I; send me (vv. 7–8)

From this it is clear that Nephi's whole record is oriented by and structured around this most crucial, clearly temple-centered theme:

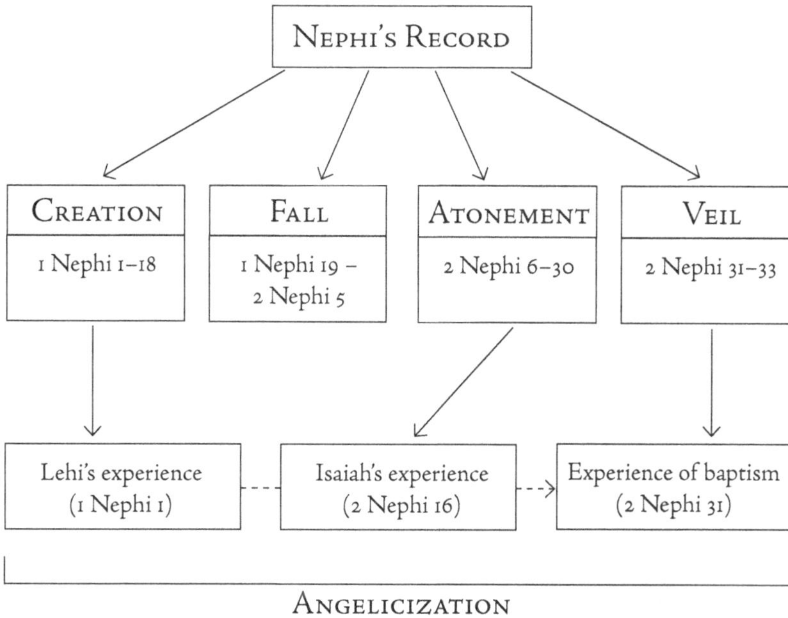

Redemption for Nephi is a question of receiving angelic messengers who, coming from the divine council and therefore knowing the unfolding history of the covenant, are sent to initiate the faithful into the angelic mysteries that will give *them* to know that same covenantal history, as well as to know the God—the God of Abraham, Isaac, and Jacob—who guides that history.

First Nephi, Second Nephi; First Isaiah, Second Isaiah

It is worth summarizing what has been outlined in this chapter so far. First and Second Nephi make up a single overarching record associated with the Nephite temple experience. Nephi organized his text into four parts associated, appropriately, with the respective themes of creation (1 Nephi 1–18), fall (1 Nephi 19 – 2 Nephi 5), atonement (2 Nephi 6–30), and passage through the veil (2 Nephi 31–33). Nephi's presentation of these themes is stretched across a covenantal framework punctuated by instances of the Isaianic motif of angelicization. Nephi privileges this motif by framing the more sacred atonement portion of his record with a less sacred contextualizing narrative, and by structurally emphasizing the "Isaiah chapters" of 2 Nephi 12–24.

Without calling the above discoveries into question, I want to ask two additional questions. First, why does this structure overlook the more obvious structural break between First Nephi and Second Nephi? Second, if Isaiah 2–14 so clearly functions as the theological core of Nephi's record, what is to be made of the other Isaiah chapters found in Nephi's text: Isaiah 48–51 (in 1 Nephi 20–21 and 2 Nephi 7–8) and Isaiah 29 (in 2 Nephi 26–27)? To answer these questions, it is necessary to take a closer look at the book of Isaiah.

The Two Isaiahs of the Nephites

Scholars generally agree that the book of Isaiah consists of three distinct parts: First Isaiah (Isaiah 1–39), Second Isaiah (Isaiah 40–55), and Third Isaiah (Isaiah 56–66). There is less agreement about how many *authors* lie behind these parts—a question I am not interested in addressing here.[32] At any rate, however many authors produced Isaiah, scholars increasingly agree that, theologically, "the book is a unity"[33] characterized by both "continuity and connectedness."[34] In short: "It is now widely held . . . that a conscious intention can be discerned toward uniting the various parts [of Isaiah] into some form of coherent literature as a whole."[35] This development does not mark an abandonment of multiple authorship theories, but a more profound investigation of how the several clearly distinct parts of the book of Isaiah do or do not mesh, theologically speaking.[36]

The Book of Mormon might be taken to weigh in on this question of Isaiah as a collection of *theologically* disparate texts.[37] Though, for example, the Nephites seem to have understood the book of Isaiah to be the work of a single author, there is evidence that they nonetheless distinguished between the themes and theological intentions of First and Second Isaiah. Moreover, as John Welch points out, "chapters 56–66, the so-called Third Isaiah, . . . do not appear in the Book of Mormon" at all.[38] In the end, I surmise that the Nephites had something like what today is Isaiah 2–55: a combined edition of First and Second Isaiah without Third Isaiah, and a volume the Nephites understood as having two separable parts with distinct theological intentions (Isaiah 2–39 and Isaiah 40–55).[39] Indeed, I think there is strong evidence that Nephi's writings collectively represent an attempt to think carefully about the relationship and tension between First and Second Isaiah—between First

Isaiah's decreed "consumption" (Isaiah 10:22) and Second Isaiah's message of "comfort" (Isaiah 40:1). For the discussion that follows, it is necessary to divide Isaiah's appearances in Nephi's record into two groups:

First Isaiah
Isaiah 2–14 in 2 Nephi 12–24
Isaiah 29 in 2 Nephi 26–27

Second Isaiah
Isaiah 48–49 in 1 Nephi 20–21
Isaiah 50–51 in 2 Nephi 7–8

Taking up Second Isaiah first, one finds that, though Isaiah 48–49 (in 1 Nephi 20–21) and Isaiah 50–51 (in 2 Nephi 7–8) do not appear together, there is reason to read these two quotations as being in continuity. Not only is Nephi behind Jacob's choice of text in 2 Nephi 7–8 (see 2 Nephi 6:4), but he seems to have asked Jacob to begin his analysis of Isaiah with the last verses of Isaiah 49—verses addressed in 1 Nephi 20–22. Thus, Nephi connects the Second Isaiah material in 2 Nephi 7–8 to that in 1 Nephi 20–21. And, of course, a single theme inspires both quotations of Second Isaiah. Both Nephi and Jacob are focused on Isaiah's message about the eventual redemption of the covenant people.

Turning next to First Isaiah, one discovers a similar continuity between the quoted chapters, though continuity of a different nature. Commentators routinely point to thematic and linguistic connections that link Isaiah 29 to Isaiah 6–8, chapters at the heart of Isaiah 2–14.[40] These connections all, significantly, turn on writing and sealing texts to be read only by a later generation. Nephi was unquestionably attuned to these themes, as is especially clear in his adaptation of Isaiah 29 in 2 Nephi 26–27. He thus appears to have taken Isaiah 29 to provide an essential key to the interpretation of the rest of First Isaiah.

Nephi recognizes thematic continuity in the chapters he quotes from First Isaiah and sequential continuity in the chapters he quotes from Second Isaiah. But he keeps First and Second Isaiah apart. It is my argument that the relationship between the two sets of Isaianic texts in Nephi's record is rooted in an implicit "theology of writing" to be found in the texts Nephi borrows from First Isaiah. A consideration of this point paves the way to a final presentation of the structure of Nephi's record.

Isaiah's Theology of Writing

Nephi's interest in Isaiah 29 calls for a rereading of Isaiah 6. In my earlier discussion of that chapter, focused on angelicization, I covered only the verses culminating in Isaiah's "Here am I; send me" (verses 1–8). Taking Isaiah 29 as an interpretive key, however, requires a return to the remainder of the chapter (verses 9–12), to the details of Isaiah's call to prophesy.[41] These verses, read alongside especially Isaiah 8 (2 Nephi 18), lay the foundation of Isaiah's theology of writing.

Isaiah 6:9–12 deserves to be quoted in full:

> And he said: Go and tell this people—Hear ye indeed, but they understood not; and see ye indeed, but they perceived not. Make the heart of this people fat, and make their ears heavy, and shut their eyes—lest they see with their eyes, and hear with their ears, and understand with their heart, and be converted and be healed. Then said I: Lord, how long? And he said: Until the cities be wasted without inhabitant, and the houses without man, and the land be utterly desolate; And the Lord have removed men far away, for there shall be a great forsaking in the midst of the land.

This text is, in the words of Brevard Childs, "one of the most difficult [passages] in the bible."[42] Hence, in commenting on these verses, I take as my companion Gerhard von Rad, who I believe has worked out the most theologically productive approach to them.

While recognizing here a genuine "theological dilemma"[43]—a command to confound Israel so that she would *not* repent and be healed—von Rad dismisses out of hand any attempt to get around the plain fact that "God erected a terrible barrier against Isaiah and his preaching."[44] In essence, if the "saying about the hardening of the heart in [Isaiah 6] sounds as if it shut the door on everyone," it does so because "it was intended to be understood this way."[45] But, as von Rad makes clear, with this Isaiah "inherited an outlook which was unchallenged in Israel." And, moreover, "the enigma of obduracy to Jahweh's offer runs through the whole of Isaiah's activity." From this it follows that Isaiah 6:9–12 "ought not to be called a 'peripheral saying.' "[46] For Isaiah, "the hardening of Israel's heart is a particular mode of Jahweh's historical dealings with her."[47]

No Protestant proclivities seem to motivate von Rad's insistence on God's hardening the hearts of Isaiah's contemporaries. Rather, he sees the significance of the hardening as tied to Isaiah's theology of history, though this significance does not emerge in the text until Isaiah 8:16–18. There, as von Rad explains, Isaiah "says paradoxically that his hope is founded precisely in this God who hardens the heart," such that the "hardening of the heart is an event from which the prophet looks out into the future."[48] The passage from Isaiah 8:

> Bind up the testimony, seal the law among my disciples. And I will wait upon the Lord, that hideth his face from the house of Jacob, and I will look for him. Behold, I and the children whom the Lord hath given me are for signs and for wonders in Israel from the Lord of Hosts, which dwelleth in Mount Zion.

What Isaiah expresses here, according to von Rad, is that

> the fact that a prophet's word is not heard [in his own time] is far from meaning that this is the end of it. The message against which Jerusalem hardened its heart is to be written down [and sealed up] for a generation to come. At *that* time—such is Isaiah's meaning—all that had fallen on completely deaf ears in his own day and generation will be fulfilled. Absolutely everything in Isaiah points out into the future—even the saying about the hardening of Israel's heart which is the action of Jahweh himself.[49]

Von Rad's brilliant interpretation complicates the centrality of Isaiah 6 in Nephi's record. On this reading, Isaiah's induction into the divine council leads directly to a frustrating mission to the hard-hearted. But the impossibility of convincing his contemporaries leads Isaiah, it seems, to look to the future, and so to focus on writing, sealing, and burying prophetic texts—all this in anticipation of a later, prepared people who would unearth, unseal, and read those texts. Nephi, as focused as Isaiah on books written for later generations, places this Isaianic theme of the *written* alongside the Isaianic theme of angelicization at the center of the center of the center of his record. First Isaiah thus serves, for Nephi, as a source for thinking carefully about both (1) the possibility of apocalyptic experience (angelicization) and (2) the inevitable turn of the apocalyptic figure to a future covenant people only addressable through writing.[50]

What, though, of Second Isaiah? Nephi's interest seems principally focused on how Second Isaiah can be appropriated ("likened") to provide a template for the prophetically anticipated events of the (latter-day) restoration of the covenant people. But because those events are, for Nephi, to be set in motion by the emergence of sealed and buried books of scripture, there is a very close relationship between First and Second Isaiah. If First Isaiah traces the production and sealing up of books directed to a later people, Second Isaiah traces the recovery of and response to precisely those books. Second Isaiah, in a word, functions as a *response* to First Isaiah—as, in the end, a *reading* of First Isaiah.

This interpretation of the First Isaiah/Second Isaiah relationship has recently been offered by Edgar Conrad in his book *Reading Isaiah*. Conrad claims that his approach is itself suggested by the book of Isaiah through a connection between Isaiah 29 and Isaiah 40:

> In 40:6 a voice reiterates the command to read (*qr'*), a command that reflects the command to read in 29:11. The usual translation of the imperative in 40:6 is 'cry,' as in the RSV [and the KJV]. 'A voice says, "Cry!" And I said, "'What shall I cry?'" There is nothing wrong with this translation, but . . . what is to be called out aloud here is what is to be read out aloud. *To read is also to cry or call.*[51]

Conrad argues, perhaps not unlike Nephi, that Second Isaiah records the history of the redemption of those who return to First Isaiah, to the book written because its message was rejected in its own time. In Conrad, as in Nephi, the distinction between First and Second Isaiah is maintained even as a crucial relationship between them emerges. The two "halves" of Isaiah are, through the structure of prophecy-and-fulfillment, essentially intertwined.

I have already shown that, with First Isaiah, Nephi picks and chooses passages that concern his theology of writing. In dealing with Second Isaiah, however, Nephi appears less choosy. Rather than picking out this or that fitting text, Nephi simply begins with Isaiah 48 and then works through Second Isaiah chapter by chapter. Interestingly, what Nephi does not get to, later Nephite prophets take up—and in the order the texts appear in Second Isaiah:

> Isaiah 48–49 in 1 Nephi 20–21
> Isaiah 50–51 in 2 Nephi 7–8
> Isaiah 52–53 in Mosiah 12–14
> Isaiah 54–55 in 3 Nephi 22[52]

Thus, while Nephi, having dealt with the relevant passages necessary to outline the Nephite theology of writing, seems to exhaust Nephite interest in *First* Isaiah, he only whets his successors' appetites for *Second* Isaiah—providing only the first stretch of a Second Isaianic trajectory that forms the backbone of the Book of Mormon.

All of this clarifies the role of the *other* Isaiah chapters that find their way into Nephi's record. What, though, has any of this to say about the obvious textual break between First and Second Nephi? It is already clear that Nephi's detailed interpretation of *First* Isaiah is located entirely in the atonement portion of *Second* Nephi. It might further be noted that Nephi's systematic work on *Second* Isaiah is to be found more or less entirely within *First* Nephi. If this "distribution" of sorts (First Isaiah in Second Nephi; Second Isaiah in First Nephi) is intended, then it is possible to suggest that there are two distinct overarching structures at work in Nephi's larger record. On the one hand, there is the four-part structure that associates the record with the temple and its concerns. On the other hand, there is the two-part structure that compartmentalizes the intertwined treatment of Isaiah in Nephi's record. These two structures overlap and intertwine, particularly in their joint emphasis on the importance of Isaiah to Nephi's project. Whichever structure one decides to privilege at any given moment, it is always clear that to dismiss Isaiah is, in essence, to miss the whole point of Nephi's project.

With the details worked out in this chapter, it is possible now to turn directly to Nephi's explicit discussions of typology and, eventually, to a full investigation of what Nephi's take on typology has to say about how the Book of Mormon, according to the Book of Mormon itself, should be read. The theological insights culled in the course of this chapter—Nephi's interest in the fourfold pattern of creation, fall, atonement, and veil, the curious idea of angelicization, the Nephite theology of writing—will prove to be as important as the basic structural and exegetical points made.

Notes

1. Frederick W. Axelgard, "1 and 2 Nephi: An Inspiring Whole," *BYU Studies* 26.4 (Fall 1986): 54–55.

2. Ibid., 54. This way of subdividing the first division of Nephi's record seems to be confirmed by the fact that Nephi places the six-verse discussion of structure between the two subdivisions, that is, in the first verses of 1 Nephi 19.

3. This is universally overlooked in the commentaries. For a fascinating example of the difficulties that result from missing the apologetic nature of verses 5–6, see Gardner, *Second Witness*, 1:360.

4. Noel B. Reynolds, "The Political Dimension in Nephi's Small Plates," *BYU Studies* 27.4 (Fall 1987): 15. See also Noel B. Reynolds, "Nephi's Outline," in Noel B. Reynolds, ed., *Book of Mormon Authorship: New Light on Ancient Origins* (Provo, UT: FARMS, 1982), 53–74.

5. Noel B. Reynolds, "Nephite Kingship Reconsidered," in Davis Bitton, ed., *Mormons, Scripture, and the Ancient World: Studies in Honor of John L. Sorenson* (Provo, UT: FARMS, 1998), 155.

6. Ibid., 178–185.

7. Ibid., 154–155.

8. It is possible that the word "kept" in 1 Nephi 19:3, 5 should be interpreted as "protected" or "guarded." But this interpretation brings with it a whole host of other questions.

9. One might object here that the presence of the fourfold pattern of creation, fall, atonement, and veil in the first verse of First Nephi unsettles the case for Nephi's subsequent alteration of his project. This does not, however, necessarily follow. It is possible to find an admittedly somewhat looser fourfold structure in 1 Nephi 1–18 as well as in the larger project of First and Second Nephi (born of goodly parents: 1 Nephi 1–2; seen many afflictions: 1 Nephi 3–7; been highly favored of the Lord: 1 Nephi 8–10; had a knowledge of the mysteries: 1 Nephi 11–15, etc.). One might thus suggest that 1 Nephi 1:1 originally spelled out in advance not the fourfold structure of the whole of Nephi's record, but an originally projected pattern behind 1 Nephi 1–18, and that when Nephi changed directions so drastically after completing his first eighteen chapters, he effectively rerouted the anticipatory first verse of 1 Nephi 1 so that it described the fourfold structure of his larger record.

10. It is common in the Book of Mormon to connect the phrase "cut off from the presence of the Lord" with the fall of Adam and Eve. See 2 Nephi 9:6; Alma 42:6–7, 14; and Helaman 14:16.

11. Hugh W. Nibley, *Teachings of the Book of Mormon: Transcripts of Lectures Presented to an Honors Book of Mormon Class at Brigham Young University*, 1988–1990, 4 vols. (Provo, UT: FARMS, 1993), 1:17–18. In a vein still more speculative than the one followed above, one might moreover suggest that Nephi—given his Egyptian connections—makes an allusion with the last line of 1 Nephi 1:1 to the temple text of the Egyptian Book of the Dead, the title of which—*rʾw nw prt m hrw*—can be translated as "the book (or record) of going forth (proceeding) by day."

12. Jon E. Levenson, *Creation and the Persistence of Evil: The Jewish Drama of Divine Omnipotence* (Princeton: Princeton University Press, 1988), 153, emphases added for clarification.

13. Ibid., 50.

14. Ibid., 92.

15. Ibid., 24.

16. Ibid.

17. Barker's version of temple theology is, in spirit, basically the same as Levenson's. Both scholars base their understanding of temple theology in close readings of the priestly tradition (P document) of the Pentateuch. As such, both Barker and Levenson place strong emphasis on the significance of the cosmic covenant, on the privileged role of the waters of chaos, on the importance of the Hebrew word חקק, and so on. In short, both Levenson and Barker are focused on a Hebraic worldview concerned at once with "the vitality of evil and the fragility of creation." Ibid., 47. It is worth pointing out that Barker has drawn a good deal of attention from Latter-day Saints. See, for example, Kevin Christensen, *Paradigms Regained: A Survey of Margaret Barker's Scholarship and Its Significance for Mormon Studies* (Provo, UT: FARMS, 2001); and Margaret Barker, "Joseph Smith and Preexilic Israelite Religion," in John W. Welch, ed., *The Worlds of Joseph Smith: A Bicentennial Conference at the Library of Congress* (Provo, UT: *BYU* Studies, 2005), 69–82.

18. Margaret Barker, *Temple Theology: An Introduction* (London: SPCK, 2004). "Creation," "Covenant," "Atonement," and "Wisdom" are, interestingly, the titles of the four chapters of *Temple Theology*.

19. It is, I think, all the more striking for me, because I had been working with the creation/fall/atonement/veil interpretation of Nephi's record for several years before I came across Margaret Barker's work for the first time.

20. Holland, *Christ and the New Covenant*, 35–36.

21. Hugh W. Nibley, *Temple and Cosmos: Beyond This Ignorant Present* (Salt Lake City: Deseret Book and FARMS, 1992), 302.

22. Scott H. Faulring, Kent P. Jackson, and Robert J. Matthews, eds., *Joseph Smith's New Translation of the Bible: Original Manuscripts* (Provo, UT: Brigham Young University Religious Studies Center, 2004), 136.

23. Levenson, *Creation and the Persistence of Evil*, 139.

24. Ibid., 91, emphasis in original.

25. Margaret Barker, *The Great High Priest: The Temple Roots of Christian Liturgy* (New York: T&T Clark, 2003), 119.

26. Some commentators neglect verse 13 entirely. See George Reynolds and Janne M. Sjodahl, *Commentary on the Book of Mormon*, 7 vols. (Salt Lake City: Deseret Book, 1955), 1:429; Daniel H. Ludlow, *A Companion to Your Study of the Book of Mormon* (Salt Lake City: Deseret Book, 1976), 154; and Monte S. Nyman, *I Nephi Wrote This Record: Book of Mormon Commentary* (Orem, UT: Granite, 2004), 747. Most tie it to one form or another of the "gift of tongues." See McConkie and Millet, *Doctrinal Commentary on the Book of Mormon*, 1:369–370; Gardner, *Second Witness*, 2:451; and Nibley, *Teachings of the Book of Mormon*, 2:361–362.

27. Note that in 2 Nephi 31, Christ serves as a model or an example, precisely as Lehi serves in 1 Nephi 1. Note also that, according to Margaret Barker, "The belief that human beings, as a result of their mystical vision, were transformed into angels was . . . what the ancient religion of Israel had been saying for many centuries" by the time Christianity was born. Barker, *Great High Priest*, 6.

28. Nephi's selection (Isaiah 2–14) is somewhat odd. There is a natural break between chapters 12 and 13 of Isaiah, but chapters 13–14 are part of the larger Isaianic collection of the "Oracles against Foreign Nations." John Gee implicitly recognizes this in his brief commentary on "Nephi's Selection of Sections" when he argues that chapters 13–14 of Isaiah function as an antithetical parallel (highlighting Babylon) to chapters 2–12 (which highlight Zion). John Gee, "'Choose the Things That Please Me: On the Selection of the Isaiah Sections in the Book of Mormon," in Donald W. Parry and John W. Welch, eds., *Isaiah in the Book of Mormon* (Provo, UT: FARMS, 1998), 73–75.

29. Marvin A. Sweeney, *Isaiah 1–39* (Grand Rapids: Eerdmans, 1996), 140.

30. Brevard S. Childs, *Isaiah* (Louisville: Westminster John Knox Press, 2001), 57.

31. Victor Ludlow mentions a series of parallels between Isaiah's account and the modern temple experience. See Victor L. Ludlow, *Isaiah: Prophet, Seer, and Poet* (Salt Lake City: Deseret Book, 1982), 128–129. See also Stephen D. Ricks, "Heavenly Visions and Prophetic Calls in Isaiah 6 (2 Nephi 16), the Book of Mormon, and the Revelation of John," in *Isaiah in the Book of Mormon*, 171–190.

32. Grant Hardy outlines the difficulties of historicity presented by the quotations of Second Isaiah in the Book of Mormon. See Hardy, *Understanding the Book of Mormon*, 66–70. Historicity is, of course, not my concern here. But see Joseph M. Spencer, "Prolegomena to Any Future Study of Isaiah in the Book of Mormon," *Claremont Journal of Mormon Studies* 1.1 (April 2011): 53–69.

33. Walter Brueggemann, *Old Testament Theology: Essays on Structure, Theme, and Text* (Minneapolis: Fortress Press, 1992), 254.

34. Ronald E. Clements, "The Unity of the Book of Isaiah," *Interpretation* 36 (1982): 129.

35. Childs, *Isaiah*, 3. But cf. Joseph Blenkinsopp, *Isaiah 40–55: A New Translation with Introduction and Commentary* (New York: Doubleday, 2000), 55. Referring to Childs's earlier work on Isaiah (in *Introduction to the Old Testament as Scripture*), Blenkinsopp writes: "It seems that none of these rather tortuous conclusions necessarily follows from accepting chs. 40–55 as a canonical text. Whatever we decide about this particular case, a biblical book is not necessarily a well-thought-out, cohesive literary unity, and there is no need to make the book the only appropriate object of theological reflection."

36. See Christopher R. Seitz, "The One Isaiah // The Three Isaiahs," in Christopher R. Seitz, ed., *Reading and Preaching the Book of Isaiah* (Philadelphia: Fortress Press, 1988), 13–22.

37. I place emphasis on the word "theologically" here to avoid the question of how the Book of Mormon might weigh in on the question of Isaiah as a collection of historically disparate texts. Again, my concerns here are not historical, but theological.

38. John W. Welch, "Authorship of the Book of Isaiah in Light of the Book of Mormon," in *Isaiah in the Book of Mormon*, 432–433. Grant Hardy suggests in a footnote that part of 2 Nephi 28:32 might be a quotation of Isaiah 65:2, but though the ideas are perhaps parallel, the language is not. Grant Hardy, ed., *The Book of Mormon: A Reader's Edition* (Urbana: University of Illinois Press, 2003), 130. Three other possible references to Third Isaiah appear in the Book of Mormon: 1 Nephi 17:39; Helaman 14:27; and Ether 13:9. Since no Book of Mormon author attributes the roughly Third Isaianic phrases in these passages to Isaiah, none of them should be taken as proof positive that the Nephites had a copy of Third Isaiah. Moreover, the omission of Isaiah 1 in the Isaiah quotation of 2 Nephi 12–24 may suggest that the Nephites had no access to Third Isaiah. Since it "is now widely held that the concluding chapters of the book (65 and 66) are closely related to the first chapter," with "chapters 65–66 repeating almost fifty words from chapter 1," Isaiah 1 is generally recognized to be the product of the same author(s)/redactor(s) who created Third Isaiah. Childs, *Isaiah*, 3; Luis Alonso Schökel, "Isaiah," in Robert Alter and Frank Kermode, eds., *The Literary Guide to the Bible* (Cambridge: Belknap Press, 1987), 165.

39. Brevard S. Childs, *Introduction to the Old Testament as Scripture* (Philadelphia: Fortress Press, 1979), 329, argues that just such a text seems to have circulated at some point in Judah, though he of course places its creation after the time the Lehites would have left Jerusalem.

40. See, for example: Joseph Blenkinsopp, *Isaiah 1–39: A New Translation with Introduction and Commentary* (New York: Doubleday, 2000), 243; Childs, *Isaiah*, 218; Edgar W. Conrad, *Reading Isaiah* (Minneapolis: Fortress Press, 1991), 130–137; Otto Kaiser, *Isaiah 1–12: A Commentary*, trans. R. A. Wilson (Philadelphia: Westminster Press, 1972), 120; Hans Wildberger, *Isaiah 28–39: A Continental Commentary*, trans. Thomas H. Trapp (Minneapolis: Fortress Press, 2002), 75, 84.

41. I have left the difficult verse 13 out of the account here for simplicity's sake.

42. Childs, *Isaiah*, 56.

43. Gerhard von Rad, *Old Testament Theology*, 2 vols., trans. D. M. G. Stalker (New York: Harper & Row, 1962), 2:153.

44. Ibid., 2:154.

45. Ibid.

46. Ibid.

47. Ibid., 2:155. It should be noted that Latter-day Saint commentators have generally been uncomfortable with this approach. Thus some commentators have relied heavily for interpretive guidance on the difference between the King James Version of Isaiah 6:9–10 and the current (1981) rendering of the passage in the Book of Mormon: "The Book of Mormon clarifies these two difficult verses. It teaches that the people to whom Isaiah was sent would fail to understand his message of their own accord. The KJV implies that the Lord did not want them to understand." Nyman, *I, Nephi, Wrote This Record*, 522; see also Gardner, *Second Witness*, 1:244. Interesting and

uniquely Mormon as this approach might be, it ignores the work of Royal Skousen. In both the printer's manuscript and the first (1830) edition of the Book of Mormon, the two verses in question stand as they do in the KJV. The change that resulted in the current rendering seems to have been rooted in an attempt to make sense of difficulties introduced into the printer's manuscript by Oliver Cowdery. See Royal Skousen, *Analysis of Textual Variants of the Book of Mormon*, 6 vols. (Provo, UT: FARMS, 2004–2009), 2:697–699; and Royal Skousen, ed., *The Book of Mormon: The Earliest Text* (New Haven: Yale University Press, 2009), 115.

48. Von Rad, *Old Testament Theology*, 2:155.

49. Ibid., emphasis added.

50. This calls for a slight emendation of my earlier characterization of the oracles of Isaiah 7–14 (2 Nephi 17–24). It is less that the oracles against Assyria and Babylon outline the full restoration of the covenant people than that they outline the events through which the *possibility* of an eventual restoration was established through the writing and sealing up of texts to be recovered during those later events.

51. Conrad, *Reading Isaiah*, 137, emphasis added.

52. Things are actually more complicated than this. Full discussion of Second Isaiah's place in Mormon's editorial work will be taken up in detail in chapter 4.

3

Typology for Nephi: Theology

My intention in this chapter is to address directly Nephi's two discussions of typology. In light of the preceding chapter, it is clear that this task is complicated by the complex structure of Nephi's record. Because the relevant passages are positioned at either end of the "Isaiah chapters" of 2 Nephi 12–24, they (2 Nephi 11:4 and 2 Nephi 25:24–27) cannot be investigated independent of the role they play in helping structurally to set off Nephi's quotation of Isaiah 2–14. This in turn implies that they cannot be interpreted without an eye to the larger role that Isaiah plays in Nephi's record, preliminarily identified in chapter 2.

Consequently, what follows first in the present chapter is a discussion of the place of Second Isaiah in First Nephi, a discussion focused principally on determining exactly what Nephi means by "likening," since evidence suggests that Nephi draws a crucial distinction between likening and typological interpretation. Likening is, for Nephi, a way of reading Isaiah, one that takes the prophet's words to Israel as a template for making sense of Israel's historical experience—wherever Israel finds herself, the New World apparently included. This discussion is followed by a detailed analysis of how Nephi might have likened one Isaianic text in particular: Isaiah 51:9–10. Included in this analysis is a study of the famous story of Nephi's obtaining the brass plates from Laban. Nephi's relationship to the Law (in part worked out in the course of his likening of the Prophets) is thus preliminarily investigated. Finally, the chapter concludes with an examination of both passages directly focused on typology. It is only in the course of this last discussion that the difference, for Nephi, between typology and likening becomes fully clear:

while likening is, for Nephi, a strategy for reading the Prophets, typology is a strategy for interpreting the Law. But whereas likening is a question of taking the prophetic text to provide a template for making sense of Israel's historical experience, typology is a question of understanding the Law through its structurally implied fulfillment. The real stakes of this approach to typology will not, unfortunately, be clarified until Abinadi's approach has also been discussed.

First Nephi, Second Isaiah

Several commentators have suggested that 1 Nephi 10 has a privileged role in First Nephi, both at the exegetical and theological levels.[1] First, 1 Nephi 10 marks the transition from Nephi's abridgment of his father's record (1 Nephi 1–9) to his own account (1 Nephi 10–22). Second, 1 Nephi 10 provides the earliest account of the Nephite understanding of the history of Israel, as well as the earliest version of Nephite Christology. This curious chapter thus lays out in almost maddening brevity the basic contours of Nephite theology. And, crucially, it turns on the interpretation of a vital passage from Second Isaiah.

According to Nephi, Lehi delivered the sermon recorded in 1 Nephi 10 just after he recounted his dream of the tree of life: "For behold, it came to pass after my father had made an end of speaking the words of his dream, and also of exhorting [Laman and Lemuel] to all diligence, he spake unto them concerning the Jews" (1 Nephi 10:2). Lehi begins his remarks by pointing out Jerusalem's wickedness and announcing anew the imminent exile to Babylon.[2] The Jews are to "be destroyed, even that great city Jerusalem, and many should be carried away captive into Babylon" (1 Nephi 10:3). Interested in moving past the sad destruction of the city to later events, Lehi then explains that after the exile, the Jews will "return again, yea, even be brought back out of captivity" so as to "possess again the land of their inheritance"—all this "according to the own due time of the Lord" (1 Nephi 10:3).

Having set the postexilic stage, Lehi populates it with two characters: (1) "a prophet" identified as the "Messiah" or the "Savior of the world" (1 Nephi 10:4), and (2) "a prophet who should come *before* the Messiah, to prepare the way of the Lord" (1 Nephi 10:7). These two characters meet in what proves to be for Nephi a central scene. The second-mentioned but first-arriving prophet (the preparer) would baptize the first-mentioned but second-arriving prophet (the Messiah) with water (1 Nephi 10:9). Nephi twice returns to this scene in his writings—first in describing his own vision of the same event (1 Nephi 11); second in the last chapters of his record (2 Nephi 31). Significantly, in 1 Nephi 11 an angelic guide heavily emphasizes the importance of the baptismal sequence, identifying it as *the* event marking "the condescension of God" (1 Nephi 11:26–27).[3] 2 Nephi 31 in turn takes the same scene as the starting point for developing a full-blown "doctrine of Christ" (2 Nephi 31:4). It is thus clear that this postexilic encounter at Bethabara is both historically and doctrinally important for Nephi.

What might be missed, though, is the fact that the description of this event in 1 Nephi 10 draws on a passage from Second Isaiah. When Lehi says that the "prophet who should come before the Messiah" will come specifically "to prepare the way of the Lord" (1 Nephi 10:7), he alludes (if not directly refers) to Isaiah 40:3. The text from Isaiah: "The voice of him that crieth in the wilderness, Prepare ye the way of the Lord, make straight in the desert a highway for our God." The Isaianic tie becomes even clearer in 1 Nephi 10:8: "Yea, even he should go forth and cry in the wilderness: Prepare ye the way of the Lord, and make his paths straight." Some conscious connection is at work here.

One might object that 1 Nephi 10:7–8 seems more directly to draw from the New Testament, from a passage that in turn draws on Isaiah 40:3. But such an approach would have to take 1 Nephi 10 to be drawing on *both* the synoptic tradition (that is, on Matthew, Mark, and/or Luke) *and* the Johannine tradition (that is, on John).[4] On the one hand, the rendering of Isaiah 40:3 in 1 Nephi 10:7–8 is identical to that of Matthew 3:3, Mark 1:3, and Luke 3:4 (and different, significantly, from that of John 1:23). But, on the other hand, the remainder of 1 Nephi 10:8 ("for there standeth one among you whom ye know not; and he is mightier than I, whose shoe's latchet I am not worthy to unloose") is identical to John 1:26–27 (but different, significantly, from Matthew 3:11; Mark 1:7; and Luke 3:16). A comparison of the passages makes this clear (italics marking synoptic sources and bold marking Johannine sources):

1 Ne. 10:8	Matt. 3:3, 11	Mark 1:3, 7	Luke 3:4, 16	John 1:23, 26–27
Yea, even he should go forth and cry in the wilderness: *Prepare ye the way of the Lord, and make his paths straight;* for **there standeth one among you whom ye know not; and he is mightier than I, whose shoe's latchet I am not worthy to unloose.** And much spake my father concerning this thing.	For this is he that was spoken of by the prophet Esaias, saying, The voice of one crying in the wilderness, *Prepare ye the way of the Lord, make his paths straight. . . .* [And John said:] I indeed baptize you with water unto repentance: but he that cometh after me is mightier than I, whose shoes I am not worthy to bear: he shall baptize you with the Holy Ghost, and with fire.	The voice of one crying in the wilderness, *Prepare ye the way of the Lord, make his paths straight. . . .* And [John] preached, saying, There cometh one mightier than I after me, the latchet of whose shoes I am not worthy to stoop down and unloose.	As it is written in the book of the words of Esaias the prophet, saying, The voice of one crying in the wilderness, *Prepare ye the way of the Lord, make his paths straight. . . .* John answered, saying unto them all, I indeed baptize you with water; but one mightier than I cometh, the latchet of whose shoes I am not worthy to unloose: he shall baptize you with the Holy Ghost and with fire.	He said, I am the voice of one crying in the wilderness, Make straight the way of the Lord, as said the prophet Esaias. . . . John answered them, saying, I baptize with water: but **there standeth one among you, whom ye know not; He it is, who coming after me is preferred before me, whose shoe's latchet I am not worthy to unloose.**

This interweaving of distinct sources into a single "quotation" is complex enough to problematize any direct tracing to the New Testament sources. And even if the *language* of 1 Nephi 10:7–8 ultimately derives from New Testament texts, it cannot be doubted that the *source* behind Lehi's words is ultimately Isaiah 40:3. However one approaches the problem of *translation* (or of *anachronistic language*), the fact that 1 Nephi 10:8 draws on Isaiah 40:3 cannot be controverted—even if the reference to Isaiah passes through the linguistic medium of the New Testament idiom.[5]

What, then, of Lehi's interest in Second Isaiah? And in particular, what of the allusion's being placed at the point of transition from abridged narrative to Nephi's account of his own experiences and his first words regarding Christology? Interestingly, Isaiah 40:3 is situated at a point of transition not only in First Nephi, but also in Isaiah. Following four chapters (Isaiah 36–39) that were, according to Brevard Childs, "intentionally inserted between First and Second Isaiah" and then "edited in such a way as to [make First Isaiah] anticipate the Babylonian exile,"[6] the first verses of Isaiah 40 *are* the transition from the devastating prophecies of First Isaiah to the comforting words of Second Isaiah.

Moreover, Isaiah 40—beginning particularly with verse 3—transitions from First to Second Isaiah specifically by restaging the prophet's encounter with the divine council portrayed in Isaiah 6. As Frank Moore Cross summarily puts it, the "parallel" between Isaiah 6 and Isaiah 40 "is remarkable."[7] Childs clarifies: "Chapter 40 does not offer a *new* independent call narrative, but rather provides a *reapplication* of [Isaiah 6]. . . . [T]he point of the prologue [in Isaiah 40] is the announcement of a divine decision that now reverses the commission of judgment assigned to Isaiah [in Isaiah 6:9–12]."[8] All of this means that the plainest reading of Isaiah 40:3—*as* the passage stands in the canonical setting of Isaiah 2–55—presents the figure Lehi identifies with the Messiah's baptizer as a kind of "Isaiah reconfigured," as an Isaiah turned from announcing destruction to the people of one era to announcing redemption to the people of a later era. Lehi, like the evangelists, takes the passage as referring to the work of John the Baptist, whom Lehi seems to have seen in vision. But Lehi is more explicit than the New Testament authors in that he does not see the passage simply as an isolated prophecy of a New Testament event. Instead, placing the appearance of the Baptist—*and* the Messiah—within the context of the exile and the return, he makes clear that he sees the New Testament events as being particularly poignant fulfillments of exactly what (Second) Isaiah had predicted about the overcoming of the Babylonian exile.

This approach to Second Isaiah, attributed to Lehi in 1 Nephi 10, is mirrored later in 1 Nephi 15. Here, in the course of reporting his attempt to explain to his brothers the meaning of their father's sermon from 1 Nephi 10, Nephi makes another passing reference to (presumably Second) Isaiah.[9] Effectively dividing the discussion concerning Lehi's sermon in two, Nephi steps away from direct dialogue to note editorially: "I did rehearse unto them the words of Isaiah, who spake concerning the restoration of the Jews, or of the house of Israel" (1 Nephi 15:20).[10] Though he provides his readers with no details, Nephi suggests here that he found it easiest to clarify Lehi's words concerning Israel's future by, like Lehi, quoting and expositing Isaiah's writings.

This return to Second Isaiah in 1 Nephi 15 sets up what exegetes call an *inclusio* that frames the whole of 1 Nephi 10–15. Opening and closing these collective chapters are the references to Second Isaiah. And Latter-day Saint scholars have not entirely overlooked the importance of the centralization, as early as 1 Nephi 10–15, of Nephi's emphasis on Isaiah. Garold Davis, for instance, reads 1 Nephi 10—Lehi's exposition of Isaiah 40:3—as laying out the basic pattern for *all* of Nephi's subsequent commentaries on (Second) Isaiah.[11] At any rate, it seems clear that 1 Nephi 10 and 1 Nephi 15 provide early if only sketchy formulations of the Lehite/Nephite understanding of Israel's covenantal history, always mediated through Second Isaiah. And, of course, more expansive—but similar—formulations follow in 1 Nephi 19–22 and 2 Nephi 6–8.

1 Nephi 19–22 deserves particular attention. In chapter 2, I raised the possibility that Nephi originally intended only to write what is now 1 Nephi 1–18. On that reading, Nephi's original project would have made only two brief references to Isaiah's writings, those in 1 Nephi 10 and 15. Given that 1 Nephi 19–22—the first chapters added to the apparently original project—are so heavily focused on Isaiah, it is possible that part of what motivated Nephi's change in direction after 1 Nephi 18 was guided by his recognition that he needed to give Isaiah's writings a more prominent role, expanding on the references of 1 Nephi 10 and 15. In short, it is possible that Nephi's original project only passingly footnoted Isaiah, and had reference only to *Second* Isaiah, while Nephi's expanded project, first envisioned about the time he completed 1 Nephi 1–18, was meant to make Isaiah—and eventually *First* Isaiah as much as Second Isaiah—absolutely central to the record he was producing. At any rate, it is only with the concluding chapters of First Nephi that Isaiah begins to take center stage.

Likening

The emergence of Second Isaiah into the limelight is curious. Immediately following 1 Nephi 19:1–6—the passage that details the basic structure of Nephi's perhaps newly revamped project—Nephi fills out the remainder of 1 Nephi 19 by weaving together a whole series of quotations from the brass plates in a kind of systematization of Nephite Christology. Though Isaiah's name goes unmentioned, he *is* quoted (1 Nephi 19:17 quotes Isaiah 52:10).[12] More importantly, when Nephi comes to the end of his Christology, he explicitly mentions Isaiah: "that I might more fully persuade [my brothers] to believe in the Lord their Redeemer *I did read unto them that which was written by the prophet Isaiah;* for I did liken all scriptures unto us, that it might be for our profit and learning" (1 Nephi 19:23). Here, not only does Nephi identify Isaiah as his source for the development of a full-blown doctrine of the Redeemer,[13] but he provides what is his first and by far most-cited account of how he reads Isaiah. The passage deserves detailed discussion.

The passage serves as an introduction to chapters 20–22. A transition to Nephi's quotation of and commentary on Isaiah 48–49 (1 Nephi 20–22) follows immediately.[14] The transition is worth quoting in full, especially because it repeats what Nephi says about how he reads Isaiah:

> Wherefore I spake unto them, saying: Hear ye the words of the prophet, ye who are a remnant of the house of Israel, a branch who have been broken off; hear ye the words of the prophet, which were written unto all the house of Israel, *and liken them unto yourselves,* that ye may have hope as well as your brethren from whom ye have been broken off; for after this manner has the prophet written. (1 Nephi 19:24)

Obviously, the operative methodological term here is "liken." It is one of the most commented-on words in the Book of Mormon. But little rigorous analysis has been given to it. Instead, the methodology it describes (or prescribes) is always *assumed,* as if it were perfectly obvious what it means to "liken" a text to oneself.[15] The term, however, is hardly self-explanatory.

The word "liken" appears often enough in the King James Bible. Jesus himself frequently uses it in the Gospels, generally when beginning a parable. More immediately relevant, though, and for obvious reasons, is the fact that the word appears several times in the King James Version of Second Isaiah. In all three instances (Isaiah 40:18, 25; 46:5), the word appears in rhetorical questions asked by the Lord to underscore the incomparability of God: "To whom then will ye liken me?" Interestingly, though, the Hebrew word here translated as "liken" can also be translated as "think" or "project."[16] The root of the word nonetheless denotes likeness or similarity in appearance,[17] but—indicating an act of sketching out or projecting—the verb is more creative than receptive.

Assuming some continuity between Second Isaiah's and Nephi's usage of the word "liken" (given that Second Isaiah is precisely what Nephi likens), to liken would be to give shape to something through a predetermined likeness. Thus, to liken Isaiah would be to take Isaiah's writings as a template for creatively interpreting something non-Isaianic, to employ an "Isaianic framework."[18]

Also important is the fact that in both verses 23 and 24 of 1 Nephi 19, Nephi speaks only of likening Isaiah's writings to a *group* of people, not to individual persons: "I did liken all scriptures unto *us*"; "liken them unto *yourselves*." This focus on likening a text to a whole people (rather than to individuals) is confirmed in every other instance of the word in Nephi's writings: "the Lord God will proceed to do a marvelous work . . . which shall be of great worth unto *our seed*; wherefore, it is likened unto *their* being nourished by the Gentiles" (1 Nephi 22:8); "The words which I shall read are they which Isaiah spake concerning *all the house of Israel*; wherefore, *they may be likened unto you, for ye are of the house of Israel*" (2 Nephi 6:5); "I, Nephi, write more of the words of Isaiah, for . . . *I will liken his words unto my people*, and I will send them forth unto *all my children*" (2 Nephi 11:2); "I write some of the words of Isaiah. . . . Now these are the words, and *ye may liken them unto you and unto all men*" (2 Nephi 11:8). All these examples—striking in their consistency—make clear that likening is for Nephi an interpretive approach founded on collective rather than individual experience. In other words, Isaiah's writings can be likened to Nephi's people less because everyone can find meaning in "applying them to everyday life" than because (1) Isaiah was writing about Israel as a people, and (2) the Nephites were collectively an Israelite people.

What, though, of typology? Indeed, in all this analysis of Nephi's manner of reading Isaiah, nothing has yet been said about typology—unless, that is, one presumes that likening *is* Nephi's typological method. But it is important to step carefully here. There is, as yet, no reason to conflate likening with typology. Indeed, I will argue later that there is an essential distinction for Nephi between likening and typology. For the moment, though, it is necessary—in order to put a finer point on what Nephi means by "likening"—to take up in more detail actual examples of Nephi's work of likening.

The Culmination of First Nephi

Returning, then, to Nephi's quotation of Isaiah 48–49, it should be noted that, in light of a basic consensus of interpretation among Isaiah scholars,

Nephi's launching of the Second Isaiah trajectory in the Book of Mormon specifically with Isaiah 48 is peculiar, and for two reasons. First, as Joseph Blenkinsopp explains, Isaiah 48 "is beset by more problems and subject to more diverse interpretations than any of the eight [chapters] that precede it," in part because it is characterized by a "denunciation of a severity encountered nowhere else in chs. 40–55."[19] That is, in the words of Claus Westermann, "These words harshly accusing Israel occur in an utterance in which they seem to have no place—this is the real difficulty."[20] Second, as Blenkinsopp again explains:

> Most commentators agree that chs. 40–48, which are bracketed with their own inclusive passage (48:20–22 cf. 40:3–5), form a section that is quite different in theme and tone from 49–55 in which we hear no more about Cyrus and the fall of Babylon, and no more satire is directed against foreign deities and their devotees. In 40–48 the focus is on Jacob/Israel, while in 49–55 Jerusalem/Zion is in the foreground.[21]

Consequently, Nephi's choice to begin his quotation of Second Isaiah with Isaiah 48 rather than, say, Isaiah 49 is odd—particularly because he clearly pairs Isaiah 48 (the strange end of the first half of Second Isaiah, chapters 40–48) with Isaiah 49 (the obvious beginning of the second half of Second Isaiah, chapters 49–55) by quoting them together in 1 Nephi 20–21. What sense can be made of this?

Nephi's selection may have its own crucial logic. Blenkinsopp himself frames the division between Isaiah 40–48 and Isaiah 49–55 by pointing to the textual connection between Isaiah 40:3–5 and Isaiah 48:20–22. And not only does the second of these two passages appear in 1 Nephi 20, the first appears in 1 Nephi 10, as discussed above. In other words, the very two passages that set up the inclusive boundaries of the first half of Second Isaiah are to be found in First Nephi, with no quotation of Isaiah to be found between them. One might therefore suggest that Nephi employs Isaiah 48 in 1 Nephi 20 precisely in order to echo the quotation of Isaiah 40:3 in 1 Nephi 10, almost as if by this move Nephi intended to include the whole of Isaiah 40–48—though with a major ellipsis—in 1 Nephi 10–20.

What, though, of the harsh denunciations of Isaiah 48, mentioned by both Blenkinsopp and Westermann? As it turns out, Nephi uses them to good effect, even if they seem "out of place" in Second Isaiah. Quoting the chapter in a discourse to his rebellious brothers and likely in order to critique harshly the people of Jerusalem, Nephi seems to find that Isaiah 48 fits his concerns. As Brevard Childs points out, whereas Isaiah 40–47 "focuse[s] on the promised deliverance of Israel, announced in prophecy and about to be fulfilled," Isaiah 48 "addresses the issue of Israel's unfaithful response to the promises, and challenges Israel to obedience in order to share in the promised salvation."[22] Nephi might well have drawn on Isaiah 48 *without* Isaiah 40–47 precisely to isolate for his own purposes the chapter's harsh message. At any rate, it is easy to see the last verses of Isaiah 48 as echoing the Lehite experience:

> Go ye forth of Babylon [Jerusalem?], flee ye from the Chaldeans, with a voice of singing declare ye, tell this, utter to the end of the earth; say ye: The Lord hath redeemed his servant Jacob [Lehi?]. And they thirsted not; he led them through the deserts [to Bountiful?]; he caused the waters to flow out of the rock for them; he clave the rock also and the waters gushed out. (1 Nephi 20:20–21)

Moreover, a still more negative word—one that, as Childs puts it, "casts a shadow on the celebration of deliverance"[23]—immediately follows these two verses that so clearly echo the deliverance of the Lehite exodus. It perfectly addresses, in Nephi's deft handling, his brothers' continued rebellion: "And notwithstanding [the Lord] hath done all this [for the Lehites as much as for Israel?], and greater also, there is no peace, saith the Lord, unto the wicked [Laman and Lemuel?]" (1 Nephi 20:22).[24]

As it turns out, it may be significant that these verses (along with Isaiah 40:3–5)[25] appear to be connected with the Lehite exodus. Kent Brown has analyzed the possibility that Nephi cited Isaiah 48–49 in 1 Nephi 20–21 precisely because of how the Isaiah text reflects the family's passage through the desert.[26] In fact, Brown lists *sixteen* connections between the Lehite wilderness journey and the text of Isaiah 48–49, some connections stronger than others:

Passage	Text	Referent
1 Nephi 20:1–2	Hearken and hear this, O house of Jacob, who are called by the name of Israel, and are come forth out of the waters of Judah, or out of the waters of baptism, who swear by the name of the Lord, and make mention of the God of Israel, yet they swear not in truth nor in righteousness. Nevertheless, they call themselves of the holy city, but they do not stay themselves upon the God of Israel, who is the Lord of Hosts; yea, the Lord of Hosts is his name.	The Lehites leave Jerusalem because of the wickedness prevailing there.

PASSAGE	TEXT	REFERENT
1 NEPHI 20:8–9	Yea, and thou heardest not; yea, thou knewest not; yea, from that time thine ear was not opened; for I knew that thou wouldst deal very treacherously, and wast called a transgressor from the womb. Nevertheless, for my name's sake will I defer mine anger, and for my praise will I refrain from thee, that I cut thee not off.	The Lord forgives Laman and Lemuel on the journey for his own reasons.
1 NEPHI 20:10–11	For, behold, I have refined thee, I have chosen thee in the furnace of affliction. For mine own sake, yea, for mine own sake will I do this, for I will not suffer my name to be polluted, and I will not give my glory unto another.	The desert experience refined Nephi.
1 NEPHI 20:14	All ye, assemble yourselves, and hear; who among them hath declared these things unto them? The Lord hath loved him; yea, and he will fulfil his word which he hath declared by them; and he will do his pleasure on Babylon, and his arm shall come upon the Chaldeans.	Jerusalem would be destroyed by Babylon.
1 NEPHI 20:17	And thus saith the Lord, thy Redeemer, the Holy One of Israel; I have sent him, the Lord thy God who teacheth thee to profit, who leadeth thee by the way thou shouldst go, hath done it.	The Lehites were led in their desert travels.
1 NEPHI 20:18	O that thou hadst hearkened to my commandments—then had thy peace been as a river, and thy righteousness as the waves of the sea.	Lehi composed poems making similar comparisons.
1 NEPHI 20:19	Thy seed also had been as the sand; the offspring of thy bowels like the gravel thereof; his name should not have been cut off nor destroyed from before me.	Nephi received promises concerning his seed.
1 NEPHI 20:20	Go ye forth of Babylon, flee ye from the Chaldeans, with a voice of singing declare ye, tell this, utter to the end of the earth; say ye: The Lord hath redeemed his servant Jacob.	Again, Jerusalem would be destroyed by Babylon.

Passage	Text	Referent
1 Nephi 20:21	And they thirsted not; he led them through the deserts; he caused the waters to flow out of the rock for them; he clave the rock also and the waters gushed out.	The Lehites were guided/protected.
1 Nephi 21:1	And again: Hearken, O ye house of Israel, all ye that are broken off and are driven out because of the wickedness of the pastors of my people; yea, all ye that are broken off, that are scattered abroad, who are of my people, O house of Israel. Listen, O isles, unto me, and hearken ye people from far; the Lord hath called me from the womb; from the bowels of my mother hath he made mention of my name.	The Lehites were driven out of Jerusalem because of the wickedness of its leaders.
1 Nephi 21:10	They shall not hunger nor thirst, neither shall the heat nor the sun smite them; for he that hath mercy on them shall lead them, even by the springs of water shall he guide them.	Again, the Lehites were guided/protected.
1 Nephi 21:13	Sing, O heavens; and be joyful, O earth; for the feet of those who are in the east shall be established; and break forth into singing, O mountains; for they shall be smitten no more; for the Lord hath comforted his people, and will have mercy upon his afflicted.	The Lehites traveled eastward on their way to the promised land.
1 Nephi 21:17	Thy children shall make haste against thy destroyers; and they that made thee waste shall go forth of thee.	The Lehites were protected from robbers.
1 Nephi 21:19–21	For thy waste and thy desolate places, and the land of thy destruction, shall even now be too narrow by reason of the inhabitants; and they that swallowed thee up shall be far away. The children whom thou shalt have, after thou hast lost the first, shall again in thine ears say: The place is too strait for me; give place to me that I may dwell. Then shalt	Brown explores the possibility that the Lehites served in captivity for a time during their travels. He even

Passage	Text	Referent
	thou say in thine heart: Who hath begotten me these, seeing I have lost my children, and am desolate, a captive, and removing to and fro? And who hath brought up these? Behold, I was left alone; these, where have they been?	suggests that the reference to children in captivity here might refer to Jacob and Joseph.
1 Nephi 21:22–23	Thus saith the Lord God: Behold, I will lift up mine hand to the Gentiles, and set up my standard to the people; and they shall bring thy sons in their arms, and thy daughters shall be carried upon their shoulders. And kings shall be thy nursing fathers, and their queens thy nursing mothers; they shall bow down to thee with their face towards the earth, and lick up the dust of thy feet; and thou shalt know that I am the Lord; for they shall not be ashamed that wait for me.	The Lehites would be gathered again.
1 Nephi 21:25	But thus saith the Lord, even the captives of the mighty shall be taken away, and the prey of the terrible shall be delivered; for I will contend with him that contendeth with thee, and I will save thy children.	The Lehites were delivered out of their afflictions into the promised land.

These connections are not surprising, since Second Isaiah "used the imagery of *a new exodus* to present the coming of a new eschatological age that would occur simultaneously with the deliverance of Israel from Babylon."[27] Thus any use of Second Isaiah in First Nephi might be tied to a larger attempt on Nephi's part to compare his family's journey to the ancient Israelite exodus.

Here it might be productive to turn to George Tate's study, mentioned in chapter 1, on the exodus pattern in the Book of Mormon. After citing studies of the importance of the exodus traditions to authors of biblical texts, Tate states his first point bluntly: "The Book of Mormon opens with an exodus."[28] And this fact, according to Tate, is not accidental: "Nephi is keenly aware of his distinct moment in history," and he "senses that he and his family are reenacting a sacred and symbolic pattern that looks back to Israel and forward to Christ—the pattern of Exodus."[29] Tate then carefully compares the exodus traditions and the story of First Nephi:

> Notice how many details of the early narrative conform to this pattern. Nephi and his family depart out of Jerusalem into the wilderness, "deliver[ed] . . . from destruction" (1 Ne. 17:14). In what might be called a paschal vision—referring fifty-six times to the Lamb (Lamb of God, blood of the Lamb, etc.)—Nephi's interpretive revelation on his father's dream recalls the Passover lamb of Exodus as it figures Christ (chs. 11–15). While a pillar of light rested upon a rock, Lehi had been warned to flee; and the Lord now provides miraculous guidance in the form of a compass-ball, the Liahona, and assures them, "I will also be your light in the wilderness; and I will prepare the way before you" (1 Ne. 1:6; 16:10; 17:13). When the family begins to murmur from hunger as had the Israelites before receiving manna, Nephi obtains food miraculously at the Lord's direction (see 1 Ne. 16:23, 31). He repeatedly receives instruction from the Lord on a mountain (see 1 Ne. 16:30; 17:7) and builds a ship not "after the manner of men; but . . . after the manner which the Lord had shown unto me"; just as Moses had received the design for the tabernacle (see 1 Ne. 18:1–3; Exod. 26). . . . Nephi and his family bear with them a sacred text, the plates of Laban, containing the law of Moses in the Pentateuch, and other prophets including Isaiah (see 1 Ne. 5:11, 13, 23). The Lord had promised them: "Inasmuch as ye shall keep my commandments ye shall be led towards the promised land; and ye shall know that it is by me that ye are led" (1 Ne. 17:13). And indeed the party crosses the ocean and reaches this land of promise, learning after their arrival that Jerusalem has been destroyed (see 2 Ne. 6:8).[30]

Tate goes on, however, to explain: "Though the correspondences between the exodus of the Israelites and this exodus are compelling, Nephi's conscious sense of reenacting the pattern is even more striking."[31] On Tate's reading, Nephi *purposefully* sets up the parallel between Laman and Lemuel and the "recalcitrant Israelites before them."[32] And it is striking that, "after describing the prosperity of the people in the new land, [Nephi] ends his account by noting that forty years have passed since their departure from Jerusalem (see 2 Ne. 5:34)."[33]

But here an unanticipated, subtle difficulty has crept in. Kent Brown's interpretation of Nephi's likening of Second Isaiah—strengthened by Tate's account of Nephi's interest in the exodus theme—turns from what Nephi himself identifies as his focus on *eschatological* (future) covenantal history to a focus on *current* (present) experiential history. In other words, rather than taking Nephi to be employing Isaiah in an attempt *to look out onto the future gathering of Israel,* Brown takes him to be reading Isaiah *to make sense of the experiences of his own life.* It is tempting simply to take Nephi's word against Brown's, especially because the latter's interpretations are, in the end, speculative—that is, Brown guesses about what interests Nephi in Second Isaiah. But one should not be so quick to abandon Brown's speculative insight. He makes, in the end, a strong case, especially in light of Tate's (and others') studies of exodus themes in Nephi's record.

How, then, might this tangle between Brown and Nephi be sorted out? To clarify this point, I will take up Brown's speculative point of view and look at another example of a Second Isaiah text quoted in Nephi's record. This example will, I believe, show that Nephi and Brown are actually reconcilable and, further, it will also make it possible to distinguish likening from typology, as Nephi understood these terms.

Nephi and the Law

The text I want to take up is Isaiah 51:9–10 (quoted in 2 Nephi 8:9–10):

> Awake, awake, put on strength, O arm of the Lord; awake, as in the ancient days, in the generations of old. Art thou not it that hath cut Rahab, and wounded the dragon? Art thou not it which hath dried the sea, the waters of the great deep; that hath made the depths of the sea a way for the ransomed to pass over?

Westermann notes by way of commentary: "God's act in creation" (the slaying of the dragon) is "put together with his salvation at the Red Sea" (making the waters a pathway), which suggests that in Second Isaiah "the way of the redeemed" is, for Israel, "now not only in the far past, but also in the immediate future."[34] But precisely because this passage roots the exodus experience (escape into the desert) in "an ancient creation myth in which the dragon who was the primeval waters was defeated" (decapitation of the primeval foe),[35] Nephi might have seen here an echo of his own most harrowing experience: the encounter with Laban.

Nephi's killing of Laban is justly famous. Immediately after his conversion to Lehi's prophetic claims, Nephi is commanded to retrieve the brass plates from the apparently wealthy and unquestionably powerful Laban—a task he only accomplishes, in the end, by decapitating Laban in a Jerusalem street. The story has raised serious ethical questions for many readers, and a number of able scholars have ventured their interpretations of the experience, ranging from John Welch's legal defense of Nephi's actions to Eugene England's theological wrestle with the story.[36] However, I will suspend ethical questions while reading the narrative in order to highlight its relevance to Nephi's relationship to Isaiah.[37] My approach is thus akin to readings offered by Steve Olsen, Gordon Thomasson, Brett Holbrook, and Ben McGuire, all of whom have set aside ethical questions to focus on a more strictly narratological interpretation.[38] However, instead of Mosaic ritual (Thomasson), ancient Near Eastern culture (Holbrook), or Hebrew royal narratives (McGuire), I will look at how the story Nephi tells plays into and complicates the relationship between First Nephi and Second Isaiah.

The basic connection is simple: Laban echoes the dragon of Isaiah 51:9–10, the figure of Rahab who is *cut* to allow the ransomed to escape into the desert. Interestingly, in both the Lehite and the ancient Israelite exodus stories, this cutting makes possible the reception of the Law (of Moses). Indeed, both the Lehites and the Israelites are described as having traveled "three days" in the wilderness (see Exodus 3:18; 5:3; 8:27; 1 Nephi 2:6) before camping at the place from which their leading figure would have to "go up" to retrieve the Law (see Exodus 19:3, 20; 1 Nephi 3:9, 29). These parallels are striking and, in the end, more important than all other parallels between the two exoduses: front and center is the Law of Moses.

Commandments and Covenant

The story of Laban's death begins, not in 1 Nephi 3 when the commandment to return to Jerusalem is first issued, but rather in 1 Nephi 2 when Nephi—feeling "great desires to know of the mysteries of God"—receives in response to his prayers a full-blown revelation from God. It is in this first conversation with the Lord that Nephi learns of the crucial Lehitic covenant that undergirds the entirety of Nephi's record: "inasmuch as ye shall keep my commandments, ye shall prosper, and shall be led to a land of promise" (1 Nephi 2:20). With this communication, the central theme of the subsequent narrative is set. It will be a question, from start to finish, of *commandment*.

Crucially, though, Nephi could not have even guessed what commandments were indicated by the covenant at first. In the beginning, he seems naturally to have taken the covenant to refer abstractly to *whatever* God happened to command at any particular moment. A crucial anxiety thus inevitably attended Nephi's earliest divine encounter, and Nephi's subsequent zeal—the constant source of tension between Nephi and his brothers—seems largely to have been a reflection of this anxiety.

This is clear from the moment Nephi receives word that he would be returning to Jerusalem. The anxiety associated with the vagueness of the covenant's conditions is suddenly transformed into an intense release of energy when Nephi returns from his revelatory experience to be confronted with a specified commandment to retrieve the brass plates. Importantly, Nephi portrays Lehi as using the word "commandment" three times in his commission:

> Behold I have dreamed a dream, in the which the Lord hath *commanded* me that thou and thy brethren shall return to Jerusalem. For behold, Laban hath the record of the Jews and also a genealogy of my forefathers, and they are engraven upon plates of brass. Wherefore, the Lord hath *commanded* me that thou and thy brothers should go unto the house of Laban, and seek the records, and bring them down hither into the wilderness. And now, behold thy brothers murmur, saying it is a hard thing which I have required of them; but behold I have not required it of them, but it is a *commandment* of the Lord. Therefore go, my son, and thou shalt be favored of the Lord, because thou hast not murmured. (1 Nephi 3:2–6)

Nephi then, in his exuberant response, matches Lehi's triple use of the word "commandment":

> And it came to pass that I, Nephi, said unto my father: I will go and do the things which the Lord hath *commanded*, for I know that the Lord giveth no *commandments* unto the children of men, save he shall prepare a way for them that they may accomplish the thing which he *commandeth* them. (1 Nephi 3:7)

This matching up of threefold mentions of "commandments" in commission and response cannot be accidental, especially after the covenantal privileging of the word in 1 Nephi 2:20. It marks a kind of zealous fixation from the beginning of the narrative: the whole story of the return to Jerusalem will be about the question of the commandments.

Unsurprisingly, the narrative itself is punctuated by consistently repeated references to "the commandments." When the first, relatively naïve attempt at retrieving the brass plates fails (Laman simply asks for them) and most of the group is ready to return to camp, Nephi "commits" his brothers to their task by delivering a sermon on, precisely, commandments: "But behold I said unto them that: As the Lord liveth, and as we live, we will not go down unto our father in the wilderness until we have accomplished the thing which the Lord hath *commanded* us" (1 Nephi 3:15). Anxious that the commandment be kept because of the covenant, Nephi here employs what Hugh Nibley long ago described as "the one oath that no [Eastern] man would dream of breaking, the most solemn of all oaths to the Semite," namely, the oath on the life of the Lord ("as the Lord liveth").[39] Making failure an act of blasphemy (punishable by death under the Law of Moses), Nephi binds his brothers to pursue their quest until they have fulfilled the commandment.

In the speech that follows the oath, Nephi again triply employs the word "commandment":

> Wherefore, let us be faithful in keeping the *commandments* of the Lord; therefore let us go down to the land of our father's inheritance, for behold he left gold and silver, and all manner of riches. And all this he hath done because of the *commandments* of the Lord. For he knew that Jerusalem must be destroyed, because of the wickedness of the people. For behold, they have rejected the words of the prophets. Wherefore, if my father should dwell in the land after he hath been *commanded* to flee out of the land, behold, he would also perish. Wherefore, it must needs be that he flee out of the land. And behold, it is wisdom in God that we should obtain these records, that we may preserve unto our children the language of our fathers; And also that we may preserve unto them the words which have been spoken by the mouth of all the holy prophets, which have been delivered unto them by the Spirit and power of God, since the world began, even down unto this present time. (1 Nephi 3:16–20)

Nephi adds, narratively: "And it came to pass that after this manner of language did I persuade my brethren, that they might be faithful in keeping the *commandments* of God" (1 Nephi 3:21).

Though this little scene seems to portray Nephi as infinitely faithful, the end of the story will make clear that it is not without a sense of irony. Nephi retroactively reveals this speech—as well as the zealous response of 1 Nephi 3:7—as uncomprehending, though obedient.[40] In particular, the reasons Nephi attributes to God for wanting them to have the brass plates are not what God actually has in mind. At this point in the story, Nephi sees the plates only as preserving (1) "the language of [their] fathers" and (2) "the words which have been spoken by the mouth of all the holy prophets." Only with the slaying of Laban will Nephi come to see what the plates are *really* for.

The second failed attempt to get the plates from Laban lands Lehi's sons in a cave outside Jerusalem, where Laman and Lemuel take to beating Nephi and Sam, only to be interrupted by an angel. Vitally, the angel, in his brief message, uses language drawn directly from the Lehitic covenant (see 1 Nephi 3:29), which could only have increased Nephi's sense of anxiety. After the angel departs, the theme of commandments again emerges, though now with a curious twist. Nephi describes his brothers as idolatrously displacing the power to command from God to Laban: "And after the angel had departed, Laman and Lemuel again began to murmur, saying: How is it possible that the Lord will deliver Laban into our hands? Behold, he is a mighty man, and he can *command* fifty, yea, even he can slay fifty; then why not us?" (1 Nephi 3:31). Thus Nephi presents his older brothers as completely missing what he took to be the whole meaning of the return to Jerusalem: the fulfillment of *God's* commandment. And of course, he responds by speaking of the commandments yet again: "Let us go up again unto Jerusalem, and let us be faithful in keeping the *commandments* of the Lord; for behold he is mightier than all the earth, then why not mightier than Laban and his fifty, yea, or even than his tens of thousands?" (1 Nephi 4:1).

It is at this point that Nephi explicitly draws on the Israelite exodus: "Therefore let us go up; let us be strong like unto Moses; for he truly spake unto the waters of the Red Sea and they divided hither and thither, and our fathers came through, out of captivity, on dry ground, and the armies of Pharaoh did follow and were drowned in the waters of the Red Sea" (1 Nephi 4:2).[41] The connection here with Isaiah 51:9–10 is at its most explicit. Nephi here compares deliverance from Laban to God's dividing the Red Sea, but it will be he himself only a moment later who has to cut Rahab and wound the dragon. It is thus significant that Nephi concludes his speech by affirming that "*the Lord is able* to deliver us, even as our fathers, and *to destroy Laban*, even as the Egyptians" (1 Nephi 4:3).

The portion of the narrative that follows is complex. Leaving his brothers outside the city, Nephi creeps into Jerusalem alone. When he discovers Laban drunk and passed out in the street, he finds himself "constrained"—by the Spirit—to kill Laban (1 Nephi 4:10). And there the climax of the narrative—in the shape of a discussion about the meaning of the word "commandments"—takes place.

Law and Covenant

The scene begins, oddly enough, with Nephi pulling Laban's sword from its sheath. Nephi says nothing about his motivations for doing this,[42] focusing his narrative efforts instead on making clear how surprised he was at the injunction from the Spirit: "But I said in my heart: Never at any time have I shed the blood of man. And I shrunk and would that I might not slay him" (1 Nephi 4:10).

Nephi's repulsion initiates a long conversation between him and the Spirit.[43] But one must not pass too quickly to that conversation, since at a point where—especially given all that has already been said—the reader naturally expects to find the word "commanded," Nephi instead employs the word "constrained": "I was *constrained* [not *commanded*] by the Spirit that I should kill Laban" (1 Nephi 4:10). Given Nephi's consistency and precision with the word "commandment," this substitution should not be treated lightly. But what does it imply? First, it may be that Nephi wants to make clear that he was not flouting a *commandment,* and so that he did *not* falter at the most crucial moment. On this reading, Nephi's hesitation is justified, but less because of the injunction's *extremity* than because it comes as a *constraint* rather than as a *commandment*—a spiritual impression rather than as a direct, spoken word. Second, because Nephi goes on to use the word "commandment" four more times in the immediately following verses, the use of the word "constrained" serves to distinguish the Spirit's injunction from the commandments implied in the covenant, perhaps precisely so that the *actual* identification of those commandments can finally emerge. Whereas to this point in the story, Nephi has taken "commandments" to refer simply to *whatever* the Lord happens to command at any given moment—through Lehi, through the Spirit, or whatever—it is precisely as the Spirit's injunction is labeled a *constraint* rather than a *commandment* that Nephi's original understanding begins to crumble.

The constraint of the Spirit appears therefore to serve primarily to get Nephi talking. The Spirit speaks first: "And the Spirit said unto me again: Behold the Lord hath delivered him into thy hands" (1 Nephi 4:11). These words hark back to the angel's words in the cave—to the angel's message that made mention also of the Lehitic covenant—thus directing Nephi's attention to the misunderstood covenant. And Nephi's response makes clear that he indeed begins to reflect on the terms of the covenant, though confusedly at first: "Yea, and I also knew that he had sought to take away mine own life; yea, *and he would not hearken unto the commandments of the Lord;* and he also had taken away our property" (1 Nephi 4:11). In this first mention of commandments in his conversation with the Spirit, Nephi is concerned only with *Laban's* relationship to the commandments; he does not yet see what relationship he *himself* sustains to the commandments—nor *what* commandments are implicated in the covenant. But this first, misguided response quickly summons a further word from the Spirit.

The Spirit next says: "Slay him, for the Lord hath delivered him into thy hands; Behold the Lord slayeth the wicked to bring forth his righteous purposes. It is better than one man should perish than that a nation should dwindle and perish in unbelief" (1 Nephi 4:12–13). Though modern sensibilities naturally balk at the idea that the Spirit would have cited "a classic statement of the scapegoating rationale" (and especially though one feels sickened—as one should—by the fact that, as Eugene England points out, two fundamentalists "even used [this] passage in court to defend their 'inspired' slaying of their sister-in-law and her baby"),[44] the role these words play in the narrative should not be missed. They emphatically do *not* serve immediately as the (ethical) "justification" for Laban's death. Rather, they serve only to point Nephi again to the Lehitic covenant: "And now, when I, Nephi, had heard these words, I remembered the words of the Lord which he spake unto me in the wilderness, saying that: Inasmuch as *thy seed* shall keep my commandments, they shall prosper in the land of promise" (1 Nephi 4:14). Rather than justifying a murderous scapegoating, the Spirit's words—however they might otherwise (unfortunately) be used under other (unfortunate) circumstances—immediately serve the purpose in the narrative of drawing Nephi's attention to the meaning of the return to Jerusalem. What mattered was not the immediate fulfillment of an arbitrary commandment, but the future history of the "nation" of Nephi's seed. The Spirit forces Nephi to see, oddly enough, that his reluctance to follow the constraint may well be simple selfishness.

The next four verses trace a drastic shift in Nephi's understanding of the commandments:

> Yea, and I also thought that that they [his seed] could not keep the *commandments* of the Lord *according to the law of Moses,* save they should have the law. And I also knew that *the law was engraven upon the plates of brass.* And again, I knew that the Lord had delivered Laban into my hands *for*

> *this cause*—that I might obtain the records *according to his commandments. Therefore* I did obey the voice of the Spirit, and took Laban by the hair of the head, and I smote off his head with his own sword. (1 Nephi 4:15–18)

Though Nephi still asserts that he had the task of retrieving the record "according to [God's] commandments," he also comes to recognize that the anxiety-inducing covenant has reference not to *those* commandments, but to "the commandments of the Lord *according to the law of Moses.*" Nephi only recognizes quite late in the game the conditions of the Lehitic covenant—and his many missteps on the way to actually obtaining the brass plates are suddenly revealed. And it is only with this much larger picture and clarification that Nephi finally has the courage to follow the Spirit's constraint.

So much for the narrative itself, but what of Isaiah 51:9–10? It is not difficult to see how Kent Brown might read the connection: Nephi's interest in the Isaiah passage is in part driven by his own harrowing encounter with Laban. But the connection, I think, turns out to be more complex.

Isaiah 51:9–10

In the Isaiah passage, the image of the decapitated dragon reflects—unlike most of Second Isaiah's message—something that happened *anciently*, rather than something happening in the (eschatological) *present*, that is, in what Nephi usually appropriates as the projected *future* of Israel:

> Awake, awake, put on strength, O arm of the Lord; awake, *as in the ancient days, in the generations of old.* Art thou not it that *hath* cut Rahab, and wounded the dragon? Art thou not it which *hath* dried the sea, the waters of the great deep; that *hath* made the depths of the sea a way for the ransomed to pass over?

Here Israel, during its eschatological exodus and restoration, calls on the Lord who anciently delivered Israel. Thus, one aspect of the "new exodus" of Second Isaiah is the community's explicit recognition that the Lord had *once before* decapitated the primordial enemy and so allowed the original exodus to take place. In other words, Second Isaiah enacts a new exodus, but a new exodus intertwined with an earlier, anticipatory exodus.

Thus, if Nephi did see his own experience reflected in Isaiah 51:9–10, he would likely have associated his own experiences only with what the eschatological community of Second Isaiah projected back into the primordial past—namely, the cutting/wounding that allowed anciently for escape. In other words, because Second Isaiah describes an eschatological exodus that keeps its eye on an earlier, essentially primordial exodus, Nephi could read himself into Second Isaiah as the embodiment of the earlier exodus to which the eschatological exodus—which Nephi consistently associates with the eventual gathering of Israel—would look back. The Lord's fidelity to Nephi in delivering him from Laban (ancient exodus) is meant to serve as a narrative source of strength to Israel struggling to trust the Lord in the eschatological events outlined in Book of Mormon prophecy (new exodus).

It might then be said that the Lehite task of likening Second Isaiah requires a kind of *double* "application" of the text. First, it recognizes in Second Isaiah the pattern to be followed in the future restoration of Israel (of the Lehites in particular)—a pattern similarly outlined in Lehi's and Nephi's visions. Second, it recognizes in Second Isaiah's occasional references to the ancient exodus the pattern through which the ancient Lehite exodus from Jerusalem should be interpreted.

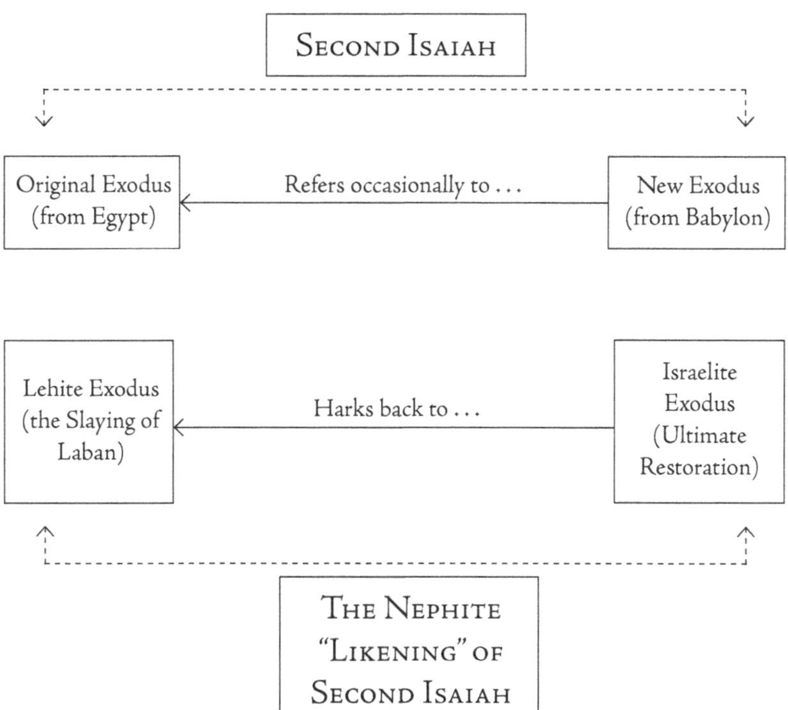

Whatever light this sheds on Nephi's notion of *likening*, it clarifies in a preliminary way Nephi's notion of *typology*. Because the Lehites looked out from the circumstances of their own exodus to an eschatological exodus, and particularly because their own exodus was predicated on an event through which they received the Law, *it seems quite natural that the Lehites should have anticipated from the very beginning that the Law of Moses would eventually be "fulfilled."* Indeed, the fact that Israelite eschatology is first mentioned in Nephi's record (1 Nephi 10) in connection with *both* the first Nephite Christology and the first word concerning interpreting Isaiah suggests that the Lehites should have seen from the very start that the Law's normative force was only temporary—*that what was received in the first, anticipatory exodus would be fulfilled in the second, eschatological exodus.* The Lehites' reading of Isaiah gave

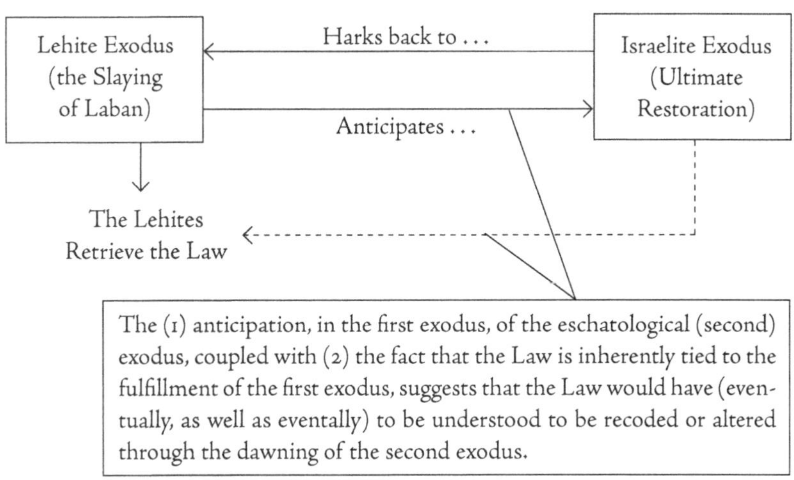

them to understand from the beginning that the Law of Moses *implied* a Messiah.

But this preliminary sketch, grounded for the moment only in a close reading of First Nephi, needs to be spelled out by a close reading of Second Nephi.

Grace

This discussion of Second Isaiah in First Nephi has come at last—and with some surprise—to address the crucial relationship between the Lehites and the Law of Moses. In effect, it appears that Nephi's likening of Second Isaiah helps to recast the Laban episode as an event that not only provided the Lehites with the Law of Moses, but also—through its connection to Isaiah 51:9–10—helped them to see from the beginning that the Law would someday be fulfilled. The logic here is complicated but crucial, and it is only worked out at any length and with any real precision in Second Nephi. There, in connection with extensive quotations from First Isaiah, Nephi explains the Lehite relationship to the Law of Moses.

I have already pointed out that one of the most important structural indications of the privileged place of the Isaiah chapters in Second Nephi is the parallel between Nephi's two discussions of grace and typology (2 Nephi 10:24–11:7 and 2 Nephi 25:23–27). But why does Nephi mark the heart of his record by taking up, specifically, grace and typology? That is, what do grace and typology have to do with each other, and what do they have to do with First Isaiah?

The first of the two passages makes clear that typology and grace have *everything* to do with each other because grace is a question of *the gift*: "Behold, my soul delighteth in proving unto my people the truth of the coming of Christ; for, for this end hath the law of Moses been *given*; and all things which have been *given* of God from the beginning of the world, unto man, are the *typifying* of him" (2 Nephi 11:4).[45] Nephi here claims that typology is connected with or follows from *a certain kind of giving*. Three questions, then, need to be

Wherefore, my beloved brethren, reconcile yourselves to the will of God, and not to the will of the devil and the flesh; and remember, after ye are reconciled unto God, that it is only in and through the grace of God that ye are saved.	For we labor diligently to write, to persuade our children, and also our brethren, to believe in Christ, and to be reconciled to God; for we know that it is by grace that we are saved, after all we can do.

addressed. First, what is grace/the gift? Second, what can be said about the role of the gift in typology? Finally, what has all this to do with First Isaiah?

First, then, grace or the gift. Two relevant passages, 2 Nephi 10:24 and 2 Nephi 25:23, should be placed side by side:
The similarity between the two texts is obvious, though they come, according to Nephi, from two different hands. The first comes at the end of Jacob's sermon recorded in 2 Nephi 6–10. The second, however, comes directly from Nephi—though apparently only after he had heard (and recorded) his brother's sermon. What do these two passages say about grace? The question, I believe, is especially important today, given the somewhat controversial status of 2 Nephi 25:23 in the wake of writers like Stephen Robinson and Robert Millet.[46] What, then, do Jacob and Nephi claim regarding salvation?

First, with the two passages side by side, the parallel between Jacob's and Nephi's uses of the word "after" can dispel the most common interpretation of 2 Nephi 25:23. Nephi *cannot* be saying that grace is only what makes up for what goes beyond an individual's "best efforts." Inasmuch as the phrase "all we can do" (in 2 Nephi 25:23) is structurally parallel to and clearly meant to echo the phrase "ye are reconciled unto God" (in 2 Nephi 10:24), it seems all one can do, in the end, *is* be reconciled to God.[47] There is no reason to assume that "all we can do" refers to a laundry list of works to be accomplished before one becomes worthy of grace,[48] nor does it appear to mean that salvation comes only to those who have consistently done the best they theoretically could given their circumstances.[49]

A minimalist reading of the two passages would likely ignore such questions entirely, pointing out instead—and much more straightforwardly—that *both* passages distinguish two operations: that of salvation (the work entirely and only of *grace*), and that of reconciliation (something the individual apparently does). In the end, this distinction is the most important aspect of these texts. Nephi and Jacob are more concerned with explaining *what humans refuse* than with outlining *what humans need to do*. And because what humans refuse is, straightforwardly, "the will of God"—the will of God being precisely that to which they must reconcile themselves—it is clear that *it is the will of God to save them*. Neither Jacob nor Nephi suggests that some identifiable list—whether large *or* small—of prerequisite steps to grace is to be sought. Rather, both state frankly that grace and its salvation remain distant because humans pretend that grace is to be earned. In other words, while God's will is precisely to save human beings from death (see 2 Nephi 10:23), *they do not want to be delivered from death*. Thus Jacob and Nephi call upon their hearers to be reconciled to the will of God—that is, to be reconciled to God's desire to deliver them from death.

To be saved by grace is thus neither to obtain grace through earning it, nor to be raptured by some irresistible sovereign God. It is—quite simply—to *stop fighting against grace*. This is implied in the word "reconciliation." To be reconciled is to cease holding a meaningless, purposeless grudge. If all that must "be done" to be "saved" is to be reconciled to the will of God, then it suffices to stop working against grace—to stop trying to save oneself (by works), to stop refusing to see that one can do nothing without God's love. In short, grace, as grace, is always a gift. Reconciliation is "all" that must be done to avail oneself of grace because one has refused, in advance, the gift of God's graceful will. Reconciliation depends on coming to see that grace has been given—and should be received—*without cause*. It was given in love and, therefore, without (compelling) reason.

God's gift, though, comes in the surprising shape of a *law* (in Jacob's terminology: God's *will*). A law, in order to be law, must be given without reason ("because I said so"), as self-justifying, as a gift. A law is only received as law when one ceases to seek an explanation for it, when one receives the law as a gift and no longer as something to be resented, rebelled against, or guilty before. The gift is the "without reason," the "without cause," the thing given in love—and love always betrays a kind of madness, a lack of reason. Saved by grace: deliverance comes when one ceases to regard the law as sovereignly guaranteed by something extralegal,when one finally regards the law as a gift in and of itself.[50]

So much, for the moment, for grace. But this leads immediately into the parallel passages dealing with typology, passages that speak not only of giving, but also—and at length—of the Law. In the end, Nephi's discussions of typology clarify what he says of grace.

Typology

In 2 Nephi 11:4, Nephi frames his discussion of typology within a discussion of proof or of proving—specifically of "proving . . . the truth of the coming of Christ."[51] Nephi's perhaps surprising but straightforward claim is that it is "for *this* end"—that is, for the purpose of proving the truth of Christ's coming—that "the law of Moses [was] given." What can this mean? A conventional approach might understand Nephi simply to mean that, because the elements of the Law of Moses can serve as so many symbols pointing to Christ—as so many embodiments of events in the life of Christ—the Law is meant to be used to prove Christ's coming. But this approach actually goes beyond what Nephi himself says. In fact, it goes beyond Nephi by drawing, specifically, on Abinadi's account of typology. While Abinadi explicitly argues that individual elements of the Law typologically anticipate Christic events, Nephi never claims this much.

Of course, one might object that while Nephi never explicitly affirms such a model of typology, he also never explicitly denies it either. True, but there is nonetheless an irreducible—and perhaps surprising—difference between Nephi's and Abinadi's models of typology. While Nephi asserts that the Law of Moses can be—indeed, is meant to be—employed to *prove* Christ's coming, Abinadi straightforwardly states that it was the Law specifically that got in the way, for Israel, of recognizing that Christ would come! For Abinadi, the Law was given, not for the "end" of proving Christ's coming, but simply "to keep [Israel] in remembrance of God and their duty towards him" (Mosiah 13:30). Abinadi does not therefore deny the typological Law, but he associates typological regard with *faith*, while Nephi associates it with *proof*.

From this it follows that either: (1) though Nephi was more optimistic than Abinadi about the force of the typological connections between the Law and Christ, the two nonetheless had a shared typological model; or (2) the difference between Nephi and Abinadi in terms of optimism is actually rooted in a structural difference between their models of typology.[52] The first of these two options seems unlikely, given Nephi's frequently expressed pessimism regarding his people's ability to understand spiritual things. In the end, it seems most likely that the difference between Nephi's and Abinadi's understandings of the purpose of the Law betrays a difference between their understandings of the typological nature itself of the Law. What is this difference? Actually, I will only come to the specifics of this difference at the end of chapter 5. For the moment, it is enough to recognize that Nephi's comments on typology need not be read *through Abinadi's*, as is perhaps common.

Coming back to Nephi alone, then, what should be said about *the gift* in 2 Nephi 11:4? The preceding discussion of grace sheds some light on this question. If a law is only fully a law when it is received as a gift, then the Law of Moses—particularly in that it was *given*—orients itself, by its very nature, to its messianic fulfillment. Unless it remains within the order of economy, within which its status as gift is obscured, the Law must come to fulfillment. Put another way, for the Law to have any genuine force, it must be bound to its *end* ("for this end . . ."), or to the messianic possibility of its suspension. The giving of the Law necessarily pointed to the coming of a Messiah—to the coming of Christ.[53]

In the remainder of 2 Nephi 11:4, Nephi broadens his claim and finally ties it to typology: "and all things which have been given of God from the beginning of the world, unto man, are the typifying of him." Here it becomes clear that, if the Law is typological, it is so only because it came as a gift since it is the *givenness* of the given that makes it typological. In general, everything given—that is, the given *as such*—is oriented to the coming of Christ. For Nephi, typology cannot be disentangled from the gift. Whatever is given and received as a gift inevitably points to messianic fulfillment.

This is further clarified in the parallel text of 2 Nephi 25:24–27, where Nephi attempts to address a problem issuing from the nature of grace as he articulates it. If the gift, as gift, *formally* points to messianic fulfillment, does the gift not *materially* disappear? That is, how can a messianic orientation not simply amount to an abandonment of the Law?[54] Nephi, in response, gives this thesis statement: "Notwithstanding we believe in Christ, we keep the law of Moses" (2 Nephi 25:24). To explain this, Nephi comes back to his claim in 2 Nephi 11:4, stating that it was precisely "for this end"—namely, to help Israel "look forward with steadfastness unto Christ, until the law shall be fulfilled"—that "the law [was] given" (2 Nephi 25:24–25). *For Nephi there is no law but the given-and-therefore-typological-law; there is no Law without the Messiah.* Or rather, for Nephi, if there is a messiah-less law, it can only be "dead," a mere set of social constraints to be kept "because of the commandments" (2 Nephi 25:25). According to Nephi, "the right way is to believe in Christ and deny him not; for by denying him *ye also deny the prophets and the law*" (2 Nephi 25:28).

Thus, to keep the Law—and so to receive it as a gift—is to live in light of its fulfillment. To teach "the law of Moses, *and* the intent for which it was given" is, in the words of a slightly later Book of Mormon author, to persuade others "to look forward unto the Messiah, and believe in him to come *as though he already was*" (Jarom 1:11). The Law itself is nothing without grace, but grace is not therefore something added to the Law. Rather, grace is given with the Law or *as* the Law itself—if it is received in the right way.[55]

First Isaiah

What, though, is to be made of the fact that Nephi employs the two passages just exposited—each dealing in turn with grace and typology—to frame the Isaiah chapters of 2 Nephi 12–24? I have already argued that, in light of a possible likening of Isaiah 51:9–10, the Nephites would have anticipated the Law's fulfillment through the eschatological intervention of the Redeemer. But that is a question of *Second* Isaiah (in *First* Nephi), while the Isaiah chapters (of *Second* Nephi) come from *First* Isaiah. Why is there a link in Nephi's text between, on the one hand, the twin themes of grace and typology and, on the other hand, the task of reading First Isaiah?

Actually, the link is not difficult to explain. I have already borrowed heavily, in chapter 2, from the work of Gerhard von Rad in interpreting Isaiah 6:9–12. But what I have not yet mentioned is that von Rad's interest in that passage—in Isaiah's turn to the future and the task of writing and sealing prophetic texts—was driven by his interest in the question of typology. Indeed, according to von Rad, *typological thought was effectively invented in the course of Isaiah's production of Isaiah 6–8.*[56] Whether von Rad is right that typology only began with First Isaiah, it seems to me that he is certainly right that its basic mechanisms are on display there and in the very chapters of First Isaiah that Nephi quotes between his two discussions of grace and typology. Indeed, in Isaiah 8:16 (2 Nephi 18:16), it is precisely "the law" that is to be bound up and sealed for a later time.[57]

One must be careful here. While the fact that Nephi places his discussions of typology on either end of the Isaiah chapters might incline one to believe that he thought Isaiah should be read typologically, things are not so simple. Nephi consistently associates *likening* with the task of reading Isaiah, and *typology* with the task of understanding the Law. (Note, for example, that in 2 Nephi 11, Nephi describes the Law as "typifying" of the Messiah, but invites his readers to "liken" First Isaiah to themselves.) But likening and typology are nonetheless entangled in an interesting way. Because the model for typological reading is itself developed within Isaiah—in fact, within the complex entanglement between First and Second Isaiah, between Isaiah as writing for a future people and Isaiah as speaking for that future people—the Lehite assumption of a typological relationship to the Law would have been a *consequence* of their likening Isaiah. Nephi seems not to have read Isaiah typologically, but to have likened Isaiah, and in likening him, to have assumed the typological regard for the Law that Isaiah himself had developed. *In likening the Prophets, Nephi developed a typological interpretation of the Law.*

In the end, then, these two interpretive operations of likening and typology are, for Nephi, distinct, and he seems to have developed them at different times. Given that he borrowed the typological understanding of the Law—that is, his theology of grace—from Isaiah, Nephi could not have discovered typology without first having taken up the work of likening Isaiah's writings. In the work of likening the Prophets, Nephi developed the possibility of typologically living the Law. Thus likening is, for Nephi, what one does *with* the book of Isaiah, while typology is what one learns *from* the book of Isaiah. One can only begin to live typologically, like Isaiah, if one positions oneself within the writings of Isaiah by likening him.

What, then, does it mean to read scripture? Complete answers can only be given after the other typological model—that of Abinadi—has been examined. For the moment, though, it is possible to distinguish in Nephi two distinct ways of approaching scripture, one Nephi associated with reading the Prophets (likening), and one Nephi associated with reading the Law (typology). And it is possible to suggest that Nephi understood the latter to have been discoverable only through the former. It can, moreover, be said that typology was for Nephi a question of recognizing the givenness of the Law, such that one recognized the inherent connection between the Law and its fulfillment.

But more needs to be said about all of this. It will prove easiest, however, to recognize the full stakes of Nephi's approach to typology only when it can be set against a rival model. For that reason, I would like to leave off direct discussion of Nephi's approach and turn instead to that of Abinadi. As is already clear, approaching Abinadi will involve sorting out his relationship to Isaiah.

Notes

1. Garold N. Davis, "Pattern and Purpose of the Isaiah Commentaries in the Book of Mormon," in Bitton, *Mormons, Scripture, and the Ancient World*, 281; Gardner, *Second Witness*, 1:187; Reynolds, "Nephi's Outline," 56–57; and Eldin Ricks, *Book of Mormon Commentary: Volume 1* (Salt Lake City: Deseret News Press, 1935), 35, 110–111.

2. The dream of the tree of life perhaps set the stage of Lehi's criticisms of Jerusalem. It seems to me most natural to see in the image of the "great and spacious

building" a reflection of the corrupt temple of Lehi's day, from which the wealthy Jerusalem elite would have mocked the wild-eyed prophets who dared to retreat into the wilderness to eat of the fruit of the tree of life. On such an interpretation, it seems clear that Lehi's dream of the tree of life was at least in part meant to be understood as a critique of the self-satisfied Jerusalem establishment.

3. No interpreter of the Book of Mormon has yet pointed out that the simplest and most straightforward way of understanding the angel's words in 1 Nephi 11 concerning "the condescension of God" is to take them as referring to the baptism of Christ.

4. Brant Gardner wagers that the text is a quotation of Isaiah 40:3 mediated through the New Testament. Gardner, *Second Witness*, 1:191. McConkie and Millet come to a rather different—and obviously somewhat strained—interpretation: "Lehi came to know by revelation that John would quote from Isaiah (40:3) regarding the coming of the Lord." McConkie and Millet, *Doctrinal Commentary on the Book of Mormon*, 1:66.

5. It might also be pointed out that in 1 Nephi 10:4, Nephi portrays Lehi as drawing also on Deuteronomy 18:15–19, the prophecy of the prophet like unto Moses who would be raised up to redeem the Jews. Von Rad, importantly, connected this same prophecy from Deuteronomy to the "servant songs" of Second Isaiah. Von Rad, *Old Testament Theology*, 2:276.

6. Childs, *Introduction to the Old Testament as Scripture*, 332–333. Childs attributes this discovery to Peter Ackroyd.

7. Frank M. Cross Jr., "The Council of Yahweh in Second Isaiah," *Journal of Near Eastern Studies* 12.4 (October 1953): 275–276. Cf. Blenkinsopp, *Isaiah 40–55*, 179–180.

8. Childs, *Isaiah*, 295–296.

9. One presumes, given Nephi's pattern elsewhere, that Second Isaiah was his basic source here. However, it should be noted that Eldin Ricks, in his selection of an exemplary Isaiah passage Nephi might have used, chose to cite Isaiah 11:11–12. Ricks, *Book of Mormon Commentary*, 179. Gardner more straightforwardly states: "Nephi does not give enough detail about what he cited from Isaiah to allow identification of the relevant passages." Gardner, *Second Witness*, 1:259.

10. The reference to Nephi's having read from Isaiah to his brothers marks a transition, in 1 Nephi 15, from discussion of Lehi's discourse about the olive tree (in 1 Nephi 10) to discussion of Lehi's dream of the tree of life (in 1 Nephi 8). 1 Nephi 15 thus reproduces the transitional markers found in the first verses of 1 Nephi 10.

11. Davis, "Pattern and Purpose of the Isaiah Commentaries," 281.

12. Among the commentators, this is only pointed out by Brant Gardner. See Gardner, *Second Witness*, 1:370. Noel Reynolds, interestingly, suggests that Nephi is actually quoting the prophet Zenos. See Noel B. Reynolds, "Nephite Uses and Interpretations of Zenos," in Stephen D. Ricks and John W. Welch, eds., *The Alle-*

gory of the Olive Tree: The Olive, the Bible, and Jacob 5 (Salt Lake City: Deseret Book and FARMS, 1994), 26–34.

13. Unfortunately, Latter-day Saints have generally understood Nephi to be saying here that Isaiah's words should be read as so many (highly specific!) prophecies of Jesus Christ's life, ministry, death, and resurrection. This is, however, to misread the word "Redeemer." Everywhere he deals with Isaiah, Nephi finds in him the basic contours of the historical redemption of Israel, not of the events of the life of Christ. 1 Nephi 19:23 thus straightforwardly explains that Nephi read Isaiah with his brothers in order to persuade them more fully to believe that the Lord would fulfill His promises to Israel, rather than simply to believe in Christ or his atonement.

14. In the 1830 (original) edition of the Book of Mormon, there was no chapter break between what are now chapters 19 and 20, marking the continuity between Nephi's words regarding Isaiah and his actual quotation.

15. The word "liken" is almost always equated, in commentary, to the word "apply," from as early as Reynolds and Sjodahl ("This I take to mean that Nephi, in his sermons explained the Scriptures and applied their teachings to their own needs and circumstances") and Eldin Ricks ("Nephi applied the lessons of scripture to his own people") to as recently as Brant Gardner ("For Nephi, the principle of 'likening' scriptures meant that, although a text was written for another time and place, it still has applicability to the present and to future events"). Reynolds and Sjodahl, *Commentary on the Book of Mormon*, 1:206; Ricks, *Book of Mormon Commentary*, 234; Gardner, *Second Witness*, 1:373.

16. It thus appears as "thought"—and in parallel with "purposed"—in Isaiah 14:24, quoted by Nephi in 2 Nephi 24:24: "The Lord of hosts hath sworn, saying, Surely as I have thought, so shall it come to pass; and as I have purposed, so shall it stand."

17. Thus a derivative of the word famously appears as "likeness" in Genesis 1:26–27, where it is distinguished from but set in parallel to "image."

18. It is at least of some interest that the English word "liken" derives from an Indo-European root (lik-) that means "body"—such that to liken is literally to give a body to, to embody. Here again it would seem that to liken Isaiah would be to allow his writings to function as a kind of spirit on which to hang the flesh of something else.

19. Blenkinsopp, *Isaiah 40–55*, 286.

20. Claus Westermann, *Isaiah 40–66: A Commentary*, trans. David M. G. Stalker (Philadelphia: Westminster Press, 1969), 195.

21. Blenkinsopp, *Isaiah 40–55*, 59.

22. Childs, *Isaiah*, 372–373.

23. Ibid., 378–379.

24. Grant Hardy suggests a reading similar to mine. See Hardy, *Understanding the Book of Mormon*, 71–76.

25. Blenkinsopp summarizes: "The final injunction to leave Babylon and the Chaldeans behind while inviting the whole world to join in the celebration of the redemptive intervention of God on their behalf (vv 20–21) serves to round off chs. 40–48" precisely "by referring back to the motif of the trek through the wilderness at the beginning of this section (40:3–4). Blenkinsopp, *Isaiah 40–55*, 295.

26. Kent S. Brown, *From Jerusalem to Zarahemla* (Provo, UT: Brigham Young University Religious Studies Center, 1998), 9–27. Brown speaks of Nephi's "poignantly personal reasons" for including Isaiah 48–49 in his record.

27. Childs, *Isaiah*, 479, emphasis added.

28. Tate, "The Typology of the Exodus Pattern," 248–249.

29. Ibid., 249–250.

30. Ibid., 249–250. Terry Szink lists (and explores in greater detail) several other parallels between Nephi's exodus and the Old Testament exodus, the most unique of which is his setting in parallel of Laman and Lemuel's "rude" dancing on the ship and the Israelites' worship before the golden calf. Terrence L. Szink, "Nephi and the Exodus," in Sorenson and Thorne, *Rediscovering the Book of Mormon*, 38–50. See also the list of twenty-one correspondences between the Moses story and First Nephi provided in Reynolds, "Nephite Kingship Reconsidered," 172–177.

31. Tate, "Typology of the Exodus Pattern," 250.

32. Ibid., 250–251.

33. Ibid., 251.

34. Westermann, *Isaiah 40–66*, 242–243.

35. Margaret Barker, "Isaiah," in James D. G. Dunn and John W. Rogerson, eds., *Eerdmans Commentary on the Bible* (Grand Rapids, MI: Eerdmans, 2003), 533.

36. John W. Welch, "Legal Perspectives on the Slaying of Laban," *Journal of Book of Mormon Studies* 1.1 (1992): 119–141; Eugene England, "Why Nephi Killed Laban: Reflections on the Truth of the Book of Mormon," *Dialogue: A Journal of Mormon Thought* 22.3 (Fall 1989): 32–51.

37. I have myself ventured a study of the ethical implications of the story. See Joseph M. Spencer, "René Girard and Mormon Scripture: A Response," *Dialogue: A Journal of Mormon Thought* 43.3 (Fall 2010): 6–20.

38. Steven L. Olsen, "The Death of Laban: A Literary Interpretation," *FARMS Review* 21.1 (2009): 179–195; Gordon Thomasson, "Madness, Differentiation and Sacrifice, or Reconciliation: Humanity's Options as Seen in 2 Maccabees and Genesis," unpublished paper presented 15 November 1984 at the Eighth Annual BYU College of Humanities Symposium, "Myth, Literature, and the Bible," discussed in England, "Why Nephi Killed Laban," 40–41; Brett L. Holbrook, "The Sword of Laban as a Symbol of Divine Authority and Kingship," *Journal of Book of Mormon Studies* 2.1 (Spring 1993): 48–54; Ben McGuire, "Nephi and Goliath: A Case Study of Literary Allusion in the Book of Mormon," *Journal of Book of Mormon and Other Restoration Scripture* 18.1 (2009): 16–31.

39. Hugh W. Nibley, *Lehi in the Desert/The World of the Jaredites/There Were Jaredites* (Salt Lake City: Deseret Book and FARMS, 1988), 104.

40. Hugh Nibley notes in passing that Nephi interprets the purposes of the Lord "incorrectly" at this point. Hugh W. Nibley, *An Approach to the Book of Mormon* (Salt Lake City: Deseret Book, 1988), 111.

41. It is perhaps worth noting that Nephi here quite explicitly attributes the might—and hence the "murder"—to the Lord, not to himself. Something similar seems to be at work in Isaiah 51:9–10.

42. The most interesting speculation on this point, it seems to me, is that of Jeffrey R. Chadwick, "Lehi's House at Jerusalem and the Land of His Inheritance," in John W. Welch, David Rolph Seely, and Jo Ann Seely, eds., *Glimpses of Lehi's Jerusalem* (Provo, UT: FARMS, 2004), 114.

43. Nephi bears a curious relationship to the Spirit. Whereas the Hebrew tradition Nephi inherited—which is reflected at important points in Nephi's record—understood the Spirit to be an influence that ecstatically carried the individual beyond her or his control, Nephi appears to have some ability, however limited, to resist that constraint. The consequence, it seems, is Nephi's strange ability to converse with the Spirit as a person, both in this narrative and, more strikingly perhaps, in 1 Nephi 11. More attention needs to be devoted to this curious pattern.

44. England, "Why Nephi Killed Laban," 40–42.

45. The theme of the gift holds a crucial place in contemporary philosophical discussions. Taking its cue from the anthropological work of Marcel Mauss, this debate has primarily been staged by Jacques Derrida and Jean-Luc Marion. See Jacques Derrida, *Given Time: I. Counterfeit Money*, trans. Peggy Kamuf (Chicago: University of Chicago Press, 1994); Jean-Luc Marion, *Being Given: Toward a Phenomenology of Givenness*, trans. Jeffrey L. Kosky (Stanford: Stanford University Press, 2002); and "On the Gift: A Discussion between Jacques Derrida and Jean-Luc Marion, Moderated by Richard Kearney," in John D. Caputo and Michael J. Scanlon, eds., *God, the Gift, and Postmodernism* (Bloomington: Indiana University Press, 1999), 54–78. My own position on these debates has been greatly influenced by Adam Miller, *Badiou, Marion and St Paul: Immanent Grace* (New York: Continuum, 2008). See my review essay on the latter: Joseph M. Spencer, "Taking Grace for Granted: A Roundabout Review of Adam Miller's Immanent Grace," *Element: The Journal of the Society for Mormon Philosophy and Theology* 4.2 (2008): 89–108.

46. See in particular Stephen E. Robinson, *Believing Christ: The Parable of the Bicycle and Other Good News* (Salt Lake City: Deseret Book, 1992), 90–92; and Robert L. Millet, *After All We Can Do . . . Grace Works* (Salt Lake City: Deseret Book, 2003), 131–132. A completely distinct approach has recently been taken by Brant Gardner, who appeals to Joseph Smith's part in the work of translation as having, through the language of modern Christian theology, obscured Nephi's original intentions: "This statement [2 Nephi 25:23] is couched in modern Christian terms that represent the way Joseph Smith understood what was on the plates."

Gardner's own demythologizing interpretation is that by "all we can do" Nephi referred to the centuries during which the Nephites would have to keep the Law of Moses, after which grace—through the finally enacted atonement—would come. Gardner, *Second Witness*, 1:343–344.

47. See Alma 24:11: "And now behold, my brethren, since it has been all that we could do, (as we were the most lost of all mankind) to repent of all our sins and the many murders which we have committed, and to get God to take them away from our hearts, for it was all we could do to repent sufficiently before God that he would take away our stain."

48. Indeed, if this were the meaning of the phrase, it would actually be completely inappropriate to speak of grace, since it would be, strictly speaking, earnable.

49. If this were the meaning of the passage, no one would be saved, because no one ultimately does one's theoretical best, even one's adjusted theoretical best.

50. Abinadi, by contrast with Nephi, claims that "it was expedient that there should be a law given" (Mosiah 13:29).

51. This is the second of three "proofs" Nephi offers in 2 Nephi 11. In verse 3, he speaks of adding Jacob's and Isaiah's words to his own in order "to prove unto [his children] that [his] words are true." And then in verse 6 he announces the delight he takes in "proving unto [his] people that save Christ should come all men must perish."

52. Perhaps a third way of approaching this would be actually to assert that there is no difference between Nephi and Abinadi, even in terms of "optimism." This approach would have to be undertaken through a reinterpretation of what Nephi means by "proof."

53. I draw here heavily on Giorgio Agamben, *The Time That Remains: A Commentary on the Letter to the Romans*, trans. Patricia Dailey (Stanford: Stanford University Press, 2005).

54. This, of course, is Sherem's question in Jacob 7.

55. The Book of Mormon—and Mormonism with it—thus wagers an importantly unique messianic theology, one that has been, for the most part, overlooked. This messianism of the Messiah who has always already come deserves full exposition elsewhere.

56. Thus, as von Rad explains, "Typological thinking has come under discussion again as one of the essential presuppositions of the origin of prophetic prediction." Von Rad, *Old Testament Theology*, 2:367, emphasis added.

57. It is doubtful that Isaiah meant by "the law" anything like "the Law of Moses," but Nephi might well have likened the text that way.

4

Typology for Abinadi: Exegesis

Close study of Nephi has brought us only halfway to the possibility of assessing what it means to read the Book of Mormon typologically, to read the Book of Mormon as the Book of Mormon itself suggests it should be read. In order to set off Nephi's approach to typology, it is necessary to look just as carefully at Abinadi's approach. At the heart of Abinadi's encounter with Noah's priests lies not only a typological theory but also a question of Isaianic interpretation. The larger importance of that encounter, though, predictably emerges only through analysis of its textual setting. The present chapter will be given entirely to exegesis, while chapter 5 will deal with Abinadi's distinct notion of typology and its complex relationship to Isaiah.

Nephi's massive record is obviously a different kind of text from Abinadi's isolable, relatively short speech. Exegesis of the former primarily involved structural analysis, focused on drawing out the contexts of and relationships between distinct discussions of typology positioned within Nephi's larger engagement with the book of Isaiah. Because Abinadi's speech is much shorter, its internal structure much simpler, its discussion of typology more direct, and its engagement with Isaiah more familiar, my exegesis will focus more on the stakes of the Abinadi episode within Mormon's larger record than on the structure of the text itself.

What follows in the present chapter, then, is first a series of attempts to situate Abinadi's discussion of Isaiah within the Book of Mormon as a whole.

First, I consider the structure of Mormon's larger editorial project, guided by connections between Abinadi's words in Mosiah and Christ's teachings in Third Nephi, particularly a shared interest in Isaiah 52:7–10. Second, I clarify both the historical setting of the Abinadi narrative and the basic structure of Mosiah. Finally, I take up the important, unexplored relationship between Abinadi's speech and the book of Jacob (from the small plates), a relationship that will shed important light on the status of Abinadi's encounter with Noah's priests. Following these three attempts to situate Abinadi within the Book of Mormon, I offer a few words on the internal structure of Abinadi's speech itself, mostly by way of transition to the more theological considerations of chapter 5.

Mormon's Project: Contentions and Disputations

After Nephi's near obsession with Isaiah in the small plates, readers can be baffled (and, all too often, relieved) to find that Isaiah effectively disappears from the Book of Mormon after the small plates—baffled, that is, *until* Jesus Christ himself, during his Third Nephi visit to the Lehites, initiates a return to Isaiah. There, Isaiah returns with a vengeance, with Christ going so far as to command his listeners to "search these things diligently; for great are the words of Isaiah" (3 Nephi 23:1). The respite from Isaiah in Mosiah, Alma, and Helaman, as well as the sudden return to Isaiah in Third Nephi, deserves critical attention. What is behind this Isaianic lacuna?

Crucially, Abinadi is the *last* figure to take up Isaiah before the apparent lapse in interest. Moreover, when Christ returns to Isaiah in Third Nephi, he takes up first *the very text Abinadi last commented on*—namely, Isaiah 52. When Noah's priests question him during his trial in Mosiah 12, Abinadi is burdened with the task of interpreting Isaiah 52:7–10. Then, Christ, at the end of his first discourse and through the whole of his second discourse in Third Nephi, interprets Isaiah 52:7–15. Abinadi and Christ both concern themselves with the same Isaianic text, though the former takes *chapter 53* of Isaiah as the key for interpreting that text, while the latter takes *chapter 54* of Isaiah as the key.[1]

This common interest in Isaiah 52 is one in a whole series of connections between Abinadi's speech and Christ's teachings. From the very beginning of his words to the Lehites, it appears that Christ makes two subtle references to Abinadi. First, his initial point of instruction in Third Nephi concerns *baptism*—an ordinance that seems to have been introduced to the Nephites only by Alma the Elder and precisely in fidelity to the teachings of Abinadi. That the "Abinadite baptism" had to be replaced by a "Christian baptism" is certainly of some significance. Second, Christ's second point of instruction concerns what he calls "the points of my doctrine" (3 Nephi 11:28)—points of doctrine he immediately clarifies as concerning the relationship between the Father and the Son (3 Nephi 11:32). As every reader of the Book of Mormon knows, any dispute over the relationship between the Father and the Son was likely to have been generated by Abinadi's difficult doctrinal discussion in Mosiah 15.

But determining the significance of these allusions is difficult. Why does the visiting Christ focus so heavily on questions connected to Abinadi's discourse and influence, to the "Abinadite institution"? It is my contention that the simplest way to make sense of the "disputations" Christ identifies—disputations that have as much to do with the practice of baptism as with doctrines concerning the Godhead—is to suggest that there had been in the Nephite ecclesiastical tradition a "Nephi faction" and an "Abinadi faction."[2] Abinadi was not the only one who had spoken on the question of the Godhead, nor was he the only one who had outlined or inspired a baptismal tradition. Nephi, in the small plates, assumed both of these otherwise distinctively Abinadite tasks. And crucially, Nephi's and Abinadi's teachings on both baptism and the Godhead are distinct, if not at odds.[3] Nephi thoroughly intertwines his doctrine of the Godhead with his understanding of baptism (in 2 Nephi 31)—from which one might conclude that Abinadi's doctrine of the Godhead came to be intertwined with Alma's Abinadite institution of baptism. At any rate, it requires little imagination to picture the Nephites contending over whether Nephi or Abinadi was right about both the doctrinal basis and the practical execution of baptism.

Latter-day Saints have long recognized that 3 Nephi 11, with its reinstitution of baptism, calls for explanation. The Nephites had been practicing some kind of Christian baptism for two centuries, but Christ dismisses that longstanding practice by authorizing and commanding his Lehite disciples to baptize in a new way. The standard explanation, expressed by Joseph McConkie and Robert Millet, posits that though previously administered baptisms were indeed valid (that is, performed under appropriate priesthood authority), a "new gospel dispensation" called for a readministration of the ordinances.[4] As helpful as this interpretation is, and as generally agreed upon as it has become, it makes little sense of the text. That Christ introduces his "new" order of baptism within the context of settling longstanding disputes suggests that a real difficulty concerning baptism had been circulating since Alma's founding of the Nephite church at the waters of Mormon. Another possibility, then, is that the "rebaptisms" of Third Nephi mark a return from the Abinadite practice to that outlined earlier by Nephi.[5]

This question of rebaptism is tied up with another much-commented-on "problem" of the Book of Mormon. How did Alma the Elder receive the "authority" to perform baptisms in the first place? Because no ordination is mentioned, and especially because the text suggests that Alma simply received authorization to baptize through prayer immediately before performing the ordinance, there has long been debate about the source of Alma's authority. But if Alma's baptisms were, as the text suggests, authorized by the Spirit (rather than by the priesthood strictly speaking), it would seem that Alma introduced a second understanding of baptism, one *supplementing* that of Nephi and Jacob. While Nephi's and Jacob's understandings of the ordinance called for priesthood authority—Jacob was, after all, a Nephite priest—Alma's notion of baptism, perhaps, did not.

So far, in dealing with these "problems" in the Book of Mormon, I have only been exploring *possibilities*. I do not intend to argue for any particular approach to the difficulties.[6] I want only to highlight possibilities opened by giving due weight to Christ's indication that there had been contentions about baptism and the Godhead, the most crucial of which is that the Nephites may have harbored two related but rival ritual and theological traditions, one associated with Nephi and one associated with Abinadi. Most important for my purposes is the possibility that the Lehites saw Abinadi's teachings as having marked a turning point in Nephite theological thinking. Because Abinadi seems to have been at the bottom of a number of theological innovations and diversions in the years between his martyrdom and the visit of Christ—innovations and diversions that mark his distance specifically from the ideas of Nephi—there is reason at least to explore the possibility that it was similarly Abinadi's teachings that effected the shift in (or away from) Nephite thinking about Isaiah.

At any rate, Third Nephi may form the climax of the Book of Mormon for more reasons than that it marks the visit of Christ to the Americas. Third Nephi seems to mark also the reconciliation—or at least the working out—of two parallel and perhaps rival theological traditions. Part of Christ's task, during his visit, appears to have been to heal what had been perceived for two centuries as a rift between Nephi and Abinadi, what readers of the Book of Mormon might see as a rift between the small and large plates. Importantly, this understanding of Christ's task in Third Nephi allows for a preliminary structuration of Mormon's larger editorial project, which can be diagrammed in two distinct ways:

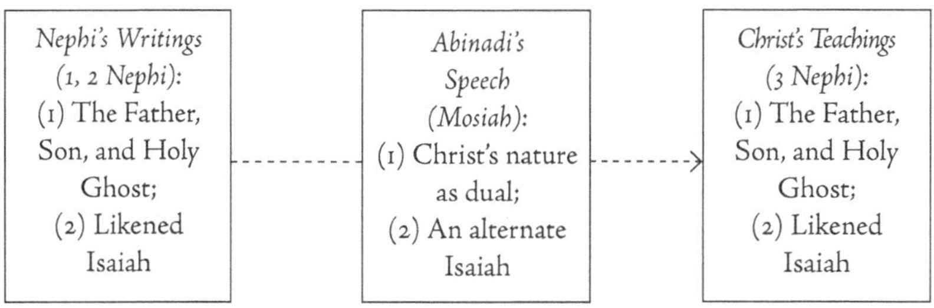

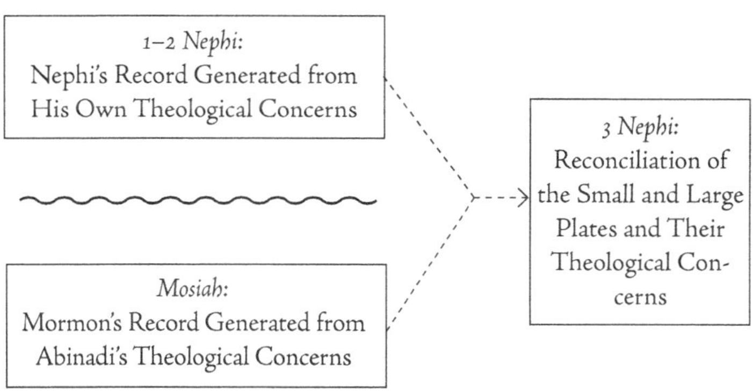

To put a finer point on this interpretation of the clearly crucial role of Abinadi—and of the whole book of Mosiah—in the larger Book of Mormon project, it is necessary to ask about everything this preliminary structuration ignores. What of the remainder of the small plates—Jacob through Omni? What of Alma and Helaman (as well as the last chapters of Mosiah and the first chapters of Third Nephi)? What of Fourth Nephi and Mormon? And what of Moroni's contributions to the volume? All these questions call for attention, and answers to them will help to clarify the stakes of Mosiah, and particularly of the Abinadi episode.

Mormon's Project: The Rest of the Book of Mormon

Quite as crucial as Third Nephi's intervention in the Nephi/Abinadi entanglement is its essentially apocalyptic role in Nephite history. Arguably, *everything* in Mormon's narrative anticipates the events of that book. There are, though, two distinct ways this anticipation unfolds in the Book of Mormon. On the one hand, of course, the visit of Christ marks the fulfillment of centuries of Nephite preaching. In this first sense, Third Nephi is a culmination because it realizes every positive Nephite yearning.[7] On the other hand, though, Third Nephi tells the story of the horrific destructions that immediately preceded Christ's visit. In this second sense, Third Nephi is a culmination because it brings the long, negative process of Nephite political deterioration to its end. Third Nephi thus realizes every negative Nephite *fear* as much as every positive Nephite *hope*.

This double culmination—positive and negative—makes Third Nephi apocalyptic. And, importantly, this double culmination is set in motion by a double inauguration in Mosiah. Every hope as well as every fear realized in Third Nephi initially entered the Nephite consciousness in the events recorded in Mosiah. In particular, this double trajectory leading from Mosiah to Third Nephi begins with the event of Abinadi's speech.

The first trajectory—that of Nephite preaching—clearly begins with Alma's organization of the Nephite church after Abinadi's martyrdom. From that initial point in Mosiah 18, Mormon's story traces the ups and downs of Nephite preaching through Alma and Helaman to its culmination in Third Nephi. Importantly, Mormon highlights the continuity of this preaching by rooting it in an unbroken dynastic line of high priests responsible for the church through the whole period leading up to the coming of Christ.[8] This dynasty acquires priestly "power" only through the strange circumstances recounted in the second half of Mosiah. Before Mosiah grants complete ecclesiastical jurisdiction to Alma the Elder—and before he awards the newly founded chief judgeship to Alma the Younger—Alma's family was anything but central to the Nephite story in Zarahemla. But, once appointed to positions of authority, Alma and his descendants quickly replace the centuries-old Nephite royal dynasty.

Moreover, the basic story of dynastic succession among Alma's descendants seems to have guided the structure of Mormon's history. The four books that trace the progress of Nephite preaching from its founding to its culmination with the visit of Christ—the books of Mosiah, Alma, Helaman, and Third Nephi—read as stories of a particular succession: (1) from the royal lineage of Mosiah$_2$ to Alma$_1$; (2) from Alma$_2$ to Helaman$_1$; (3) from Helaman$_2$ to Nephi$_2$; and (4) from Nephi$_3$ to Christ himself.[9]

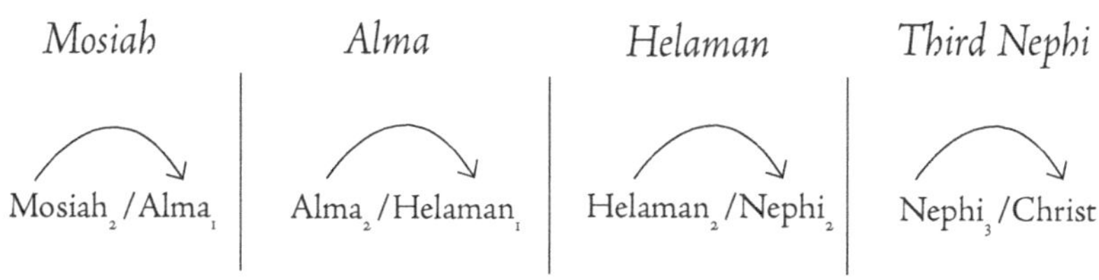

Of course, while each book in Mormon's history recounts a particular succession, each break between books also marks a succession. At the same time, Mormon softens the impact of these breaks by having all cross-book successions be those in which the successor shares his name with his father: (1) the break between Mosiah and Alma marks the succession from Alma$_1$ to Alma$_2$; (2) the break between Alma and Helaman marks the succession from Helaman$_1$ to Helaman$_2$; and (3) the break between Helaman and Third Nephi marks the succession from Nephi$_2$ to Nephi$_3$:

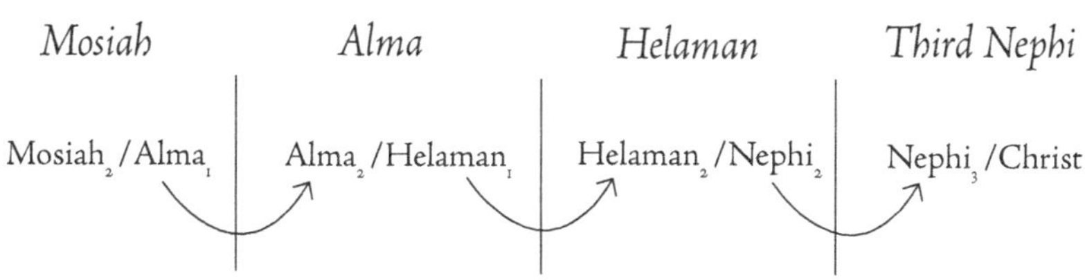

That Mormon highlights dynastic continuity even at points of historical transition makes clear his interest in maintaining the essential progression of the trajectory of Christian preaching that underlies his history.

This first trajectory of continuous Nephite preaching is, however, coupled with a second trajectory—that, namely, of the progressive political collapse of the Nephite state. This second trajectory, like the first, takes its bearings from Mosiah 18, where the narrator emphasizes the possibility of understanding Alma's Abinadite church as politically revolutionary. I will justify this interpretation later. For the moment, it is only necessary to recognize that the initiation of Nephite preaching cannot be separated from the beginning of the collapse of the centuries-old Nephite state—just as the culmination of Nephite Christian anticipation cannot be disentangled from the culmination of Nephite political deterioration.

As with the first trajectory, the points of the second trajectory are tied to the basic structure of Mormon's history. But whereas the story of Christian preaching is a story of essential continuity, the story of Nephite political dissolution is clearly marked by political crises and reversals. The largest and most crucial of these crises are, interestingly, always located at the breaks between historical books (that is, at the moment of the strongest indications of continuity in the first trajectory): (1) the dismantling of the Nephite monarchy (both the lines of Mosiah and Zeniff) and the organization of the system of judges marks the transition from Mosiah to Alma; (2) the effective dissolution of the system of judges and the rise of the Gadianton robbers marks the transition from Alma to Helaman; and (3) the dissolution of the Gadianton robbers and the complete collapse of Nephite politics marks the transition from Helaman to Third Nephi:

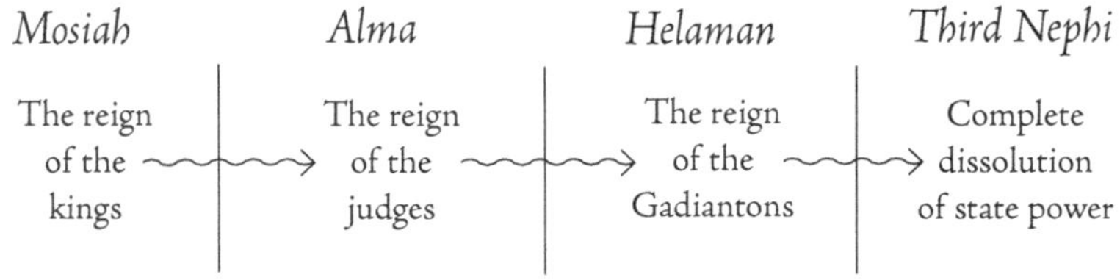

That these major breaks in Nephite political history take place at the transitions from one book to another makes clear that, in Mormon's history, each book is meant in part (1) to recount the establishment of a political system, (2) to trace the process through which that system's internal problems emerge, and (3) to detail the essential collapse of that particular system. And, importantly, whatever system of government replaces its failed predecessor is always weaker or more fragmented, from the perspective of the state, than what went before it—until, that is, the state completely collapses in the first chapters of Third Nephi.[10]

Two trajectories, then, but what must not be missed is the way the two trajectories are actually one and the same—the way, that is, each trajectory is ultimately just the reverse side of the other. It seems to have been the establishment of the church and its preaching that set the dissolution of the state in motion, and it is arguably the continuity of that preaching that consistently pushes the state toward collapse. How and why it does so will be explored in the sections that follow. For the moment, though, the double trajectory of Mormon's history might be worked into a single diagram:

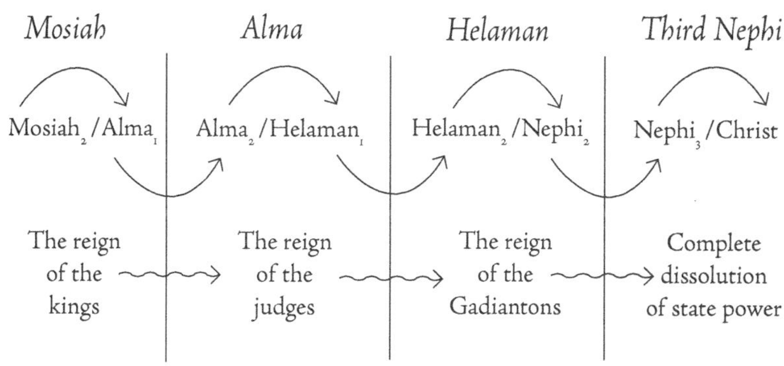

In essence, each of Mormon's four historical books tells the story of a priestly succession that both sustains the basic continuity of Nephite preaching but presses forward the essential fragmentation of the Nephite state; and each of the breaks between these books tells the story of a break in the dissolution of the Nephite state even as it marks the unbroken succession of the Nephite priestly dynasty.

If these comments do justice to Alma and Helaman, what remains to be said of what follows Third Nephi and, apart from Nephi's record, precedes Mosiah? I will address the as-yet-untreated parts of the small plates later in this chapter. As for the rest, it is perhaps best to deal with it summarily. In light of what I have just said about Mosiah, Alma, Helaman, and Third Nephi, it seems best to understand Fourth Nephi and Mormon to be an epilogue to Mormon's overarching project. And, so far as Moroni's contributions go, they are concerned with details so foreign to Mormon's immediate concerns that I will simply excuse myself from commenting on them.[11] At any rate, it seems clear that, for Mormon, Mosiah, Alma, Helaman, and Third Nephi were most central to his project.[12]

The Book of Mosiah: The Context of the Abinadi Episode

A few attempts have been made to discover a basic structure in Mosiah, the most productive of which is Gary Sturgess's "The Book of Mosiah: Thoughts about Its Structure, Purposes, Themes, and Authorship."[13] Pointing to the obvious antithesis between King Benjamin and King Noah—as also to the abandonment of monarchy at the end of the book—Sturgess suggests that the book forms "a loosely chiastic structure built around the three great royal ceremonies of King Mosiah in 124, 121, and 92 or 91 B.C."[14] But commentators generally—Sturgess included—tend to ignore the larger importance of Alma's church in Nephite history, as well as in Mosiah more narrowly. Here, then, I will start from the question of, not the Nephite *monarchy*, but the Nephite *church* in Mosiah. But because Alma's church is clearly founded in direct fidelity to Abinadi's words,[15] the following analysis of Mosiah takes its bearings primarily from the Abinadi episode. Of course, sorting out Abinadi's place in Mosiah—structurally *or* historico-politically—is hard work. I will first address the historical circumstances surrounding the Abinadi episode, so that all the relevant details are on the table from the start. Building on that foundation, I will then attempt to sort out the textual structure of Mosiah.

The Abinadi story is woven into the intricate history of the land of Nephi. That story began shortly after the death of Lehi, essentially at the beginning of Nephite history. To avoid further conflicts with Laman and Lemuel, Nephi was told to "depart from them and flee into the wilderness" (2 Nephi 5:5). Traveling into the mountains from their original settlement, the newly separated Nephites established the land of Nephi as a permanent settlement. Some three and half centuries of increasing apostasy ensued, until a man named Mosiah was, as Nephi had been before, "warned of the

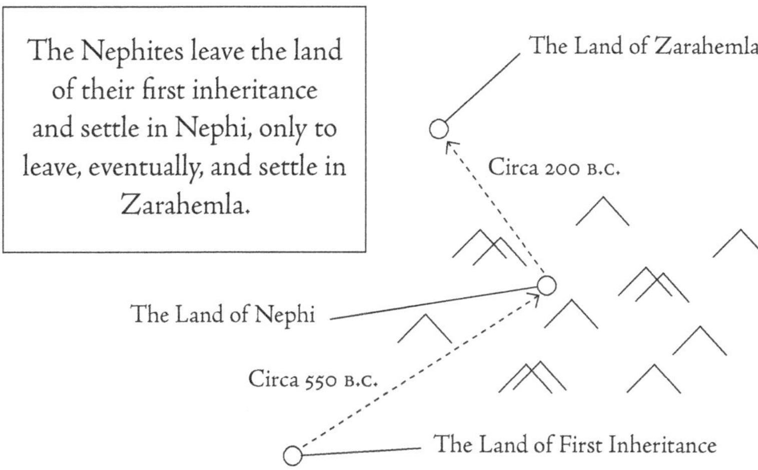

Lord that he should flee out of the land," since destruction had become imminent (Omni 1:12). Leaving this *second* "land of their inheritance," Mosiah and his followers came down out of the mountains into an already populated valley to the north—the land of Zarahemla—where Mosiah soon became king over both the Nephites and the already-settled people of Zarahemla. In the meanwhile, the promised destruction came to the land of Nephi, apparently in the shape of a Lamanite conquest. By the time of Benjamin's accession to the throne (only a few years before Abinadi's speech), the Nephites were established in the valley of Zarahemla and in the mountainous land of Nephi.

Textual clues (see Omni 1:24, 27–30; Words of Mormon 1:12–18) suggest that Nephite control of power in Zarahemla was at first insecure. But King Benjamin eventually established a political unification—a Nephite/Zarahemlaite fusion that laid the foundation for two hundred years of Lehite history. Uniting the Nephites and the people of Zarahemla, Benjamin came to wield the military strength to "drive [the Lamanites] out of the land of Zarahemla" when they tried to claim the valley as well as the mountains (Omni 1:24). Benjamin's victory against the Lamanites—associated on the one hand with his political unification and on the other hand with his retrenchment of Nephite religion (see Words of Mormon 1:15–18) and followed by his marvelous speech—led to the longest season of peace in pre-Fourth Nephi history.

Apparently taking advantage of peacetime, a group of Nephites announced their intention to return to the land of Nephi in hopes of again "possess[ing] the land of their inheritance" (Omni 1:27). Their purposes at first appear to have been violent. They hoped, it seems, to reclaim their lands by force. Allowed to do so by Benjamin, the group traveled up into Lamanite territory and sent out spies to "spy out their forces, that [their] army might come upon them and destroy them" (Mosiah 9:1). One of these spies, Zeniff by name—chosen for the job because he had "a knowledge of the land of Nephi, or of the land of our fathers' first inheritance" (Mosiah 9:1)—upset plans when he "saw that which was good among [the Lamanites]" and so became "desirous that they should not be destroyed" (Mosiah 9:1).[16]

A group of Nephites desire to reclaim the land of Nephi ("the land of their inheritance"), and so travel back up to the mountains.

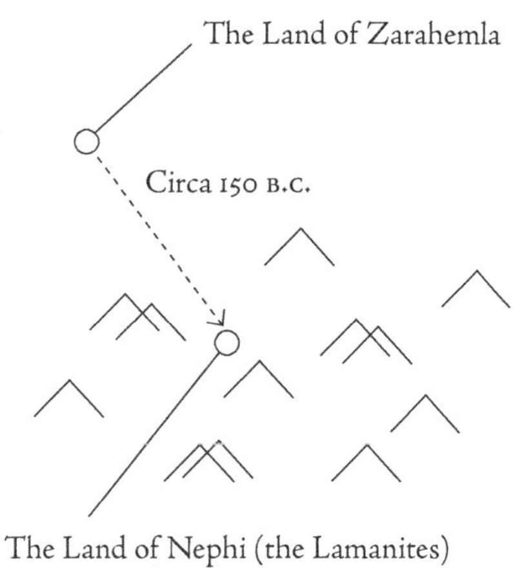

Zeniff's pacifistic report to his "blood-thirsty" commander caused a violent contention, in which "father fought against father, and brother against brother, until the greater number of [their] army was destroyed in the wilderness" (Mosiah 9:2). The survivors—Zeniff among them—returned to Zarahemla, but Zeniff seems to have become convinced that, because of the goodness he had seen among the Lamanites, the Nephites' lands could be reclaimed peacefully. He assembled a group of followers, and they again traveled up into Lamanite territory. Once there, Zeniff worked out an arrangement with the Lamanite king, and his people settled in the city of Lehi-Nephi. (The king actually removed Lamanites from the city to make this settlement happen.) Though he would soon enough claim that "it was the cunning and the craftiness of king Laman, to bring my people into bondage, that he yielded up the land that we might possess it" (Mosiah 9:10), in the meanwhile Zeniff seems to have believed he had, in reclaiming the land of Nephi, effectively restored the "original" Nephite kingdom.

With Zeniff's kingdom established in Lehi-Nephi, the Nephite regime was divided between two kingdoms, one in Nephi, and one in Zarahemla.[17] But while Zarahemla continued in peace (Mosiah$_2$ inherited from Benjamin a kingdom quite prepared to follow him), things in Lehi-Nephi quickly deteriorated. Zeniff's successor Noah used his royal prerogatives to turn his followers into an idolatrous and effectively enslaved people. It was into *this* situation that Abinadi came with his message.

The Nephite kingdom is divided into two separate kingdoms.

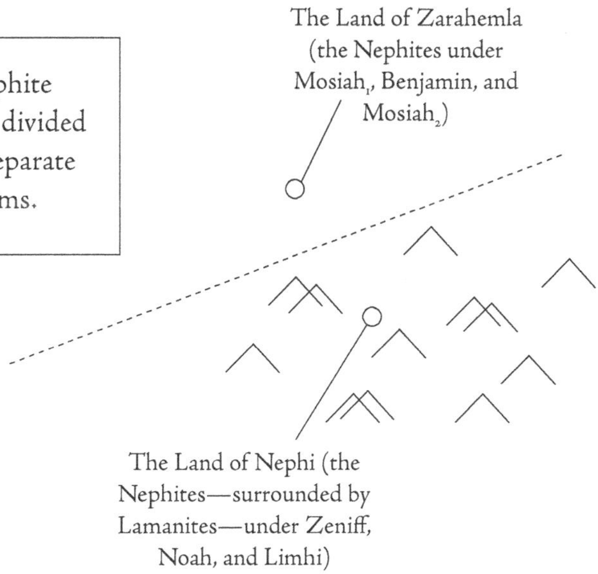

Abinadi's words would have been without effect had there not been present the one sympathetic listener he found in Noah's court—Alma$_1$. Because he was one of Noah's royal priests, Alma nearly lost his life for defending Abinadi. After escaping from Noah's servants and going into hiding, Alma began secretly to spread Abinadi's teachings, soon founding a church in the

The Nephite kingdom is reunited as the groups return to Zarahemla.

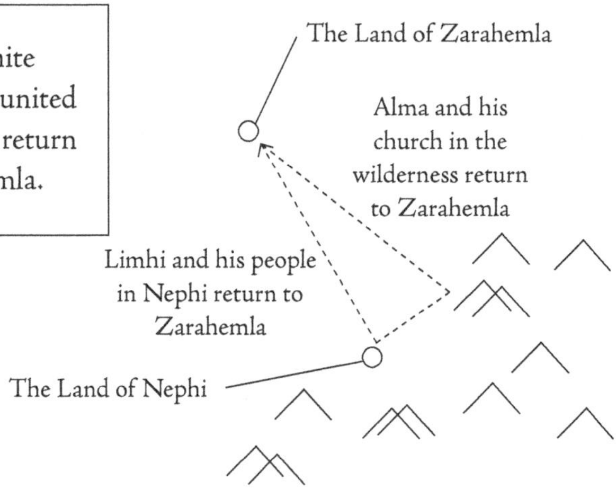

forest at the border of Noah's kingdom, and eventually taking the whole church into exile to escape Noah's army. Abinadi was in the meanwhile put to death by Noah and his priests, but soon Noah's people grew tired of Noah's excesses, such that he in turn was killed, while his corrupt priests escaped into the wilderness.[18] Limhi, Noah's son, reluctantly assumed the throne only to become soon thereafter a vassal king under harsh Lamanite rule. At the height of despair, Limhi's people were joined by an unsolicited relief company from Zarahemla who helped them to escape the land of Nephi and to return to Zarahemla. Alma's people also eventually found their way back to Zarahemla, where Alma's church flourished, though this flourishing led inexorably to a major restructuring of Nephite government—the first major step in the dissolution of the Nephite state.

The Book of Mosiah: Alma and Abinadi

If the story is complex, the way it is organized in Mosiah—as a series of flashbacks and flashforwards—is more so. But the book might be outlined as follows:

Part I: In Zarahemla
- Chapters 1–6: Benjamin's coronation of Mosiah
- Chapters 7–8: The envoy to Lehi-Nephi

Part II: In Lehi-Nephi
- Chapters 9–10: The reign of Zeniff

Chapters 11–17: Abinadi's speech
Chapters 18: The formation of the church
Chapters 19–20: From Noah to Limhi

Part III: Back to Zarahemla
Chapters 21–22: Limhi's return to Zarahemla
Chapters 23–24: Alma's return to Zarahemla

Part IV: Of the Church
Chapters 25–29: The dissolution of the kingdom

Is there, though, any order behind this basic list? I believe it is possible to detect a basic chiastic structure at work here—one that Mormon could only set up by dechronologizing the events in Mosiah:

Establishment of the kingdom (Mosiah's coronation)
On the road (from Zarahemla to Lehi-Nephi)
Zeniff's reign (wars and contentions)
Abinadi's speech
Alma's formation of the church
Limhi's reign (wars and contentions)
On the road (from Lehi-Nephi to Zarahemla)
Dissolution of the kingdom (establishment of the judges)

Thus, Mosiah seems to trace a road from the establishment to (only a few years later) the thorough dissolution of the kingdom under Mosiah. Paving this road is an entanglement between peaceful Zarahemla and turbulent Lehi-Nephi, at the heart of which lies Abinadi's encounter with Noah's priests and Alma's faithful establishment of the Abinadite church.

Abinadi and Alma are entangled not only narratively and structurally, but also textually. The narrative explicitly states that Alma reconstructed Abinadi's words. After he pled on Abinadi's behalf and so had to go into hiding to save his life, Alma assumed the responsibility to "write all the words which Abinadi had spoken" (Mosiah 17:4). Presumably, it was Alma's definitive account that Mormon employed, not only because it would have been the most authoritative account, but also because it would likely have been the *only* favorable account. The Abinadi of Mosiah 11–17 is, in the end, Alma's Abinadi.[19]

It appears that Mosiah should be read as the story of how the ecclesiastical entanglement between Abinadi and Alma in the land of Nephi came to alter the status of the monarchical state in the land of Zarahemla. In other words, the book is heavily political because Abinadi's speech led to the founding of a church that came quickly into conflict with the Nephite state and so eventually led to its dissolution.[20] Actually, this conflict between the Nephite monarchy and the Abinadite church takes two distinct shapes in the narrative. A first period of conflict occurs right in Mosiah 18, at the time of the church's founding. Here, though, the conflict is between the Abinadite church and *the monarchy in the land of Nephi under Noah*. In this first period of conflict, it *almost* appears as if the church was organized for specifically political ends—that questioning the state was part of the church's essential program (see Mosiah 23:6–16). Abinadi's original prophetic announcements have a clearly seditious nature (see Mosiah 12:10–12) and Noah's first reaction to the discovery of Alma's church is to assume that a political coup is being organized (see Mosiah 18:33).

The second period of conflict unfolds only after the monarchy in the land of Nephi ceases to exist—the whole kingdom having abandoned their lands and returned to Zarahemla—and Alma's church/people find their way also to Zarahemla. In this second period, the conflict is between the Abinadite church and *the monarchy in Zarahemla under Mosiah*. Because of Mosiah's official support of the church and its expansion, however, this second period of conflict is much friendlier, so to speak, but it is no less conflictual. The difficulties resulting from the copresence of the church and the monarchy—which had previously united church and state—are the principal focus of the last chapters of Mosiah (chapters 25–29), and they culminate in Mosiah's official call for a complete dissolution of the Nephite monarchy. Abinadi's subversive prophetic activity in the land of Nephi thus ultimately leads—through Alma's militant fidelity to Abinadi's teachings—to the complete, though official, subversion of the Nephite state in the land of Zarahemla. Without question, Abinadi and Alma make up the heart of the Mosiah narrative.

The Book of Mosiah: Benjamin and Abinadi

This privileging of Abinadi and Alma is unusual. I have already noted that most commentators focus principally, in analyzing Mosiah, on the obvious antithetical parallel between Benjamin and Noah and the way this parallel itself leads Mosiah to shift from monarchy to a system of judges. Though this familiar approach overlooks the crucial role of the Abinadi/Alma entanglement, there is nonetheless something obviously correct about its identification of the antithesis between Noah and Benjamin. What, then, should be said about this antithetical relationship?

Greatly complicating this antithesis is a striking correspondence between the speeches of Benjamin and Abinadi. Both explicitly teach, in Abinadi's words, that "God himself shall come down among the children of men and shall redeem his people" (Mosiah 15:1) or, in Benjamin's words, that "the time cometh and is not far distant, that with power, the Lord Omnipotent who reigneth, who was, and is from all eternity to all eternity, shall come down from heaven among the children of men, and shall dwell in a tabernacle of clay" (Mosiah 3:5). While this teaching seems to be what inspired Benjamin's people to set aside political and cultural differences so as definitively to unite, it is also this teaching that Noah officially cited in order to justify the execution of Abinadi (see Mosiah 17:7–8). Benjamin thus seems at once (positively) to parallel Abinadi and (negatively) to parallel Noah.

But the just-cited parallel between Benjamin's and Abinadi's speeches, both in Mosiah, is only the first of a remarkable series of similarities:

Benjamin	Abinadi
For behold, the time cometh and is not far distant, that with power, the Lord Omnipotent who reigneth, who was, and is from all eternity to all eternity, shall come down from heaven among the children of men, and shall dwell in a tabernacle of clay. (3:5)	I would that ye should understand that God himself shall come down among the children of men, and shall redeem his people. (15:1)
[Christ] shall go forth amongst men, working mighty miracles, such as healing the sick, raising the dead, causing the lame to walk, the blind to receive their sight, and the deaf to hear, and curing all manner of diseases. And he shall cast out devils, or the evil spirits which dwell in the hearts of the children of men. (3:5–6)	And after all this, after working many mighty miracles among the children of men . . . (15:6)
And lo, he shall suffer temptations, and pain of body, hunger, thirst, and fatigue, even more than man can suffer, except it be unto death; for behold, blood cometh from every pore, so great shall be his anguish for the wickedness and the abominations of his people. (3:7)	[Christ] suffereth temptation, and yieldeth not to the temptation, but suffereth himself to be mocked, and scourged. (15:5)

Benjamin	Abinadi
And even after all this they shall consider him a man, and say that he hath a devil. (3:9)	[Christ is also] cast out, and disowned by his people. (15:5)
And [they] shall scourge him, and shall crucify him. (3:9)	Yea, even so he shall be led, crucified, and slain. (15:7)
And he shall rise the third day from the dead. (3:10)	And thus God breaketh the bands of death, having gained the victory over death; giving the Son power to make intercession for the children of men—having ascended into heaven. (15:8–9)
And behold, he standeth to judge the world; and behold, all these things are done that a righteous judgment might come upon the children of men. (3:10)	[Christ] stand[s] betwixt them and justice; having broken the bands of death, taken upon himself their iniquity and their transgressions, having redeemed them, and satisfied the demands of justice. (15:9)
For behold, and also his blood atoneth for the sins of those who have fallen by the transgression of Adam, who have died not knowing the will of God concerning them, or who have ignorantly sinned. (3:11)	These are they that have died before Christ came, in their ignorance, not having salvation declared unto them. And thus the Lord bringeth about the restoration of these; and they have a part in the first resurrection, or have eternal life, being redeemed by the Lord. (15:24)
But wo, wo unto him who knoweth that he rebelleth against God! For salvation cometh to none such except it be through repentance and faith on the Lord Jesus Christ. (3:12)	But behold, and fear, and tremble before God, for ye ought to tremble; for the Lord redeemeth none such that rebel against him and die in their sins; yea, even all those that have perished in their sins ever since the world began, that have wilfully rebelled against God, that have known the commandments of God, and would not keep them; these are they that have no part in the first resurrection. (15:26)

Benjamin	Abinadi
And the Lord God hath sent his holy prophets among all the children of men, to declare these things to every kindred, nation, and tongue, that thereby whosoever should believe that Christ should come, the same might receive remission of their sins, and rejoice with exceedingly great joy, even as though he had already come among them. (3:13)	Yea, and are not the prophets, every one that has opened his mouth to prophesy, that has not fallen into transgression, I mean all the holy prophets ever since the world began? I say unto you that they are his seed. And these are they who have published peace, who have brought good tidings of good, who have published salvation; and said unto Zion: Thy God reigneth. (15:13–14)
Yet the Lord God saw that his people were a stiffnecked people, and he appointed unto them a law, even the law of Moses. And many signs, and wonders, and types, and shadows showed he unto them, concerning his coming; and also holy prophets spake unto them concerning his coming; and yet they hardened their hearts, and understood not that the law of Moses availeth nothing except it were through the atonement of his blood. (3:14–15)	And now I say unto you that it was expedient that there should be a law given to the children of Israel, yea, even a very strict law; for they were a stiffnecked people, quick to do iniquity, and slow to remember the Lord their God. Therefore there was a law given them, yea, a law of performances and of ordinances, a law which they were to observe strictly from day to day, to keep them in remembrance of God and their duty towards him. But behold, I say unto you, that all these things were types of things to come. (13:29–31)
And even if it were possible that little children could sin they could not be saved; but I say unto you they are blessed; for behold, as in Adam, or by nature, they fall, even so the blood of Christ atoneth for their sins. (3:16)	And little children also have eternal life. (15:25)

These parallels suggest on close analysis that it is not, strictly speaking, Abinadi and Benjamin that are parallel. Because all of the quotations from Benjamin given above come specifically from chapter 3 of Mosiah, they are not Benjamin's words but the words of the *angel* who visited Benjamin before his speech (see Mosiah 3:1–3). Consequently, it is the angel who visits Benjamin rather than Benjamin himself whose words are parallel to Abinadi's,[21] and Benjamin is in fact parallel, not to Abinadi, but to Noah. The Benjamin and Abinadi narratives thus do, as the commentators suggest, set up an antithetical parallel between the righteous King Benjamin

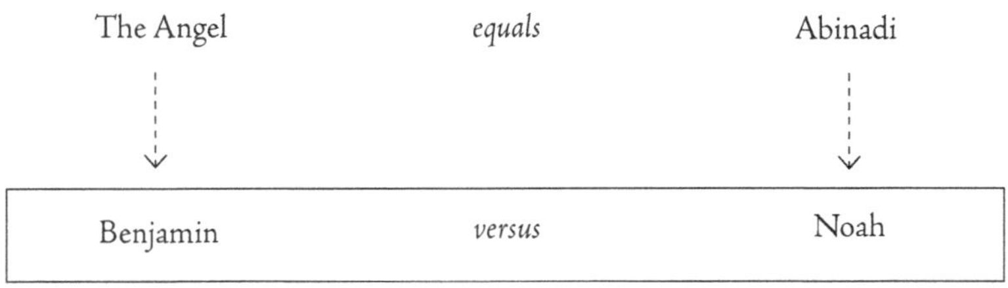

and the wicked King Noah. But the parallel is actually stronger and deeper than is usually recognized—stronger because both Benjamin and Noah receive the same message from a divinely appointed messenger (the angel for Benjamin and Abinadi for Noah) and deeper because all the apparently political differences between Noah and Benjamin are less a question of simple moral goodness or badness than a question of how they respond to the divine message.[22]

But a further complication must be addressed. Though I have, to this point, argued that Benjamin's speech effected a crucial political unification in Zarahemla, a closer look at Benjamin's words shows that he anticipated and effectively laid the foundation for the eventual dismantling of the Nephite monarchy under Mosiah. He begins by disavowing sacral kingship—"I am like as yourselves, subject to all manner of infirmities in body and mind" (Mosiah 2:11)—and by subtly inviting his listeners themselves, through language borrowed from coronation ritual, to become kings and priests: "you should hearken unto me, and *open your ears that ye may hear,* and *your hearts that ye may understand,* and *your minds that the mysteries of God may be unfolded to your view*" (Mosiah 2:9). Moreover, he goes on to invite his hearers to do exactly what he has done as their king, that is, to be lost in the *service* of God (see Mosiah 2:16–18). Benjamin's speech might thus be interpreted as an attempt, however subtle, to demonarchize the monarchy, to flatten the political hierarchy.

It seems all the clearer, then, that what is on display in Mosiah is less a comparison between ways of deploying monarchical power than a comparison between monarchical responses to a message that in itself calls earthly power into question. While Benjamin responded to the angel by planting the seeds of demonarchization—seeds that would bear fruit only a few years later when Alma's church arrived in Zarahemla—Noah responded to Abinadi by attempting futilely to secure his control of the state, something that resulted in short order in Noah's death, the enslavement of the Nephites, and finally the complete abandonment of the settlement and its monarchy. And, in the last chapters of the book, Mosiah himself is presented with these two alternatives, and with the necessity of emulating one of them. Wisely, he chose to follow his father's example.

Finally, it must be pointed out that the message in each case took the shape of an announcement of the coming Christ. Thus, throughout Mosiah, it is the core of Nephite preaching itself—whether in a demonarchizing monarchical address or in the consistent preaching of an ecclesiastical organization—that calls Nephite political power into question. What unsettles earthly things for the Nephites is the return, after so many years of effective apostasy, to the small plates vision of the coming Christ. But in order to clarify the stakes of this return—and the political questions associated with it throughout Mosiah—it is necessary to turn to the relationship between Abinadi and Jacob, the brother of Nephi.

Abinadi and Jacob

It is difficult to ascertain the relationship between the small plates and Mosiah. The one gives way rather suddenly—perhaps too suddenly—to the other.[23] Turning from the short books of the later small plates to the robust history of Mosiah, the reader of the Book of Mormon feels a bit lost. That the small plates are never specifically mentioned again and are seldom quoted is somewhat confusing and one wonders how the small plates had become so marginalized over the course of the centuries.

As it turns out, though, there are important connections to the small plates in Mosiah, though they may be easy to miss. In order to spell out the connection between Abinadi and the small plates author Jacob, it is necessary to look at some of these in detail.

Scholars have noted the connection between Mosiah 9:1–2 and 1 Nephi 1:1.[24] The two passages should be seen side by side:

1 Nephi 1:1	Mosiah 9:1–2
I, Nephi,	*I, Zeniff,*
having been born of goodly parents, therefore I was *taught* somewhat *in all the* learning *of* my father;	*having been taught in all the* language *of* the Nephites,
and having seen many afflictions in the course of my days, nevertheless, having been highly favored of the Lord in all my days;	
yea, *having had a* great *knowledge of the* goodness and the mysteries of God,	and *having had a knowledge of the* land of Nephi, or of the land of our fathers' first inheritance,
	and having been sent as a spy among the Lamanites that I might spy out their forces, that our army might come upon them and destroy them—but when I saw that which was good among them I was desirous that they should not be destroyed.
therefore I make a record of my proceedings in my days.	*Therefore, I* contended with my brethren in the wilderness.

At first, the obvious similarity between these two passages appears to be a straightforward borrowing—evidence, perhaps, of a Nephite royal tradition. But there may be reason, in light of the history surrounding the return to the land of Nephi, to take the connection more seriously. Given the uniqueness of Zeniff's situation, it may be advisable to assume that Zeniff's borrowing from the opening of the small plates was also unique. Indeed, one might suggest that the borrowing is meant to mark the return to the land of Nephi as a restoration or at least reenactment of the beginnings of Nephite civilization. As a kind of "latter-day Nephi," Zeniff may have seen himself as reviving his ancestor's settlement of the mountainous land of Nephi through a glorious conquest. And indeed, the whole of Mosiah 9–10—written entirely in the first person and therefore apparently by Zeniff himself—betrays a kind of self-conscious spirit of historical reenactment. A whole series of parallels with 1 Nephi 18 and 2 Nephi 5 deserves attention:

From the Record of Zeniff	From the Small Plates
We started again on our journey into the wilderness to go up to the land; but we were smitten with famine and sore afflictions; for we were slow to remember the Lord our God. (Mosiah 9:3)	And it came to pass that after they had bound me insomuch that I could not move, the compass, which had been prepared of the Lord, did cease to work. (1 Nephi 18:12) [And it did work for them according to their faith in God; therefore, if they had faith to believe that God could cause that those spindles should point the way they should go, behold, it was done; therefore they had this miracle, and also many other miracles wrought by the power of God, day by day. Nevertheless, because those miracles were worked by small means it did show unto them marvelous works. They were slothful, and forgot to exercise their faith and diligence and then those marvelous works ceased, and they did not progress in their journey; Therefore, they tarried in the wilderness, or did not travel a direct course, and were afflicted with hunger and thirst, because of their transgressions. (Alma 37:40–42)]
After many days' wandering in the wilderness we pitched our tents. (Mosiah 9:4)	And it came to pass that when [Lehi] had traveled three days in the wilderness, he pitched his tent in a valley by the side of a river of water. (1 Nephi 2:6) And it came to pass that after we had sailed for the space of many days we did arrive at the promised land; and we went forth upon the land, and did pitch our tents; and we did call it the promised land. (1 Nephi 18:23) And after we had journeyed for the space of many days we did pitch our tents. (2 Nephi 5:7)

From the Record of Zeniff	From the Small Plates
The land of Lehi-Nephi. (Mosiah 9:6)	An account of Lehi and his wife Sariah and his four sons, being called, (beginning at the eldest) Laman, Lemuel, Sam, and Nephi. (headnote to 1 Nephi)
And we began to build buildings, and to repair the walls of the city. (Mosiah 9:8)	And I did teach my people to build buildings, and to work in all manner of wood, and of iron, and of copper, and of brass, and of steel, and of gold, and of silver, and of precious ores, which were in great abundance. (2 Nephi 5:15)
And we began to till the ground, yea, even with all manner of seeds, with seeds of corn, and of wheat, and of barley, and with neas, and with sheum, and with seeds of all manner of fruits; and we did begin to multiply and prosper in the land. (Mosiah 9:9) I did cause that the men should till the ground, and raise all manner of grain and all manner of fruit of every kind. (Mosiah 10:4)	And it came to pass that we did begin to till the earth, and we began to plant seeds; yea, we did put all our seeds into the earth, which we had brought from the land of Jerusalem. And it came to pass that they did grow exceedingly; wherefore, we were blessed in abundance. (1 Nephi 18:24) And the Lord was with us; and we did prosper exceedingly; for we did sow seed, and we did reap again in abundance. (2 Nephi 5:11).
Now they were a lazy and an idolatrous people; therefore they were desirous to bring us into bondage, that they might glut themselves with the labors of our hands; yea, that they might feast themselves upon the flocks of our field. (Mosiah 9:12)	And because of their cursing which was upon them they did become an idle people, full of mischief and subtlety, and did seek in the wilderness for beasts of prey. (2 Nephi 5:24)
There began to be wars and contentions in the land. (Mosiah 9:13)	And it sufficeth me to say that forty years had passed away, and we had already had wars and contentions with our brethren. (2 Nephi 5:34)

From the Record of Zeniff	From the Small Plates
[My people] did call upon me for protection. (Mosiah 9:15)	Nephi, unto whom ye look as a king or a protector, and on whom ye depend for safety. (2 Nephi 6:2)
I did arm them with bows, and with arrows, with swords, and with cimeters, and with clubs, and with slings, and with all manner of weapons which we could invent. (Mosiah 9:16) And I caused that there should be weapons of war made of every kind, that thereby I might have weapons for my people against the time the Lamanites should come up again to war against my people. (Mosiah 10:1)	And I, Nephi, did take the sword of Laban, and after the manner of it did make many swords, lest by any means the people who were now called Lamanites should come upon us and destroy us. (2 Nephi 5:14)
I and my people did cry mightily to the Lord that he would deliver us out of the hands of our enemies. (Mosiah 9:17)	Wilt thou deliver me out of the hands of mine enemies? . . . O Lord, wilt thou make a way for mine escape before mine enemies! Wilt thou make my path straight before me! Wilt thou not place a stumbling block in my way—but that thou wouldst clear my way before me, and hedge not up my way, but the ways of mine enemy. (2 Nephi 4:31–33)
[The Lamanites] believ[ed] that they were driven out of the land of Jerusalem because of the iniquities of their fathers, and that they were wronged in the wilderness by their brethren, and they were also wronged while crossing the sea. (Mosiah 10:12)	And thou art like unto our father, led away by the foolish imaginations of his heart; yea, he hath led us out of the land of Jerusalem, and we have wandered in the wilderness for these many years; and our women have toiled, being big with child; and they have borne children in the wilderness and suffered all things, save it were death; and it would have been better that they had died before they came out of Jerusalem than to have suffered these afflictions. (1 Nephi 17:20)

From the Record of Zeniff	From the Small Plates
	And I, Nephi, began to fear exceedingly lest the Lord should be angry with us, and smite us because of our iniquity, that we should be swallowed up in the depths of the sea; wherefore, I, Nephi, began to speak to them with much soberness; but behold they were angry with me, saying: We will not that our younger brother shall be a ruler over us. (1 Nephi 18:10)
And again, [Nephi's brethren] were wroth with him when they had arrived in the promised land, because they said that he had taken the ruling of the people out of their hands; and they sought to kill him. (Mosiah 10:15)	Yea, they did murmur against me, saying: Our younger brother thinks to rule over us; and we have had much trial because of him; wherefore, now let us slay him, that we may not be afflicted more because of his words. For behold, we will not have him to be our ruler; for it belongs unto us, who are the elder brethren, to rule over this people. (2 Nephi 5:3)
And again, [Nephi's brethren] were wroth with him because he departed into the wilderness as the Lord had commanded him, and took the records which were engraven on the plates of brass, for they said that he robbed them. (Mosiah 10:16)	Wherefore, it came to pass that I, Nephi, did take my family, and also Zoram and his family, and Sam, mine elder brother and his family, and Jacob and Joseph, my younger brethren, and also my sisters, and all those who would go with me. And all those who would go with me were those who believed in the warnings and the revelations of God; wherefore, they did hearken unto my words. . . . And I, Nephi, had also brought the records which were engraven upon the plates of brass. (2 Nephi 5:6, 12)

From the Record of Zeniff	From the Small Plates
And thus [the Lamanites] have taught their children that they should hate them, and that they should murder them, and that they should rob and plunder them, and do all they could to destroy them; therefore they have an eternal hatred towards the children of Nephi. (Mosiah 10:17)	I knew their hatred towards me and my children and those who were called my people. (2 Nephi 5:14)
And now I, being old, did confer the kingdom upon one of my sons; therefore, I say no more. (Mosiah 10:22)	Now Nephi began to be old, and he saw that he must soon die; wherefore, he anointed a man to be a king and a ruler over his people now, according to the reigns of the kings. (Jacob 1:9)

These parallels suggest that Zeniff consciously borrowed from the small plates and, in light of these borrowings, it seems that Zeniff saw himself as a kind of Nephi reborn, reproducing the Nephite beginnings in his own time, right down to gaining superiority over the Lamanites and claiming the land over which Nephi himself had originally ruled.

Curiously, as soon as Zeniff's record (Mosiah 9–10) comes to an end, the voice of a third-person narrator, rather than the first-person voice of Zeniff's royal successor, takes over (in Mosiah 11). This sudden distance from the king's perspective, though, also reproduces the spirit of the small plates. After Nephi's contribution to the small plates, the priestly—rather than kingly—line assumes responsibility for the record, such that the small plates, like the "record of Zeniff," turn abruptly from a first-person account *of* the king to a third-person account *about* the king. Moreover, in both Mosiah and the small plates, the succeeding third-person account about the king is critical. Nephi's successor, like King Noah, is unfaithful. Indeed, both succeeding kings are described in the respective records as given to the same sins:

King Noah	Nephi's Successor
He had *many wives and concubines.* And he did cause his people to commit sin, and do that which was abominable in the sight of the Lord.	And now it came to pass that the people of Nephi, under the reign of the second king, began to grow hard in their hearts, and indulge themselves

Yea, and they did commit whoredoms and all manner of wickedness. And he laid a tax of one fifth part of all they possessed, a fifth part of their *gold and* of their *silver*, and a fifth part of their ziff, and of their copper, and of their brass and their iron; and a fifth part of their fatlings; and also a fifth part of all their grain.... And it came to pass that king Noah built *many elegant and spacious buildings*; and he ornamented them with fine work of wood, and of all manner of precious things, *of gold, and of silver*, and of iron, and of brass, and of ziff, and of copper. And he also built him a spacious palace, and a throne in the midst thereof, all of which was of fine wood and was ornamented with gold and silver and with precious things. And he also caused that his workmen should work all manner of fine work within the walls of the temple, of fine wood, and of copper, and of brass. (Mosiah 11:2–3, 8–10)

somewhat in wicked practices, such as like unto David of old desiring *many wives and concubines*, and also Solomon, his son. Yea, and they also began to search much *gold and silver*, and began to be lifted up somewhat in *pride*. (Jacob 1:15–16)

(See also Jacob 2–3.)

This connection between Noah's sins and the sins of Nephi's successor makes clear that the parallel between the small plates and the story of the return to the land of Nephi runs deep. If the Zeniff narrative is an intentional echo of First and Second Nephi, it appears that the Noah/Abinadi narrative is similarly an intentional echo of the book of Jacob.

The book of Mosiah thus reenacts not only the original settling of the land of Nephi but also—unfortunately—the corruption of the founding king's successor. This allows for a more critical reading of the shift from first-person narration in Mosiah 9–10 to third-person narration beginning in Mosiah 11. It seems that the editor of the Noah narrative intended with this shift to highlight an implicit problem in Zeniff's apparent belief that he was restoring the original Nephite kingdom. Though Zeniff would seem to have been justified in seeing himself as an eschatological figure—a kind of end-times character bringing back the golden age and so, in some sense, bringing Nephite history to its end—the editor of the narrative makes clear that such a vision would be badly mistaken, because Zeniff's restoration led only to the same problematic excesses that followed the original monarchical establishment in the land of Nephi. The editor, in other words, emphasized what Zeniff himself began to suspect by the end of his life—that the "restoration" was the result of an "over-zealous" and therefore romantic/nostalgic desire to restore a paradise that had never really existed as such in the first place (see Mosiah 9:3).

What, though, of Jacob in all this? Crucially, just as Jacob in the small plates prophetically disrupts the second Nephite king's royal excesses, Abinadi in Mosiah prophetically disrupts Noah's similar actions. If Zeniff is Nephi reborn and Noah Nephi's successor reborn, Abinadi is Jacob reborn. But, one might object, did not Jacob—as a priest and teacher, ordained by Nephi himself—wield far more institutional power than Abinadi? Not necessarily. Jacob's own book, carefully read, seems to trace a trajectory of increasing disincorporation. If Jacob seems to have a strong influence when he gives his speech against the king's excesses in Jacob 1–3, his writings in Jacob 4–6 suggest that he subsequently retreated from (or was forced out of) the public sphere and focused his efforts on writing, Isaiah-like, to future generations. At any rate, Jacob's marginal social position in Jacob 7 is unmistakable, and he describes himself there as having had to use Sherem's demise to his prophetic advantage. And Jacob's descendants Enos and Jarom appear to have been even further marginalized institutionally. If Jacob was not at first an outsider like Abinadi, there is nonetheless some evidence that he became such, perhaps precisely because of his witness against the king.[25]

But Jacob and Abinadi are connected still more profoundly. Abinadi not only reembodies Jacob narratively, he also clearly inherits Jacob's *doctrinal* legacy. Jacob actually occupies a strange place in the small plates. Nephi's doctrinal concerns focus almost exclusively on what might be called "covenantal theology." Likely because of his apocalyptic visions—not to mention his way of reading Isaiah—Nephi always looked to the future history of Israel. Nephi never leaves this theme to discuss its soteriological underpinnings (to discuss, that is, what the covenant implies about *individual* salvation). In short, because Nephi's vision is consistently trained on the covenant, he says nothing about Christ's atoning sacrifice as such. But while *Nephi* never deals with these "practical" details, Jacob does—and, interestingly, he does so right in Nephi's record. The first word on the subject comes from Lehi in 2 Nephi 2, but the words offered there are directed specifically to Jacob. And so it is unsurprising that it is Jacob who offers the only systematic discussion of the theme in the small plates, located in 2 Nephi 9—a chapter long celebrated for its doctrinal exposition of the atonement. Interestingly, Nephi's only close-to-explicit statement about soteriology—"we are saved by grace, after all we can do"—is actually just a reformulation of something said by Jacob.[26]

Abinadi is Jacob's unquestionable doctrinal heir. Faced with Noah's priests who seem, as will be seen, to have inherited (and likely distorted) *only* Nephi's covenantal focus, Abinadi criticizes them by setting forth the soteriology that they apparently overlooked through their focus on a strictly covenantal theology. Moreover, Abinadi's discourse borders on being a commentary on 2 Nephi 9 (as well as on 2 Nephi 2), revealing his familiarity with Jacob's teachings. And Abinadi—through his influence on Alma—seems thereby to have launched a two-centuries-long Nephite focus on soteriology.[27] Abinadi thus appears in Mosiah as the double heir of Jacob, as much doctrinally or theologically as narratively or historically.

The Structure of Abinadi's Speech

The analysis so far wagered locates Abinadi's speech both within the framework of the larger Book of Mormon project and within the framework of the book of Mosiah itself. The importance of these contextual details will become clear in chapter 5. However, before finally turning to less exegetical, more theological reflection, it is necessary to take up one last question: What is the basic structure of Abinadi's speech itself?

Abinadi's speech is responsive and interpretive from the start. Taken before Noah and his priests because he criticized the king and his people, Abinadi's words are a bold defense of his actions. Moreover, because his condemnation of the king was a *prophetic* intervention (rather than a merely *political* move), Abinadi's trial has a thoroughly religious character. Noah's priests force Abinadi to defend himself by, oddly enough, interpreting scripture, and the text they ask him to interpret happens to be, of all things, a passage from Second Isaiah (Isaiah 52:7–10). The way this develops deserves close attention.

The verses leading up to the priests' challenge read as follows:

> And it came to pass that king Noah caused that Abinadi should be cast into prison; and he commanded that the priests should gather themselves

> together that he might hold a council with them what he should do with him. And it came to pass that they said unto the king: Bring him hither that we may question him; and the king commanded that he should be brought before them. And they began to question him, that they might cross him, that thereby they might have wherewith to accuse him; but he answered them boldly, and withstood all their questions, yea, to their astonishment; for he did withstand them in all their questions, and did confound them in all their words. And it came to pass that one of them said unto him: What meaneth the words which are written, and which have been taught by our fathers, saying . . . (Mosiah 12:17–20)

Several points here call for comment.[28]

First, does verse 19 ("they began to question him . . . but he answered them boldly," etc.) refer to an event separate from the speech recorded at length, or is it meant to summarize the recorded speech itself? In other words, does the *whole* passage just quoted lay out the chronology leading up to the encounter over Second Isaiah, or does only *the first half* do so, the remainder being a summary of Abinadi's recorded speech? In the end, I think that this passage describes *two* distinct events—a first, unnarrated interrogation in which Abinadi withstands the priests (verses 17–19), and only thereafter the question about Isaiah and Abinadi's chapters-long response (verse 20 and what follows). If this is right, then it appears that the question about Isaiah was the priests' trump card—their final, most difficult question, saved to the last because they believed Abinadi could not maneuver out of its trap. This is important, I believe, because it indicates that Noah's priests, despite being physically lazy (as described in Mosiah 11:6), were anything but theologically lazy. Though it is perhaps common to see the priests as crafty but simply wrong—as if they had no theological leg to stand on, no actual scriptural or even logical defense for their ideology—it may prove important to see them as having believed they had a watertight case that would settle the whole Abinadi affair to everyone's—perhaps even Abinadi's—satisfaction.[29] The priests' "astonishment" may well have been more of a question of their being completely unprepared for the radically "unorthodox" position Abinadi would take than of their being unprepared to defend their own position in generally convincing terms.

That Abinadi's defense was launched from grounds that were drastically distinct from those on which the priests stood is perhaps confirmed by the roundabout nature of Abinadi's speech. Abinadi does not come to the actual work of interpreting the Isaiah passage until relatively late in his remarks (the question comes in Mosiah 12:20–24, but Abinadi's actual interpretation does not appear until Mosiah 15), making clear that he had first to establish the grounds on which his interpretation was to be built, or at least to call into question the priests' problematic presuppositions. Only after so much preliminary work is it possible for Abinadi's interpretation to have any purchase for his audience.

In light just of this first remark, Abinadi's speech can be divided into two major parts:

1. Mosiah 12:25 – 15:9: Reworking Presuppositions

2. Mosiah 15:10 – 16:15: Interpreting Second Isaiah

Interestingly, this basic division of the speech turns out to be significant in light of chapters 2 and 3 of the present study. While the second part of the speech is unquestionably focused on the question of *how Isaiah is to be interpreted,* Abinadi only comes to this second part after a preliminary discussion focused—in the work of questioning the priests' basic presuppositions—on the relationship between the Law (of Moses) and the Prophets. In other words, in order to come to the task of sorting out how to read Isaiah, Abinadi first clarifies the status of the (typological) Law.

Narrowing in, then, on the first half of Abinadi's speech, one can further subdivide the discussion of the Law:

1a. Mosiah 12:25 – 13:26: On Obeying the Law

1b. Mosiah 13:27–33: From the Law to the Prophets

1c. Mosiah 13:34 – 15:9: The Message of the Prophets

At the level of the outline, things seem relatively simple. At the level of the details, however, things are not. After first discussing the necessity of obeying the Law—something Abinadi addresses primarily, it seems, to point out his hearers' hypocrisy—Abinadi talks about the typological Law in a way that might at first seem to echo Nephi. But as he turns from the Law to the Prophets, Abinadi proposes an understanding of the prophets that is clearly distinct from Nephi's, the result being that Abinadi's typological Law takes a shape structurally different from that articulated by Nephi. These details and their significance will be worked out in chapter 5.

In the meanwhile, what about the second half of Abinadi's speech? Importantly, Abinadi straightforwardly divides his interpretation of Isaiah into two parts. When he finally comes to Isaiah, he first addresses only Isaiah 52:7 (in Mosiah 15:10–18). It is only after an excursus of sorts that he comes (beginning with Mosiah 15:28) to Isaiah 52:8–10. It is thus possible also to outline the basic structure of the second half of Abinadi's speech:

2a. Mosiah 15:10–18: Interpretation of Isaiah 52:7

2b. Mosiah 15:19–27: Excursus on the First Resurrection

2c. Mosiah 15:28 – 16:15: Interpretation of Isaiah 52:8–10

It is in the excursus that divides his discussion of Isaiah in two that Abinadi introduces into the Book of Mormon the doctrine of what he calls the "first resurrection." That he takes up an excursus of such length in the middle of his interpretive work indicates that the doctrine there discussed is, for Abinadi, necessary to his interpretation of Isaiah. Without that doctrine, Abinadi's interpretation of Isaiah 52:7 cannot be linked up with his interpretation of Isaiah 52:8–10. Again, these details and their significance will have to be worked out in chapter 5.

Abinadi's speech, then, can be read as having two major parts: (1) a revisionary discussion of the relationship between the Law and the Prophets that (2) allows for a further revisionary discussion of how Isaiah should be read. Whatever else Abinadi's speech accomplishes, it reworks the meaning of the Law for the Nephites and opens the way for the church that then shapes Nephite religious thought up until the visit of Christ in Third Nephi.

Notes

1. Among the commentators, only one both mentions that Abinadi and Christ comment on the same passage from Isaiah and notes that there are differences between their interpretations. Nonetheless, he makes no actual comparison between the two interpretations. See Dana M. Pike, "'How Beautiful upon the Mountains': The Imagery of Isaiah 52:7–10 and Its Occurrences in the Book of Mormon," in Parry and Welch, *Isaiah in the Book of Mormon*, 260–271.

2. Among the standard commentaries, none attempts to identify the nature of the disputations to which Christ refers. While most simply ignore the question entirely, two specifically warn against any attempt to identify the disputations. See McConkie and Millet, *Doctrinal Commentary*, 4:57; and Gardner, *Second Witness*, 5:346.

3. See Gardner, *Second Witness*, 3:327–328, for instance: "Alma's baptism . . . differs from Nephi's." Cf. also 2:433–436. That McConkie and Millet, on the other hand,

see no fundamental difference between Nephi's and Alma's notions of baptism is clear when, in their commentary on Mosiah 18, they quote 2 Nephi 31 in order to exposit Alma's understanding. McConkie and Millet, *Doctrinal Commentary on the Book of Mormon*, 2:254.

4. McConkie and Millet, *Doctrinal Commentary on the Book of Mormon*, 4:55–56.

5. Sidney B. Sperry offers another approach to these questions, suggesting, on the strength of 3 Nephi 5:12 (which speaks of Alma's church as "the first church" but perhaps qualifies the word "first" when it adds "*after* their [the Nephites'] transgression"), that Alma's church was a *restoration* of Nephi's, an organization lost during the apostate years of the later small plates writers. See Sidney B. Sperry, *Book of Mormon Compendium* (Salt Lake City: Bookcraft, 1968), 312.

6. Indeed, there is a good deal of textual work that has never been fully and responsibly undertaken that would have to be done before any definitive interpretation of these questions could be offered. My treatment here has skimmed over the surface of the difficulties at best.

7. Cf., though, Hardy, *Understanding the Book of Mormon*, 180–183.

8. The only quasi-interruption of this lineage is to be found in Alma 63 and is brilliantly analyzed by Grant Hardy. See Hardy, *Understanding the Book of Mormon*, 142–144.

9. Wherever it might be unclear which Book of Mormon character is referred to, I have used the subscript numbering system employed in Hardy's *Reader's Edition* of the Book of Mormon.

10. Brant Gardner's structuration of Mormon's editorial project emphasizes this story of disintegration. Brant A. Gardner, "Mormon's Editorial Method and Meta-Message," *FARMS Review* 21.1 (2009): 83–105.

11. I do, however, highly recommend the analysis of Moroni in Hardy, *Understanding the Book of Mormon*, 217–267.

12. I have ignored here the so-called "book of Lehi," Mormon's lost abridgment of the history of the Nephites up to the reign of King Benjamin. While this material would obviously have been important to Mormon, it is difficult to know what it would have looked like, since Mormon wrote it before he discovered the small plates. Speculation about the contents of the book of Lehi seems to me to be unhelpful.

13. Gary L. Sturgess, "The Book of Mosiah: Thoughts about Its Structure, Purposes, Themes, and Authorship," *Journal of Book of Mormon Studies* 4.2 (1995): 107–135.

14. Ibid., 134. See also Gordon C. Thomasson, "Mosiah: The Complex Symbolism and Symbolic Complex of Kingship in the Book of Mormon," *Journal of Book of Mormon Studies* 2.1 (1993): 21–38.

15. See Mosiah 26:15–17.

16. On Zeniff's personality, see Hardy, *Understanding the Book of Mormon*, 123–132.

17. Because of the distance between them, the two kingdoms were completely out of touch with one another. Their histories became entirely independent for two generations.

18. The parallel deaths of Abinadi and Noah mirror the parallel escapes of Alma and Noah's priests.

19. The most systematic discussion of the authorship of the Abinadi narrative is John W. Welch, *The Legal Cases in the Book of Mormon* (Provo, UT: BYU Press and The Neal A. Maxwell Institute for Religious Scholarship, 2008), 140–145.

20. On this conflict, see John L. Sorenson, "Religious Groups and Movements among the Nephites, 200–1 B.C.," in Stephen D. Ricks, Donald W. Parry, and Andrew H. Hedges, eds. *The Disciple as Scholar: Essays on Scripture and the Ancient World in Honor of Richard Lloyd Anderson* (Provo, UT: FARMS, 2000), 163–208.

21. See Todd B. Parker, "Abinadi: The Man and the Message," retrieved October 10, 2009, from http://mi.byu.edu/publications/transcripts/?id=41; and Todd B. Parker, "Abinadi: The Message and the Martyr," retrieved October 10, 2009 from http://mi.byu.edu/publications/transcripts/?id=42. Parker mentions twenty-five parallels between Abinadi's and the angel's words.

22. That Benjamin receives a heavenly messenger while Noah receives an earthly messenger is important, but not decisive. It will be remembered that Abinadi takes on an angelic—or at least certainly supernatural—appearance during his speech (see Mosiah 13:5).

23. See Sturgess, "Book of Mosiah," 108; Royal Skousen, *The Printer's Manuscript of the Book of Mormon: Typographical Facsimile of the Entire Text in Two Parts*, 2 vols. (Provo, UT: FARMS, 2001), 1:284; Gardner, *Second Witness*, 3:97–98; and, for a revisionary approach, Brent Lee Metcalfe, "The Priority of Mosiah: A Prelude to Book of Mormon Exegesis," in Brent Lee Metcalfe, ed., *New Approaches to the Book of Mormon: Explorations in Critical Methodology* (Salt Lake City: Signature Books, 1993), 395–444.

24. Brant Gardner states straightforwardly of Mosiah 9:1–2: "This introduction echoes [1] Nephi 1:1–2." He goes on, however, to suggest that the passages are "sufficiently different" that one should not regard Zeniff as "copying Nephi." Curiously, he goes on to suggest that perhaps Nephi had "introduced his large plates in a similar way," such that Zeniff would have been copying from those, rather than the small plates. Gardner, *Second Witness*, 3:227. Alan Goff, on the other hand, places Mosiah 9:1–2 and 1 Nephi 1 side by side much in the manner I do here, asserting their interdependence. Alan Goff, "Historical Narrative, Literary Narrative—Expelling Poetics from the Republic of History," *Journal of Book of Mormon Studies* 5.1 (Spring 1996): 85–86.

25. Radicalizing the parallel between Jacob and Abinadi, one might suggest that Abinadi was one of the deposed when Noah "put down all the priests that had been consecrated by his father, and consecrated new ones in their stead, such as were lifted up in the pride of their hearts" (Mosiah 11:5). Incidentally, John Tvedtnes has outlined

this possibility: "It is possible that [Abinadi] was one of the deposed priests who had served under the righteous king Zeniff, but, alas, the record is silent on this matter." John A. Tvedtnes, *The Most Correct Book: Insights from a Book of Mormon Scholar* (Salt Lake City: Cornerstone, 1999), 324.

26. I do not intend to suggest, though, that Jacob was unconcerned with covenantal theology. Indeed, he seems to have been quite as concerned with the covenant as with constructing a working soteriology. The point to emphasize is Jacob's uniqueness in focusing *at all* on soteriology in the small plates.

27. A Jacob-like focus on Christ's atoning sacrifice saturates the Book of Mormon from Abinadi's speech up until the visit of Christ. During the same period, interestingly, covenantal theology seems effectively to have disappeared.

28. The only detailed treatment of this "preliminary council" is in Welch, *Legal Cases in the Book of Mormon*, 166–169.

29. John Welch presents a picture of the priests "spen[ding] a fair amount of time discussing the law, if for no other purpose than to justify their conduct and to get as close to the edge of legality as they possibly could." Welch, *Legal Cases in the Book of Mormon*, 147.

5

Typology for Abinadi: Theology

After so much preparation, it is possible at last to turn to what Abinadi has to say about typology and to differentiate Abinadi's approach from Nephi's. Only with these two models of typological interpretation set side by side will it be possible to draw conclusions about what the Book of Mormon means by its claim—derived from Alma 36—that it, the Book of Mormon itself, is to be read typologically. The task of the present chapter is, then, to tackle Abinadi's discussion of typology quite directly.

I begin with a brief discussion, drawing heavily on the exegetical findings of chapter 4, of what seems to have motivated Noah's priests to give Abinadi the task to interpret, of all things, a passage from Second Isaiah. Through this preliminary discussion, the stakes of Abinadi's approach to Isaiah are clarified: the only way Abinadi could challenge the charges brought against him was to question the dominant approach to Isaiah he encountered in Noah's regime. This is followed by a close analysis of Abinadi's initial response to the question, which was not to address the meaning of Isaiah, but to call into question the priests' presumptions about the relationship between the Law and the Prophets. Through an audacious reworking of the meaning of the spirit of prophecy, coupled with an interpretation of Deuteronomy 18 that is clearly distinct from Nephi's much earlier interpretation, Abinadi presents himself to the priests as a radical revisionist.

In the next part of the chapter, I turn with Abinadi from Deuteronomy to Isaiah, looking at how Abinadi connects his understanding of Moses's role as prophet with Isaiah's role as prophet. This connection lays the foundation for what becomes Abinadi's understanding of typology, but it does not yet make clear exactly what his typological methodology is. That becomes clear only when we look in great detail at Mosiah 13:29–32, Abinadi's direct discussion, carefully contextualized by its placement in the midst of his discussion of Moses, of typology. There Abinadi clearly understands the typological nature of the Law to be a question of its symbolic anticipation of events in the life of the coming Christ.

Finally, I close the chapter with a look at how Christ, in Third Nephi, calls for a "return to Nephi" and privileges Nephi's approach to typology (together with its covenantal focus) over Abinadi's. Crucially, there are hints, both in Third Nephi and in the Mosiah account of Abinadi's speech, that the privileged role of Nephi's typological methodology is not to be understood as dismissing or simply dispensing with the Abinadite model. Rather, there seems to be a hierarchical relationship between them.

Motivations

In chapter 4, I argued not only that Abinadi's speech lays the foundation for a massive theological shift in Nephite thinking—a shift addressed by Christ himself in Third Nephi—but also that Abinadi lays that foundation through his approach to interpreting (Second) Isaiah. Consequently, the question to be asked in launching a theological interpretation of Abinadi's words is: Why do Noah's priests ask Abinadi to interpret Isaiah? If their intention was, as the text says, to "cross him, that thereby they might have wherewith to accuse him" (Mosiah 12:19), what do Noah's priests see in Isaiah 52:7–10, such that Abinadi's expected answer would allow them to condemn him? If this question has any real purchase, the priests must have anticipated a specific response from Abinadi. Noah's priests apparently assumed that Isaiah 52:7–10 had a single, obvious, incontrovertible meaning—a meaning that everyone in the land of Nephi would immediately see. Such an interpretation would have to have been well-known and rooted in a culture-wide ideology.

I begin, then, with these two assumptions. First, Isaiah 52:7–10 had, in the time of King Noah and at least in the land of Nephi, a standard interpretation, one secure enough to blind Noah's priests to the possibility of any other (justifiable) interpretation. Second, that standard interpretation—once extracted from or agreed to by Abinadi—would itself have condemned

Abinadi's prophetic intervention. With this background in mind, here is the Isaiah passage Abinadi was asked to interpret:

> How beautiful upon the mountains are the feet of him that bringeth good tidings; that publisheth peace; that bringeth good tidings of good; that publisheth salvation; that saith unto Zion, Thy God reigneth; Thy watchmen shall lift up the voice; with the voice together shall they sing; for they shall see eye to eye when the Lord shall bring again Zion; Break forth into joy; sing together ye waste places of Jerusalem; for the Lord hath comforted his people, he hath redeemed Jerusalem; The Lord hath made bare his holy arm in the eyes of all the nations, and all the ends of the earth shall see the salvation of our God. (Mosiah 12:21–24)

What was the standard interpretation of this text in Abinadi's time and place, and how would that interpretation have been used to condemn the prophet?

The most common approach among the commentators is to suggest that Abinadi's actions contradicted the first verse of the Isaiah passage. Whereas Isaiah speaks of bringing "good tidings," "peace," and "salvation" (Mosiah 12:21), Abinadi had prophetically spoken only of bondage, destruction, and punishment for wickedness. Perhaps the difference between Abinadi's negative character and Isaiah's positive picture of the prophet was meant to be used against Abinadi in the trial.[1] On this approach, Abinadi's speech could be read as reinterpreting Isaiah 52:7 along the following lines: the prophet did indeed, as Isaiah claims, have a positive message, the message that Christ is coming. Unfortunately, the prophet discovers few who desire to hear *that* good news, and so his positive announcement gives way to negative denunciation.

Without question, this first approach takes a step in the right direction, but it is hardly robust enough as it stands. First, it would be extreme to justify capital punishment by claiming, on the interpretation of a single verse, that prophets should always bring messages of joy. Second, the approach has no obvious connection to the historical and political circumstances in Noah's land of Nephi. And third, had the priests meant only to condemn Abinadi through verse 7 of Isaiah 52, why would they have bothered to quote verses 8–10 as well? This last point is crucial, since Abinadi himself does not finish his response with his counterinterpretation of Isaiah 52:7, but goes on—after an excursus on the first resurrection—to provide a full interpretation of Isaiah 52:8–10 as well. Abinadi himself makes clear that there is more at stake than the definition of prophecy.

How, then, might Isaiah 52:8–10 have been interpreted at that time and place? In a recent study, John Welch identifies the following vital point:

> This passage of scripture quoted to Abinadi by the priests could very well have been one of the theme texts that had been used often by Zeniff's colony as they rejoiced over their redemption of the land of their inheritance and temple. . . . In the face of Isaiah's prophecy and *its apparent glorious fulfillment by Zeniff's people,* how did Abinadi dare to accuse both the king and his people of falling under God's worst judgments?[22]

I believe Welch is exactly right here. That Noah's priests expected a particular answer to their question would likely imply that they themselves had often publicly expounded the text, and it is not difficult to imagine that they had presented it as a prophecy that Zeniff's return to the land of Nephi had gloriously fulfilled. *They* had witnessed the Lord "bring[ing] again Zion"; *they* had watched as the Lord "comforted his people" and "redeemed [a likened] Jerusalem"; and because these events had taken place through successful wars against *the Lamanites,* the Lord had "made bare his holy arm in the eyes of all the nations" and "all the ends of the earth . . . [had seen] the salvation of [their] God."

The pieces fit. Zeniff seems to have seen himself as the major player in a remarkable restoration—the refounding of the original Nephite monarchy in the land of Nephi. Among his revitalizations of Nephi's original project and through his obvious familiarity with the small plates, *Zeniff may well have also attempted to reintroduce Nephi's interpretive strategy of likening Isaiah.* Of course, because Zeniff seems to have seen himself as an eschatological figure, he likely would have seen Isaiah less as spelling out the *still-future* history of Israel than as detailing the *present* history of Israel—the history he and his people had lived out. In other words, there is reason to suggest that Zeniff took his own refounding to fulfill the likened writings of Second Isaiah. Indeed, when Noah's priests introduce the text to Abinadi, it is described as "the words . . . *which have been taught by our fathers*" (Mosiah 12:20). And if Isaiah had described perfectly and in advance Zeniff's restoration of Nephi's original kingdom, who could question the excesses of Noah's regime? Having received a land flowing with milk and honey, who could deny them their rightful enjoyment of that bounty?[23]

If Zeniff's people had come to interpret Isaiah 52:8–10 as connected to the refounding of the land of Nephi, they would naturally have come to interpret Isaiah 52:7 as claiming that, from the restoration onward, prophets were in essence no longer needed. The good tidings of the eschatological restoration of Nephi's kingdom had been definitively delivered, prophets (Isaiah, Nephi) and kings (Zeniff, Noah) had finally seen eye to eye and together lifted up the voice to sing praises. It appears that the employment of Isaiah 52:7–10 in Abinadi's trial was not opportunistic proof-texting that took advantage of a single scriptural passage suggesting that prophets are happy, positive characters. Rather, Noah's people and priests were apparently baffled by Abinadi's prophetic intervention simply because he claimed to be a prophet when prophets were no longer needed.

Thus, it would have been easy for the priests to put Abinadi away by making him interpret Isaiah 52:7–10. By the time of Abinadi's trial, that passage seems to have been interpreted for a full generation in such a way that the priests could—once Abinadi had dutifully repeated what had come to be the obvious (or only?) interpretation of the text in that time and place—condemn his intervention as the work of a religious radical, of someone who dismissed not only *Isaiah* (the likened prophet), but also *Nephi* (the provider of the method of likening). Blasphemy and sedition were the crimes on the docket, not merely unscriptural negativity.

From all this, a crucial point follows: *the only way Abinadi could avoid the charge and defend his prophetic intervention was to question the priests' understanding of Isaiah—of what it means to liken Isaiah.* This point guides the whole theological interpretation to follow.

The Law and the Prophets: Recasting the Situation

Abinadi's speech is thus principally a question of articulating a method for interpreting Isaiah. As already indicated in chapter 4, Abinadi takes up his task first by clarifying in detail *his* understanding of the relationship between the Law and the Prophets. It is therefore necessary to take up the task of interpretation here by beginning with Abinadi's discussion of that relationship.

Abinadi begins his response to Noah's priests with a poignant question: "Are you priests, and pretend to teach this people, and to understand the spirit of prophesying, and yet desire to know of me what these things mean?" (Mosiah 12:25). Here, through the wording of his counterquestion, together with its obvious sarcasm, Abinadi brutally exposes the subtle play of power at work in the priests' question. At the level of the word, Abinadi both

(1) affirms the priests' superiority and his own inferiority and, (2) by "coloring their question as a [genuine] request for information they did not possess,"[4] indicates that the priests themselves, through their question about Isaiah, have inverted their relationship with Abinadi (making him superior and themselves inferior). Of course, given Abinadi's sarcasm, it is clear that he actually neither believes in the priests' superiority nor assumes their question to be honest. But through the boldness of his sarcasm, as well as his charade of taking the priests quite literally at their word, Abinadi takes complete control of the situation, such that he becomes the asker—and the priests the answerers—of questions.

By seizing rhetorical control, Abinadi also introduces an idea that he regards as central to interpreting Isaiah—and the Prophets more generally—namely, "the spirit of prophesying." Coupling this "spirit" with "understanding," he makes his initial accusation against the priests:

> Are you priests, and pretend to teach this people, and to *understand* the spirit of prophesying, and yet desire to know of me what these things mean? I say unto you, wo be unto you for perverting the ways of the Lord! For if ye *understand* these things ye have not taught them; therefore, ye have perverted the ways of the Lord. Ye have not applied your hearts to *understanding;* therefore, ye have not been wise. (Mosiah 12:25–27)

Abinadi here refers three times to "understanding." First, as already mentioned, he refers to understanding the spirit of prophesying—something the priests apparently profess to do. Second, he speaks of understanding Isaiah, suggesting that there is some direct connection between understanding the spirit of prophesying and understanding the Prophets.[5] In making this connection, moreover, Abinadi, while leaving open the possibility that the priests actually *do* understand Isaiah correctly, nonetheless makes clear that the priests have never *taught* him correctly. And Abinadi thus can, third, accuse the priests of "not appl[ying their] hearts to understanding," that is, to the specifically prophetic work of interpreting the prophet.[6]

In these verses, Abinadi sets out two possible approaches to the fact that Noah's priests have not taught Isaiah correctly. Either they have not taught Isaiah correctly because they lack the spirit of prophesying, and therefore their question is actually an honest plea for interpretive help—whether they know it or not. Or they have not taught Isaiah correctly because, while through the spirit of prophesying they actually *do* know the meaning of

Isaiah, they nonetheless deliberately misinterpret his words, and therefore their question is deceptive through and through. Either they mistakenly believe they understand the spirit of prophesying, in which case they need correction; or they deliberately deceive the public, in which case they simply deserve condemnation.

Abinadi next asks the first of a series of questions that he intends the priests actually to answer: "Therefore, what teach ye this people?" (Mosiah 12:27). Given what has just been said, it seems Abinadi asks this question in order, through the priests' answer, to determine which of the two possibilities outlined is correct. Are the priests simply ideologically blinded to their misunderstanding of the spirit of prophesying, or are they deliberately deceiving the people in their interpretation of Isaiah? But the priests' response is, in essence, a dodge: "We teach the law of Moses" (Mosiah 12:28). Attempting, it would seem, to get around the issue of prophetically interpreting the Prophets, Noah's priests turn to the Law. But there they find another impasse when Abinadi asks his next question: "If ye teach the law of Moses why do ye not keep it?" (Mosiah 12:29). Certainly it is as problematic to interpret the Prophets without the spirit of prophesying as it is to teach the Law without obeying it.

But more importantly, Abinadi's second question also blocks the priests' attempted retreat by making clear that there is no clean disconnect between the Law and the Prophets: "If ye teach the *law* of Moses why do ye not keep it . . . , [such] that the Lord has cause to send me to *prophesy* against this people?" (Mosiah 12:29). The connection Abinadi here asserts between the Law and the Prophets is crucial. For him, it seems, prophets appear precisely when and where the Law is being misunderstood or abused, as if the prophets are sent specifically to clarify the status or meaning of the Law. The Law, it seems, is not without the Prophets, nor the Prophets without the Law.

But this connection between the Law and the Prophets is subtle at this point in the narrative, and Abinadi, instead of belaboring the point, returns to the priests' hypocritical flouting of the Law that they claim to teach: "it shall come to pass that ye shall be smitten for your iniquities, for ye have said that ye teach the law of Moses" (Mosiah 12:31). In fact, making his accusations more specific, Abinadi begins to recite the Ten Commandments, announcing in the middle of the recitation: "Have ye done all this? I say unto you, Nay, ye have not. And have ye taught this people that they should do all these things? I say unto you, Nay, ye have not" (Mosiah 12:37).

But Abinadi's interrogation is disrupted at this point. Noah, likely sick of this carnivalesque showdown, interjects with a diagnosis of Abinadi as obviously "mad" and a command that he be hauled away and killed (Mosiah 13:1). But Abinadi famously commands Noah's servants not to touch him, because he has "not delivered the message which the Lord sent [him] to deliver" (Mosiah 13:3). Rather than confirming Abinadi's madness, this resistance convinces the court to leave him alone—apparently principally because his face is reported to have "shone with exceeding luster, even as Moses' did while in the mount of Sinai, while speaking with the Lord" (Mosiah 13:5). The crucial significance of this turn of events will be discussed in some detail later. For the moment, it is only important to note that the miracle allows Abinadi to continue his speech. He quickly finishes his recitation and thus completes his basic accusation.

However, as Abinadi comes to the end of the Ten Commandments, he returns to the subtle point of connection between the Law and the Prophets: "It came to pass that after Abinadi had made an end of these sayings that he said unto them: Have ye taught this people that they should observe to do all these things for to keep *these commandments*? I say unto you, Nay; for if ye had, the Lord would not have caused me to come forth and *to prophesy* evil concerning this people" (Mosiah 13:25–26). But whereas Abinadi passed over this connection rather quickly before, he now takes it up explicitly and at length.

At this point, with only the subtle affirmation of an implicit connection between the Law and the Prophets, it might appear that Abinadi understands the prophets to have the task—as they often enough do in the Old Testament—of interrupting popular attempts to *totalize* the Law, of ensuring that the Law does not become a "Said" rather than a "Saying."[7] That is, it appears at first that Abinadi means only to say what has been explained by Paul Beauchamp (and nicely summarized by Paul Ricoeur):

> The Torah [Law], inasmuch as it is indivisibly law and narrative tradition, establishes what could be called the ethico-narrative identity of the people; and this identity is grounded in the security and the stability of a tradition. Prophecy, in turn, confronts this identity with the hazards of a strange and hostile history. Harbingers and witnesses of the destruction, the Prophets establish an essentially threatened [cultural] identity.[8]

However, beginning from the very next verses (Mosiah 13:27–33), Abinadi clarifies at length that he has in mind a rather distinct notion of prophetic intervention.

He begins:

> And now ye have said that salvation cometh by the law of Moses. I say unto you that it is expedient that ye should keep the law of Moses as yet; but I say unto you, that the time shall come when it shall no more be expedient to keep the law of Moses. And moreover, I say unto you, that salvation doth not come by the law alone; and were it not for the atonement, which God himself shall make for the sins and iniquities of his people, that they must unavoidably perish, notwithstanding the law of Moses. (Mosiah 13:27–28)

Here it becomes clear that Abinadi does not mean, in his intertwining of the Law and the Prophets, just to "establish an essentially threatened identity" through announcements of apocalypse. Rather, what calls narrow understandings of the Law into question for Abinadi is the prophetic anticipation of the *atonement*. For Abinadi, a prophet is through and through the figure who looks forward to the coming of the Messiah, the coming of "*God himself*" who "shall make [atonement] for the sins and iniquities of his people." The prophet's task is to make clear that obedience to the Law is not, in the end, what saves the people—whether as a "Saying" or a "Said"—because, "were it not for the atonement, . . . they must unavoidably perish, notwithstanding the law of Moses."

The Law and the Prophets: Deuteronomy 18

At exactly this moment, Abinadi begins to mark his distinction from Nephi—less, at first, in terms of the Law than in terms of the Prophets. Where Nephi took the Prophets to be concerned primarily—if not exclusively—with the eschatological redemption of Israel, Abinadi takes them to be concerned primarily—if not exclusively—with the redemption worked out in Christ's atonement. Thus, though both Nephi and Abinadi understand the Law to be aimed at its fulfillment in Christ, each holds a distinct notion of the Prophets. But in order to make this point sharper, it is necessary to look more closely at what Abinadi has to say about the relationship between the Law and the Prophets.

Distinguishing most sharply between Nephi's and Abinadi's understandings of the Prophets is Moses's own status *as a prophet*. Both Nephi and Abinadi call Moses a prophet, but they seem to understand this in different ways. In

Mosiah 13:33, Abinadi asks rhetorically: "For behold, did not Moses prophesy unto them concerning the coming of the Messiah, and that God should redeem his people?" Presumably, Abinadi here has reference to Deuteronomy 18:15–19:

> [Moses says:] The Lord thy God will raise up unto thee a Prophet from the midst of thee, of thy brethren, like unto me; unto him ye shall hearken. . . . And the Lord said unto me, . . . I will raise them up a Prophet from among their brethren, like unto thee, and will put my words in his mouth; and he shall speak unto them all that I shall command him. And it shall come to pass, that whosoever will not hearken unto my words which he shall speak in my name, I will require it of him.

By alluding to this Deuteronomic text, Abinadi joins a venerable tradition of Nephite interest in it. Lehi first makes reference to it in 1 Nephi 10:4, and that quotation launches a trajectory that passes through Nephi's reference to it 1 Nephi 22:20–21 and Abinadi's in Mosiah 13:33 to Christ's in 3 Nephi 20:23 and 21:11.

The reference in 1 Nephi 10:4 is of particular importance. There Nephi describes Lehi as teaching that "six hundred years from the time that [he] left Jerusalem, *a prophet would the Lord God raise up among the Jews*—even *a Messiah*, or, in other words, a Savior of the world." While the first part of this prophecy—the raising up of a prophet among the Jews—clearly echoes the Deuteronomy passage, Lehi adds the explicitly messianic element ("even a Messiah"), which never appears in Deuteronomy. But because Deuteronomy 18 itself speaks only of a *prophet* and never of a *Messiah*, it is likely that Abinadi's reference to the text has passed through the mediating, messianic lens of Lehi in 1 Nephi 10. This likelihood is, in fact, stronger still, given the fact that Nephi describes Lehi (in the next verse) as further describing "this Messiah" as the "Redeemer of the world" (1 Nephi 10:5). Abinadi not only speaks of Moses's "prophet" as "the Messiah," but also as the figure who "should redeem [God's] people" (Mosiah 13:33).

There thus seems to be a kind of trajectory of both textual abridgment and theological expansion that passes from Deuteronomy 18 through 1 Nephi 10 to Mosiah 13. Moses's original prophecy is summarized but also theologically augmented by Lehi; and Abinadi in turn further summarizes Lehi's summary while retaining his theological expansions:

Deuteronomy 18	1 Nephi 10	Mosiah 13
The Lord thy God will raise up unto thee a Prophet from the midst of thee, of thy brethren, like unto me [Moses]; unto him ye shall hearken. (v. 15) And the Lord said unto me, . . . **I will raise them up a Prophet from among their brethren,** like unto thee [Moses], and will put my words in his mouth; and he shall speak unto them all that I shall command him. And it shall come to pass, that whosoever will not hearken unto my words which he shall speak in my name, I will require it of him. (vv. 17–19)	Yea, even six hundred years from the time that my father left Jerusalem, **a prophet would the Lord God raise up among the Jews—** *even a Messiah,* or, in other words, a Savior of the world. And he also spake concerning the prophets, how great a number had testified of these things, concerning *this Messiah,* of whom he had spoken, *or this Redeemer of the world.* (vv. 4–5)	For behold, did not **Moses** [in Deuteronomy 18] prophesy unto them concerning *the coming of the Messiah,* and that *God should redeem his people?* (v. 33)

It thus seems that it is Nephi specifically, through his recording of Lehi's teachings, who provides Abinadi with his interpretation of Deuteronomy 18. For Abinadi, Moses prophesied of the Messiah who, having been God, would "come down among the children of men, and take upon him the form of man, and go forth in mighty power upon the face of the earth," only to be "oppressed and afflicted" and then put to death (Mosiah 13:34–35). Ironically, though, when Nephi himself—that is, not in reporting his father's teachings, but in outlining his own—quotes the same Deuteronomy passage in 1 Nephi 22, he understands it quite differently. Whatever Lehi might have seen in the Deuteronomy 18 prophecy, *Nephi* takes it to refer not to the Messiah's mortal advent, but to the Redeemer's eschatological intervention.

The context of Nephi's quotation of and commentary on Deuteronomy 18 (in 1 Nephi 22) is pivotal: *Nephi takes up Deuteronomy 18 immediately after quoting—and thus in the context of commenting on—two full chapters from Second Isaiah.* Nephi's focus, consequently, is not on Christ's coming in the flesh to accomplish the atonement and resurrection, but on the much later restoration of Israel. Here, as elsewhere, Nephi assumes that Moses and his Law are to be understood through the careful work of likening Isaiah. The passage from 1 Nephi 22 is worth citing at length:

> For behold, saith the prophet, the time cometh speedily that Satan shall have no more power over the hearts of the children of men; for the day soon cometh that all the proud and they who do wickedly shall be as stubble; and the day cometh that they must be burned. For the time soon cometh that the fulness of the wrath of God shall be poured out upon all the children of men; for he will not suffer that the wicked shall destroy the righteous. Wherefore, he will preserve the righteous by his power, even if it so be that the fulness of his wrath must come, and the righteous be preserved, even unto the destruction of their enemies by fire. Wherefore, the righteous need not fear; for thus saith the prophet, they shall be saved, even if it so be as by fire. Behold, my brethren, I say unto you, that these things must shortly come; yea, even blood, and fire, and vapor of smoke must come; and it must needs be upon the face of this earth; and it cometh unto men according to the flesh if it so be that they will harden their hearts against the Holy One of Israel. For behold, the righteous shall not perish; for the time surely must come that all they who fight against Zion shall be cut off. And the Lord will surely prepare a way for his people, *unto the fulfilling of the words of Moses,* which he spake, saying: A prophet shall the Lord your God raise up unto you, like unto me; him shall ye hear in all things whatsoever he shall say unto you. And it shall come to pass that all those who will not hear that prophet shall be cut off from among the people. And now I, Nephi, declare unto you, that this prophet of whom Moses spake was the Holy One of Israel; wherefore, he shall execute judgment in righteousness. (1 Nephi 22:15–21)[9]

There is a tendency among Latter-day Saints to read Nephi's words here (as elsewhere!) through an Abinadite lens—that is, to read Nephi's quotation as a straightforward reference to Christ's mortal sojourn. However, in context, Nephi *does not at all* appear to have reference to the mortal mission of the Messiah. Rather, he clearly takes the passage as referring to the eschatological gathering of Israel. Among the commentators, only George Reynolds and Janne Sjodahl note this fact, explaining Nephi's meaning thus: "Our Lord will, himself, have charge of the preparations for his *second* advent."[10] Moreover, when

Nephi boldly "declares" the identity of the "prophet of whom Moses spake," he says nothing of "Jesus Christ" or even "the Messiah," instead employing the title "the Holy One of Israel." This title is almost entirely unique in the Old Testament *to the writings of Isaiah,* where it refers to the sovereign Lord of history, not to the mortal Christ.

The upshot of these comments is hopefully clear. While Abinadi regards Moses as a prophet because he prophesied of the (mortal) coming of Christ, Nephi takes Moses as a prophet because he prophesied of the eschatological gathering of Israel—and, of course, both Abinadi and Nephi root these distinct understandings in *the same Deuteronomic passage.* Hence the irony of Abinadi's drawing his reading of Deuteronomy 18 from Nephi's writings. While Abinadi uses Nephi's words as justifying a Christic interpretation of Moses's prophecy, Nephi himself understands Moses's prophecy to refer to the Israelite eschaton.

However, it is not only Nephi who connects his interpretation of Moses's prophecy to his reading of Isaiah. While Nephi frames his eschatological interpretation of Deuteronomy 18 with an interpretation of Second Isaiah, Abinadi takes up his passing interpretation of the same passage only in order to introduce his own extensive discussion of Second Isaiah. Thus, immediately after he wagers his interpretation of the Deuteronomy passage, Abinadi universalizes his claim:

> Yea, and even *all the prophets* who have prophesied *ever since the world began*—have they not spoken more or less concerning *these things?* Have they not said that *God himself should come down among the children of men, and take upon him the form of man,* and go forth in mighty power upon the face of the earth? Yea, and have they not said also that *he should bring to pass the resurrection of the dead,* and that he, himself, should be oppressed and afflicted? (Mosiah 13:33–35)

Having made this universal claim, Abinadi turns immediately to Isaiah.

Deuteronomy and Isaiah

Most striking about Abinadi's assertion that all prophets have looked to Christ's mortal ministry is the way it opens onto his exposition of *one* prophet in particular. Mosiah 13 ends with the passage quoted immediately above. Mosiah 14 then begins with one last rhetorical question: "Yea, even doth not *Isaiah* say: Who hath believed our report, and to whom is the arm of the Lord revealed?" (Mosiah 14:1). Abinadi makes what looks like a simple turn from Moses to Isaiah, but, perhaps unsurprisingly, this pivot has deep implications.

Gerhard von Rad long ago identified an important connection between Deuteronomy 18 (the passage alluded to in Mosiah 13:33) and Isaiah 53 (the chapter Abinadi quotes at length in Mosiah 14). After outlining "Deuteronomy's picture of Moses" as "a suffering intercessor,"[11] von Rad suggests that the idea, in Deuteronomy 18, "that Israel should expect just such a prophet as [Moses] in the future," marks an intentional relationship between Deuteronomy and the famous portrait of the suffering servant in Second Isaiah (most poignantly, of course, in Isaiah 53).[12] More specifically, recognizing this connection, von Rad claims that it is possible to recognize that Isaiah 53 is meant, in part, *to answer* Deuteronomy 18: the expectation of the one (Deuteronomy 18) is fulfilled in the described events of the other (Isaiah 53). Thus, as von Rad concludes, "what [Isaiah 53] says was prepared long beforehand."[13]

Given this connection, Abinadi's direct turn from Moses's prophecy to Isaiah's Suffering Servant Song is unsurprising. But the significance of the connection between the two passages *as Abinadi understands it* is crucial. For von Rad, as a modern biblical theologian, the connection between Deuteronomy and Second Isaiah is in itself only a question of Israelite understandings of the prophet's assumption of an "intercessory office"; it has nothing to do, immediately, with the coming of the Messiah.[14] That is, von Rad predictably does *not* take Isaiah 53 as a prophecy of Christ, but as an account of a prophet's murder several centuries before Christ. Of course, it is standard in biblical scholarship to regard the *typological* connection between Isaiah 53 and Christ's death to have been imposed on the text only after the dawn of Christianity.[15] Thus, for von Rad, the connection between Deuteronomy 18 and Isaiah 53 is not a question of their jointly looking forward to Christ's mortal advent, but of their sharing a certain notion of the prophet as a suffering intercessor, the one (Deuteronomy 18) anticipating such an intercessor's appearance, and the other (Isaiah 53) describing such an intercessor's actually having been historically raised up.

Abinadi, though—apparently because he understands Deuteronomy 18 to refer to the coming of Christ—takes the obvious connection between Deuteronomy and Isaiah as justification for reading into *Isaiah,* as much as into Moses, an anticipation of the Savior's earthly ministry. Thus, Nephi and Abinadi differ not only on Moses's role as prophet, but also on Isaiah's.

Abinadi's quotation of Isaiah 53 thus does not really serve as proof that Moses looked prophetically to the coming of the Christ. Rather, it seems best to take Abinadi's understanding of prophecy *as such* as lying behind his interpretations of *both* Moses and Isaiah.[16]

This wrinkle in Abinadi's turn from Moses to Isaiah is only the first. Abinadi's interpretation of Isaiah is further complicated by the performative quality of his chosen text. Because Isaiah 53 describes, according to scholars, the intercessory suffering of a specifically prophetic figure, Abinadi could easily have cited it to describe his own experience in Noah's court. Abinadi himself was "despised and rejected of men," was "a man of sorrows, and acquainted with grief" (Mosiah 14:3)—and soon enough would be "wounded for [the Nephites'] transgression" and "bruised for [their] iniquities" (Mosiah 14:5). Abinadi was apparently aware of this connection: "But this much I tell you, what you do with me, after this, shall be as a type and a shadow of *things which are to come*" (Mosiah 13:10).[17]

This last claim obviously bears on Abinadi's approach to typology. Indeed, a first point might here be made about Abinadite typology. *Typology is, for Abinadi, as much a question of reading the Prophets as of interpreting the Law.* It thus seems that Abinadi's notion of typology is, so to speak, broader than Nephi's. While typology for Nephi is a question of seeing that a "present" law, given and received as a gift, implies its own "future" fulfillment, typology for Abinadi is rooted in a series of discernible *correlations* between the present—apparently the individual's contingent experiences as much as the community's necessary relation to the law—and the future advent of Christ. This is, though, of course only a preliminary formulation. It will have to be clarified through further investigation of Abinadi's discourse.

Abinadite Interpretation of Isaiah

Abinadi unambiguously interprets Isaiah 53 in terms of the event of Christ's atonement, but what has this to do with his further interpretation of Isaiah 52:7–10? The thrust of his argument is that the obviously messianic message of Isaiah 53 makes clear that Isaiah 52:7–10 also has reference to the coming of the Messiah.[18] In essence, then, Abinadi's response to the priests is a reprimand concerning their unwillingness to look at scriptural *context*. Because Isaiah 52 and Isaiah 53 are so proximate in Isaiah's writings, they should be read as having similar points of reference, and who could miss the messianic spirit of Isaiah 53?

Abinadi claims that prophets, as the announcers of Christ's coming and atonement (Mosiah 14; Isaiah 53), are those "who have published peace, who have brought good tidings of good, who have published salvation; and said unto Zion: Thy God reigneth!" (Mosiah 15:14; Isaiah 52:7). Moreover, he uses the same text of Isaiah 52:7 to indicate a typological connection between the prophet and the Prophet, between suffering servant figures like himself and the Messiah:

> And O how beautiful upon the mountains were [the ancient prophets'] feet! And again, how beautiful upon the mountains are the feet of those that are still [like Abinadi] publishing peace! And again, how beautiful upon the mountains are the feet of those who shall hereafter [in Alma's church?] publish peace, yea, from this time henceforth and forever! And behold, I say unto you, this is not all. For O how beautiful upon the mountains are the feet of him that bringeth good tidings, that is the *founder* of peace, yea, *even the Lord*, who has redeemed his people; yea, him who has granted salvation unto his people. (Mosiah 15:15–18)

The prophets—Abinadi among them—are all types of Christ.

Such is Abinadi's straightforward interpretation of Isaiah 52:7. But before turning to Isaiah 52:8–10, he introduces his doctrine of the first resurrection, of "a resurrection of [the uncondemned] that have been, and who are, and who shall be, even until the resurrection of Christ" (Mosiah 15:21). According to Abinadi, there are two ways to fall under the category of "the uncondemned." On the one hand, one can believe in the words of the prophets and keep the commandments of God (see Mosiah 15:22); but on the other hand, one can simply never have heard the prophetic message of salvation: "These are they that have died before Christ came, in their ignorance, not having salvation declared unto them. And thus the Lord bringeth about the restoration of these; and they have a part in the first resurrection, or have eternal life, being redeemed by the Lord"; and, significantly, "little children also have eternal life" (Mosiah 15:24–25). Thus it is only those who have "wilfully rebelled against God, that have known the commandments of God, and would not keep them" who will be excluded (Mosiah 15:26).

What seems most important to Abinadi in this aside about the first resurrection, it turns out, is the question of knowledge. In addition to dividing the knowingly obedient from the knowingly disobedient, Abinadi identifies a third group, the unknowingly obedient/disobedient, which also have a place in the first resurrection. Each of these three groups embodies a particular relationship (or nonrelationship) to the prophetic message of Christ's coming:

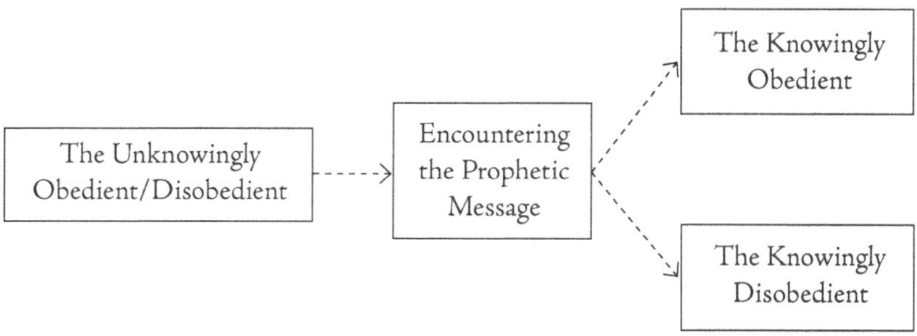

Moreover, this threefold distinction sets up Abinadi's return to the Isaiah passage. In large part, Abinadi uses Isaiah 52:8–10 to make clear that the unknowingly obedient/disobedient will, at some point, all encounter the prophetic message, such that this third group will cease to exist: "the time shall come that the salvation of the Lord shall be declared to every nation, kindred, tongue, and people" (Mosiah 15:28). That is, because the prophets will announce the atonement to all, everyone "shall see eye to eye" (Mosiah 15:29), and the Lord will "ma[k]e bare his holy arm in the eyes of all the nations; and all the ends of the earth shall see the salvation of our God" (Mosiah 15:31). With none left ignorant, only the obedient will be saved.

It is clear, then, that Abinadi's critique of the priests is *methodological* in character. If the priests would note how close Isaiah 52:7–10—through which they were apparently justifying their self-satisfied wickedness in the land of Nephi—is situated to the obviously Christological prophecy of Isaiah 53, the priests would see that they have wrested the text in their likening of it. Their blindness follows from their narrow focus, from their inability to see larger contexts. In the end, however, this methodological critique forms only the outer shell of Abinadi's deeper worry, which is less a question of interpretive methodology than of Christology. Because both Isaiah 53 and Deuteronomy 18 *can* be read in non-Christological terms, Abinadi's reference to the broader context of Isaiah 52:7–10 does more than merely point out overlooked facts. That is, Abinadi attempts to draw the attention of Noah's priests, not to a textual something about which they ought already to have *knowledge,* but to an evental something in which they must have *faith.* In effect, while Abinadi shares a common past with Noah's priests, his present is drastically different from theirs because—unlike them—he believes that something remains to happen in the future.

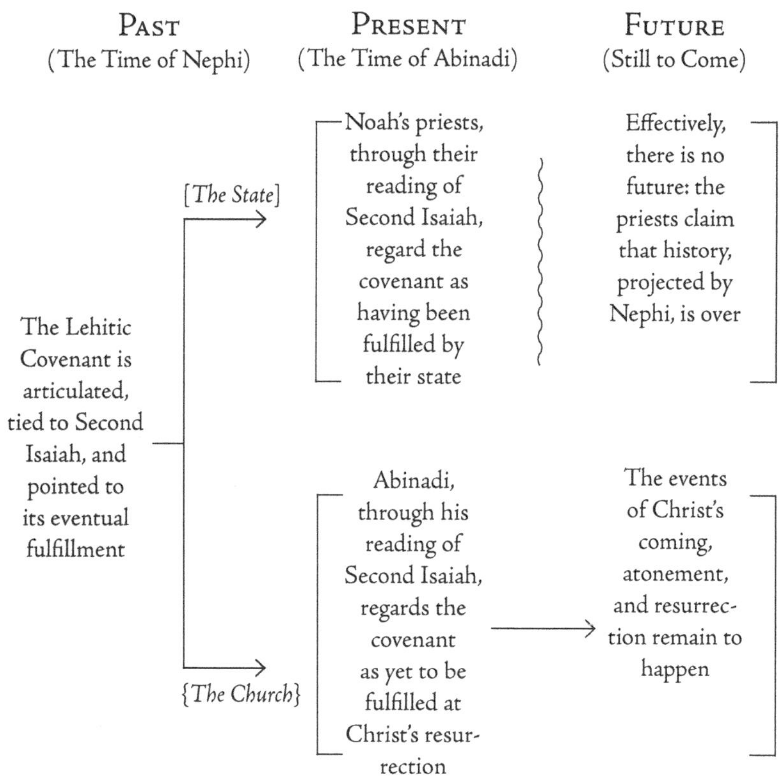

That Abinadi regarded the closure of the Law as a question of faith and not a question of knowledge (of provability) will become clear in a moment. Folding that question within itself is the larger question: Why does Abinadi invent a distinct approach to Isaiah—distinct, that is, from Nephi's? Obviously, to answer this question, it is necessary to turn to the status of the Law in Abinadi's speech. It is necessary, that is, finally to flesh out completely Abinadi's notion of typology and to compare it with Nephi's.

The Prophets and the Law

The bulk of Abinadi's discussion of the Law is found in Mosiah 13:29–32. These verses come relatively early in the speech and just after Abinadi bluntly announces that "the time shall come when it shall no more be expedient to keep the law of Moses" because "salvation doth not come by the law alone" (Mosiah 13:27–28). Notably, they also immediately precede Abinadi's interpretation of Deuteronomy 18 (Mosiah 13:33). Suspended between the insufficiency of the Law and Moses's prophetic anticipation of Christ, Abinadi's discussion of the Law carries a heavy theological burden. Its task is to explain how the reality of Christ's coming—announced by Moses the Lawgiver himself—marks within the Law itself an essential insufficiency.

But even before turning to the details, a major point of difference between Abinadi and Nephi is obvious. For Nephi, the Law's temporal limitation follows from its givenness, from the necessity of its fulfillment. That is, Nephi understands the Law as temporary because of its participation in the much broader logic of the gift (of God). All things given of God, because they were given by the infinitely faithful, will be fulfilled, and therefore the Law, received as a gift, points away from its own locality to the universality of its Giver. For Abinadi, on the other hand, the temporary character of the Law is a consequence of the prophetic lawgiver's—that is, Moses's—anticipation of something more comprehensive than the Law: a higher law. Thus, while fulfillment of the Law is for Nephi *internally* prescribed by the Law itself (as a gift), its fulfillment is for Abinadi *externally* imposed on the Law by Christ's singular atonement. Put another way, Nephi sees the atonement and the Law as two (perhaps parallel) instances of God's grace, either of which can be problematized by being treated as something other than a gift, while Abinadi takes the atonement as genuinely graceful but the Law as a circumstantial expediency problematic by its very nature.

This initial formulation, however, needs to be fleshed out through a careful interpretation of Mosiah 13:29–32.

The Law according to Abinadi

Abinadi begins with the question of circumstantial expediency: "And now I say unto you that it was expedient that there should be a law given to the children of Israel, yea, even a very strict law; for they were a stiffnecked people, quick to do iniquity, and slow to remember the Lord their God" (Mosiah 13:29). Though Abinadi uses the word "given" to describe the inauguration of the Law, he clearly uses it differently than Nephi. While Nephi emphasizes that the givenness of the Law reveals its graceful character—Nephi follows his first discussion of the Law by saying that his "soul delights in [God's] grace" (2 Nephi 11:5)—Abinadi emphasizes the *expedient circumstances* under which the Law was "given," as if any rational person would have ordained such a law in such a situation. (Indeed, it should be noted that Abinadi never specifically attributes the giving of the Law to God. Might his emphasis on Moses in verse 33 suggest that Abinadi believed Moses to be the principal author of the Law?) The fact that Abinadi apparently can give reasons for the establishment of the Law, while it may not cancel the compassionate intentions with which the Law was given, nonetheless indicates that the Law was not fully graceful. For Abinadi—as verse 30 makes especially clear—the Law is about *works* rather than *grace.*

But even before verse 30, Abinadi marks the ungraceful nature of the Law still more radically. When he actually outlines the reason for the Law, he explains that Israel had become "a stiffnecked people, quick to do iniquity, and slow to remember the Lord their God." Not only, then, does Abinadi regard the Law as a response rather than as an unprecedented gift, he sees it as a response to wickedness. Though he clearly understands the Law as given out of love, since he says it was given in order to curb iniquity and to aid remembrance, Abinadi nonetheless appears to see the Law as an *unfortunate* necessity—as anything but a happy moment in the unfolding history of God's engagement with Abraham's children.

Verse 30: "Therefore there was a law given them, yea, a law of performances and of ordinances, a law which they were to observe strictly from day to day, to keep them in remembrance of God and their duty towards him." As already pointed out above, there is a clear emphasis here on the Law as a system of *works,* as so many "performances" and "ordinances" to be "observe[d] strictly from day to day" if the Law is to serve its purpose. Abinadi thus frankly describes the Law as an intentionally massive burden, one unwieldy enough to ensure that Israel could not ignore it. But more important is the fact that, whereas the Law is for Nephi a *singular* manifestation of grace, it is for Abinadi a *multiplicity* of works. This difference is vital. The internal fulfillment of the Law in Nephi's account seems to follow from the Law's singularity. But precisely because Abinadi understands the Law as a proliferating plurality of more or less disconnected performances and ordinances, it has no unifying center *in itself.* For Nephi, the Law of Moses organizes itself into a coherent order through its very giftedness. But for Abinadi, the Law of Moses, left to itself, falls apart into a self-disseminating mass of legislative attempts to curb what would, without the Law, inevitably be the falling apart and self-dissemination of Israel itself.

If the instability of the Law in verse 30 is problematic, though, Abinadi goes on in verse 31 to suggest that this is because the Law *should* have a unifying center: "But behold, I say unto you, that all these things were types of things to come." Abinadi's contrastive "but" here is vital, as if his statement in verse 31 is meant to stop the process of proliferation and dissemination of the Law that follows from verse 30. And inasmuch as the various performances and ordinances of the Law are "types of things to come," it would seem that Abinadi gives the Law—*in Christ*—its unifying center, though a center ultimately *external* to the Law as such.

But, strictly speaking, Abinadi's verse 31 lacks the force necessary to hold the Law together. Technically, Abinadi does not actually orient the self-disseminating Law to a *single* unifying center. Rather, Abinadi can only assign to the various performances and ordinances of the Law ("these things") the status of "types" (in the plural) of "things to come" (also, crucially, in the plural). Thus, though typology would seem to have the potential to unify the Law for Abinadi, the Law nonetheless remains a system of so many types. Even the typological Law is, for Abinadi, a still-proliferating mass, though of "symbolic precursors"[19] rather than mere performances and ordinances. Because he does not unify the life of Christ, but leaves it as a plurality of activities perhaps irreducible to a single storyline, Abinadi creates a system of typological plurality.[20]

The difference between Nephi and Abinadi is embodied in the words themselves. While Abinadi speaks explicitly of "types" (a plural noun), Nephi speaks of "typifying" (a gerund).[21] Whereas Abinadi understands the individual laws, performances, and ordinances of the Law to be *individually* typical of the various individual events of Christ's mortal ministry, Nephi focuses primarily on the whole Law as indicative of Christ's coming. In short: Abinadi's Law of Moses was called for because of the atonement still to come; Nephi's Law of Moses calls for the atonement to come.

Significantly, Abinadi goes on in verse 32 to claim that Israel seldom—if ever—understood the Law as typological: "And now, did they understand the law? I say unto you, Nay, they did not all understand the law; and this because of the hardness of their hearts; for they understood not that there could not any man be saved except it were through the redemption of God." Even if the Law did have something like a unifying center in its typological referents, it was seldom experienced as such. For Abinadi, regardless of its actual meaning, the Law remained for Israel a scattering of disparate rules and ordinances.

Here again the difference between Abinadi and Nephi is clear. Because for Abinadi the messianic meaning of the Law of Moses is only externally imposed by the Prophets, it never takes hold for Israel. For Abinadi, the Law and the Prophets are inseparable because the Law cannot be understood without the Prophets' key to the Law's *real* meaning. In Nephi's model, however, no external hermeneutical key is necessary because the Law is not a multiplicity without a center. For Nephi, the Law is simply a gift to be received. For this reason, Nephi regards the Prophets as effectively separate from the Law, as given to the task, not of announcing the Law's meaning and fulfillment in Christ's *first* coming, but of outlining the gathering of Israel before his *second* coming. While Nephi sees the fulfillment of the Law—the coming of the Messiah—as thus provable or *knowable*, Abinadi sees in the insufficiency of the Law the need for prophetically instigated *faith*. Of the two, only Nephi's soul could delight in "proving" the coming of Christ through the givenness of the Law of Moses.

The differences between Nephi and Abinadi are sharpest, however, at the level of methodology. It is, more than anything else, the relationship between the Law and the Prophets that determines the details of methodology. Nephi and Abinadi work out, in the end, two distinct interpretive strategies, one associated with the Law and the other with the Prophets. For both, it is the reading of the Prophets that gives shape to the reading of the Law, and so, even though both describe their ways of interpreting the Law as typological, their different approaches to the Prophets lead them to distinct understandings of typology. For Nephi, the Prophets are to be *likened*, to be taken as providing a template for interpreting Israelite history—particularly Israelite eschatology. And because he focuses his attention most heavily on the complex of First and Second Isaiah, a complex that both works out its own typological methodology and roots that methodology in a highly developed theology of history, Nephi adopts a model of typology that roots the Law in a strong theology of grace. Abinadi, on the other hand, claims that the Prophets are to be read *Christologically*, to be read as consistently prophesying of the coming

Messiah and the larger soteriological consequences of that advent.[22] Accordingly, Abinadi develops a model of typological interpretation that focuses on how the details of the Law can be taken as symbols both of the events of Christ's mortal advent and of its larger soteriological consequences. Whereas for Nephi, the Prophets ultimately speak to a community, for Abinadi, they speak to the individual who desires salvation.

The difference between these two interpretive approaches is critical. Nephi's approach to the Prophets leads him to a typological method characterized by *literalism*. Nephi is little given to reading scripture symbolically or allegorically. Instead, he intertwines the spiritual and the temporal in a likening that reveals God's grace (see 1 Nephi 22, for example). Abinadi's approach leads him to a typological method that takes scripture to be primarily *symbolic*. Because scripture for him points inevitably to "things to come," and especially because—as the larger Abinadite tradition makes clear (see, for example, Alma 36–37)—those "things to come" consist not only of Christ's actual mortal advent but also the abstract doctrinal soteriology derivable from that advent, Abinadi's typological approach to scripture lends itself to symbolic and even allegorical interpretation of scripture. Thus while Nephi essentially takes the scriptures as an end unto themselves, something to delight *in*, Abinadi takes the scriptures as a means to a separable end, something to look forward *from*.[23]

Interestingly, though, as Jacob's heir, Abinadi arguably and ironically derives his approach to the Prophets from Nephi's own record. Not only is Abinadi's interpretation of Deuteronomy 18 to be found in Lehi's words recorded in 1 Nephi 10, but his larger interest in Christological soteriology derives from his familiarity with Jacob's sermon in 2 Nephi 9 (as well as with Lehi's sermon to Jacob in 2 Nephi 2). And Abinadi likely would never have been able to see Christological elements in Isaiah 53 had he not been familiar with Nephi's passing comments on the mortal ministry of Christ. Thus, for all the obvious differences between Nephi and Abinadi at the abstract level of methodology, there is no question that the two come from the same tradition, and that the one remains largely the heir of the other.

But at the same time, there is also no question that Abinadi marks a crucial turning point in Nephite theology. Though Abinadi may well have drawn his soteriological focus from certain portions of Nephi's record, he does so only by privileging soteriology over what is clearly Nephi's principal concern in the small plates: the covenant. Whereas Nephi's writings concern themselves obsessively with the Abrahamic and Lehitic covenants, Mormon's abridgment—detailing the aftermath of the Abinadite intervention—almost entirely ignores covenantal themes, providing instead sermon after sermon about the atonement of the coming Christ. Making these differences all the more important is the fact that Christ himself, during his visit to the Lehites, addresses the Abinadite shift.

Christ and Abinadite Typology

In chapter 4, I only introduced the possibility that Christ's words in 3 Nephi 11 speak directly to a Nephite/Abinadite divide among the Lehites. But here I will argue that Christ says far more about the differences between Nephi and Abinadi than might at first appear. The question, then, to be asked is this: What should be read into Christ's effective reversal of the Abinadite project?

In chapter 4, I suggested that Christ's expressed concern, in 3 Nephi 11, about doctrinal "disputations" were connected to Abinadi's difficult teachings in Mosiah 15—a chapter that still baffles readers of the Book of Mormon. It is now necessary, however, to point out that Christ not only identifies these disputations, he weighs in on them, and he does so by spelling out a doctrine of the Godhead that is unquestionably cast in terms of 2 Nephi 31 rather than Mosiah 15. If Christ favors an approach during his visit to the Lehites, his approval clearly goes to Nephi rather than Abinadi. Similarly, when Christ reinstitutes baptism during the same initial discourse, he not only effectively sets aside the Abinadite baptismal tradition, he also articulates the ordinance's meaning in terms strikingly reminiscent of Nephi's teachings.

But this is only the beginning of what becomes a robust return to Nephi. The Abinadite (and Jacobite) emphasis on soteriology—saturating the Book of Mormon from Abinadi's time to the arrival of Christ—is *also* trumped through a definitive return to the covenantal focus of Nephi's record. Pointing with his pierced hands to the Old Testament, and especially to Isaiah, Christ practically says nothing about his sacrificial atonement. Like Nephi, Christ's gaze is trained on the eschatological covenant rather than on the already-past atonement. There is something anti-climactic about this after Mosiah, Alma, and Helaman. Rather than coming to confirm all their Christological speculations, and rather than coming just to stand before them in all his prophesied glory,[24] Christ comes to the Lehites to point them back to the small plates and forward to the covenant's fulfillment.

Still more, when Christ comes to the task of reading the Prophets with the gathered Nephites and Lamanites, not only does he read them (Isaiah, Micah, and Malachi) employing Nephi's (rather than Abinadi's) methodological approach,[25] *he addresses himself first to the very verses Abinadi addressed at the request of Noah's priests.* And, crucially, he takes these verses to refer, not to his mortal advent, but to the covenant's fulfillment and Israel's gathering:

> And then will I remember my covenant which I have made unto my people, O house of Israel, and I will bring my gospel unto them. And I will show unto thee, O house of Israel, that the Gentiles shall not have power over you; but I will remember my covenant unto you, O house of Israel, and ye shall come unto the knowledge of the fulness of my gospel. But if the Gentiles will repent and return unto me, saith the Father, behold they shall be numbered among my people, O house of Israel. . . . Verily, verily, I say unto you, thus hath the Father commanded me—that I should give unto this people this land for their inheritance. And *then* the words of the prophet Isaiah shall be fulfilled, which say: Thy watchmen shall lift up the voice; with the voice together shall they sing, for they shall see eye to eye when the Lord shall bring again Zion. Break forth into joy, sing together, ye waste places of Jerusalem; for the Lord hath comforted his people, he hath redeemed Jerusalem. The Lord hath made bare his holy arm in the eyes of all the nations; and all the ends of the earth shall see the salvation of God. (3 Nephi 16:11–20)

For Christ—as for Nephi—Isaiah 52:8–10 has reference to the eventual covenantal inheritance of the promised land by the Lehites.

Significantly, Christ comes back to the same passage in 3 Nephi 20, during the second day of his visit. There the difference between his own approach and Abinadi's is even sharper. Like Abinadi, who had clarified his interpretation of Isaiah 52:7–10 by quoting it alongside the obviously Christological prophecy of Isaiah 53, Christ couples Isaiah 52:7–10 with another chapter from Second Isaiah. But instead of coupling it with an obviously Christological prophecy, Christ couples it with Isaiah 54, emphasizing his covenantal approach to the text that Abinadi had interpreted otherwise for Noah's priests.

3 Nephi 15 contains yet another indication of Christ's "return to Nephi." There he outlines the relationship between the Law and the Prophets in a way that echoes Nephi rather than Abinadi:

> Behold, I say unto you that the law is fulfilled that was given unto Moses. Behold, I am he that gave the law, and I am he who covenanted with my people Israel; therefore, the law in me is fulfilled, for I have come to fulfil

> the law; therefore it hath an end. Behold, I do not destroy the prophets, for as many as have not been fulfilled in me, verily I say unto you, shall all be fulfilled. And because I said unto you that old things have passed away, I do not destroy that which hath been spoken concerning things which are to come. For behold, the covenant which I have made with my people is not all fulfilled; but the law which was given unto Moses hath an end in me. (3 Nephi 15:4–8)

Joseph McConkie and Robert Millet comment on this verse: "Many of the Nephites, as they heard the Lord speak of the fulfillment of the law of Moses, must have wondered whether the words and teachings of . . . the Old World prophets, whose teachings they had from the brass plates, were no longer relevant to them."[26] Such confusion on the part of the Lehites, it would seem, could only result from the interweaving of the Law and the Prophets outlined by Abinadi. Of course, because Christ also suggests that some of the prophecies had indeed been "fulfilled in [him]," he nicely accommodates Abinadi's understanding of the Prophets while nonetheless canceling its exclusivity. That is, while Christ allows for the Abinadite approach, he also places specific limits on it, making clear that the Prophets more fundamentally had their eyes on the covenant's fulfillment.

One final but especially illustrative indication of the "return to Nephi" must be mentioned: Christ, like both Nephi and Abinadi, quotes and interprets Deuteronomy 18. And yet again he clearly privileges Nephi's interpretation over Abinadi's:

> And it shall come to pass that I will establish my people, O house of Israel. And behold, this people will I establish in this land, unto the fulfilling of the covenant which I made with your father Jacob; and it shall be a New Jerusalem. And the powers of heaven shall be in the midst of this people; yea, even I will be in the midst of you. Behold, I am he of whom Moses spake, saying: A prophet shall the Lord your God raise up unto you of your brethren, like unto me; him shall ye hear in all things whatsoever he shall say unto you. And it shall come to pass that every soul who will not hear that prophet shall be cut off from among the people. Verily I say unto you, yea, and all the prophets from Samuel and those that follow after, as many as have spoken, have testified of me. (3 Nephi 20:21–24)

These words are plain enough in themselves. But, as if to make it clearer still, Christ returns to the same text in 3 Nephi 21:11:

> Therefore it shall come to pass that whosoever will not believe in my words, who am Jesus Christ, which the Father shall cause him to bring

> forth unto the Gentiles [in the shape of the Book of Mormon at the dawn of the gathering], and shall give unto him power that he shall bring them forth unto the Gentiles, (it shall be done even as Moses said) they shall be cut off from among my people who are of the covenant.

What should be made of this remarkable reversal, this return—by Christ himself—from Abinadi back to Nephi? More specifically, what does this reversal suggest about Nephi's and Abinadi's notions of typology? Does Third Nephi imply that Nephi's typological method is to be preferred over Abinadi's?

Nephi and Abinadi

First, it is necessary—in the spirit of Christ's above-mentioned subtle approbation of Abinadi in 3 Nephi 15—to notice a few points that counter any strong indictment of Abinadi. (1) Christ never, in Third Nephi, explicitly mentions *either* Abinadi *or* Nephi. That is, he never directly instructs his hearers to abandon the Abinadite tradition in a return to the small plates. The return to Nephi is entirely implicit. (2) Similarly, Mormon never suggests that the Abinadite tradition was misguided, either in his abridgment or in his editorial asides. Moreover, he includes words of divine approbation throughout the Abinadite tradition, making clear that the Abinadite shift was one God (rather than Abinadi) instigated. (3) Finally, there is no return, after Christ's visit, to the early Nephite monarchy. Instead, at Christ's own behest in 3 Nephi 27, the tradition of the church is continued, though some of its doctrines and rituals—as well as its hermeneutical focus—were altered (or at least clarified). It may in fact be, in the end, that 3 Nephi 27 marks a rehabilitation of the Abinadite tradition that heals the Nephi/Abinadi breach.

As a result, any idea that Christ came to undo the Abinadite tradition or to rescue Lehi's children from two centuries of ecclesiastical apostasy is misguided. Some other, more nuanced approach is called for. But how could Abinadi be both right and, it seems, wrong?

A place to start, I believe, is this: Christ's sermons mark a return to Nephi, not to Noah's priests. Abinadi seems to have broken with the small plates tradition, but he did so because Nephi's tradition, ideologically usurped by Noah and his priests, had become fully corrupted. Abinadi was—as any faithful figure in his position would have been—backed into a theological corner by the circumstances of his time and place, and thus his reinterpretation of the small plates may well have been the only way to salvage the tradition. In other words, it may have been that the only way to rescue what Nephi had begun was for Abinadi to read the small plates against themselves, retrieving the soteriological thread running through the small plates material associated with Jacob, and making this thread the whole focus of the Nephite tradition. Abinadi, in short, seems to have seen it necessary—*expedient*, Abinadi himself might say—to replace the "higher law" of likening Isaiah with the "lower law" of soteriological interpretation.

This approach to the difficulty places unprecedented importance on the moment when Abinadi's "face shone with exceeding luster, even as Moses's did while in the mount of Sinai, while speaking with the Lord" (Mosiah 13:5). Whatever other significance that moment may hold—and commentators have found a good deal of significance in it—its greatest significance may yet have been overlooked. Under what circumstances specifically did Moses's face shine? The story is recorded in Exodus 32–34. It begins with Moses "delay[ing] to come down out of the mount," in response to which the Israelites ask Aaron to "make [them] gods" (Exodus 32:1). Meanwhile, the Lord, speaking with Moses in Sinai, decides to "consume" Israel and begin again with Moses, until Moses intervenes and reminds the Lord of the Abrahamic covenant (Exodus 32:9–14). Moses then hurries down from the mountain with "the two tables of the testimony" in his hand (Exodus 32:15).

Arriving at the camp, Moses finds Israel worshipping a golden calf, and "he cast the tables out of his hands, and brake them beneath the mount" (Exodus 32:19). After a harsh purging of Israel, Moses returns to Sinai and offers himself as a sacrifice for all of Israel: "Yet now, if thou wilt forgive their sin—; and if not, blot me, I pray thee, out of thy book which thou hast written" (Exodus 32:32). After some further exchange, the Lord instructs Moses to create *new* "tables of stone like unto the first," a law apparently to replace the law the idolaters were unprepared to receive (Exodus 34:1). Moses produces the tables, returns to Sinai, and receives "the words of the covenant," but "when he came down from the mount, . . . Moses wist not that the skin of his face shone" (Exodus 34:29). It is thus, *at the very moment that Moses returns to Israel with the replacement Law*, that "the skin of his face shone; and [all the children of Israel] were afraid to come nigh to him" (Exodus 34:30).

A whole series of parallels between this story and the narrative of Abinadi's speech deserves attention: the idolatry of Israel and Noah's people, the apostasy in each case of the priesthood, the parallel announcements of destruction, the willing sacrifice of the prophet, etc. But the most crucial parallel is the one most likely to be missed. Just as Moses's face shines at the very moment he replaces the first, higher law—written by the hand of God himself—with a lower law, it is precisely when Abinadi's face shines that he replaces covenantal theology and its associated "higher" approach to the Law with a strictly soteriological theology and its associated "lower" approach to the Law. I do not believe this is a coincidence. (Indeed, it is obviously significant that Paul also uses this same Old Testament story to draw a distinction between two ways of reading scripture, one "higher" and one "lower" in 2 Corinthians 3).

At once right and "wrong," the Abinadite turn—significantly reversed by Christ himself in Third Nephi—was expedient. Ironically, it is thus possible to see in Abinadi's discussion of the Law an outline not only of what Abinadi took to be Moses's relationship to Israel, but also of Abinadi's relationship to the Nephites. Indeed, Mosiah 13:29–32 might be paraphrased (with changes in italics) to highlight this point:

> And now I say unto you that it was expedient that there should be *a new typological methodology* given to the children of *Nephi*, yea, even a very strict *version of anticipatory Christianity*; for they were a stiffnecked people, quick to do iniquity, and slow to remember the Lord their God. Therefore there was *this new way of making sense of the small plates* given them, yea, *an understanding of the small plates as laying out an interpretation of the Law focused on typological* performances and ordinances, *making the Law of Moses* a law which they were to observe *and typologically interpret* strictly from day to day, to keep them in remembrance of *the coming Christ* and their duty towards him. *Thus*, behold, I say unto you, that all these things were types of things to come—*specifically of the event of the visit, to the Lehites, of Christ himself.* And now, did *the Nephites* understand *what had thus taken place?* I say unto you, Nay, they did not all understand *(really, it was only the few consistently righteous—mostly the high priests—who understood what Abinadi had done)*; and this *lack of general understanding was* because of the hardness of *the Nephites'* hearts; for they understood not—*despite all that had been told them*—that there could not any man be saved except it were through the redemption of God. (Mosiah 13:29–32)

Perhaps it was Abinadi's inspired desire to help the Nephites survive long enough to witness the coming of Christ.

Notes

1. See McConkie and Millet, *Doctrinal Commentary,* 2:208; Hugh Nibley, *Teachings of the Book of Mormon,* 2:71; Dana Pike, "'How Beautiful upon the Mountains,'" 264; Welch, *Legal Cases in the Book of Mormon,* 176. This kind of case against negative prophets seems to have been relatively common among the Nephites, at least common enough for Samuel the Lamanite to make it a basic formula some decades later (see Helaman 13:24–28).

2. Welch, *Legal Cases in the Book of Mormon,* 176, emphasis added.

3. It is important that, as John Welch notes, Noah and his priests were innocent of *direct* violation of the (letter of the) Law of Moses. Welch, *Legal Cases in the Book of Mormon,* 147–151. This is even true, shocking as this might sound to modern ears, of the royal and priestly employment of prostitutes. As Roland de Vaux explains: "The man who goes after prostitutes [according to the wisdom writings of the Old Testament] dissipates his wealth and loses his strength (Pr 29:3; 31:3), but he commits no crime in the eyes of the law." Roland de Vaux, *Ancient Israel: Its Life and Institutions,* trans. John McHugh (Grand Rapids, MI: Eerdmans, 1997), 36–37. Tikva Frymer-Kensky, moreover, points out that "In the ancient Near East, prostitutes could be hired as surrogate wombs as well as sexual objects. . . . A man could acquire a child in many ways—with his wife, by using a slave as surrogate womb, by marrying a second wife, by going to a prostitute, by adopting a foundling," all this without violating the Law of Moses. Tikva Frymer-Kensky, *Reading the Women of the Bible: A New Interpretation of Their Stories* (New York: Schocken, 2002), 103.

4. Gardner, *Second Witness,* 3:271.

5. Note that the phrase "these things" clearly refers to the Isaiah passage presented by the priests. Thus, to "understand these things" in verse 26 is to understand Isaiah 52:7–10.

6. It is unlikely that the priests would have countered the claim that Isaianic interpretation was a question of the "spirit of prophesying." In their own small plates, Nephi had written that Isaiah's words "are plain unto all those that are filled with the spirit of prophecy" (2 Nephi 25:4).

7. I borrow this language from the philosophy of Emmanuel Levinas. See, in particular, Emmanuel Levinas, *Otherwise Than Being or Beyond Essence,* trans. Alphonso Lingis (Pittsburgh: Duquesne University Press, 1998).

8. Paul Ricoeur, "Experience and Language in Religious Discourse," in Dominique Janicaud, et al, *Phenomenology and the "Theological Turn": The French Debate* (New York: Fordham University Press, 2000), 144–145. See Paul Beauchamp, *L'un et l'autre testament: Accomplir les écritures* (Paris: Éditions de Seuil, 1990).

9. Brant Gardner points out: "This text as written [in 1 Nephi 22] paraphrases Deuteronomy 18:18–19, but more closely resembles the paraphrase in Acts 3:22–23." Gardner, *Second Witness,* 1:413. Gardner is unquestionably correct that Nephi's

paraphrase of Deuteronomy reflects the New Testament rendering of the text; but Nephi also introduces phrases as distinct from the rendering in Acts as from the rendering in Deuteronomy.

10. Reynolds and Sjodahl, *Commentary on the Book of Mormon*, 1:225, emphasis added. Even Reynolds and Sjodahl here make a problematic claim, since Nephi speaks of the eschatological gathering but never says anything about the *Second Coming*. Indeed, the Book of Mormon's relationship to the Second Coming is quite complex.

11. See Deuteronomy 3:23–28; 4:21–27; 9:19.

12. Von Rad, *Old Testament Theology*, 2:276.

13. Ibid., 2:277.

14. Ibid.

15. See the discussion in Childs, *Isaiah*, 420–423. Note, however, that most Latter-day Saint scholars take Abinadi's understanding of Isaiah 53 to be *proof* that Isaiah had direct reference to Christ's suffering. Exemplary is Daniel Ludlow: "Biblical scholars have long disputed whether or not chapter 53 of Isaiah really pertained to the life and mission of Jesus Christ. The fact that Abinadi quotes this chapter in an attempt to convince the people of the coming of the Messiah would indicate that these particular writings of Isaiah definitely do pertain to Jesus Christ." Ludlow, *Companion to Your Study of the Book of Mormon*, 183. See also Sperry, *Book of Mormon Compendium*, 301; and Reynolds and Sjodahl, *Commentary on the Book of Mormon*, 2:152–153. Against this stands the more recent, careful discussion of the point by John Welch: It is "much easier for Christian readers to perceive the relevance of Isaiah 53 on the mission and passion of Jesus Christ. . . . [However, certain] ambiguities [in the text] would have been . . . a source of uncertainty about the meaning of Isaiah 53 in the minds of people like the priests of Noah, who lived before the time of Christ. . . . Because of the open texture of Isaiah 53 in this regard, *Abinadi was textually vulnerable on this very point*." John W. Welch, "Isaiah 53, Mosiah 14, and the Book of Mormon," in Parry and Welch, *Isaiah in the Book of Mormon*, 309–310, emphasis added.

16. This is not to say, importantly, that Nephi would not have seen in Isaiah 53 an anticipation of the life/death of Christ. Indeed, it is significant—from the perspective of Nephi—that Isaiah 53, like Isaiah 51:9–10, speaks in the *past tense*. It is quite possible that Nephi would have seen Isaiah 53 as an eschatological looking back to Christ's life/death, as a song to be sung by Israel at the end of history. If this speculation is not without merit—Nephi unfortunately never says anything about Isaiah 53 in his own writings—it must be recognized that Nephi as much as Abinadi breaks with the perspective of modern scholarship embodied in von Rad's interpretation. While Abinadi links Moses and Isaiah because he sees them as jointly announcing the coming of Christ, Nephi links Moses and Isaiah because he sees them entangled in a relationship much more complex than the one von Rad identifies.

17. Readers have long noted the series of typological connections between Abinadi and Christ. See, for example, Richard Dilworth Rust, "The Book of Mormon, Designed for Our Day," *FARMS Review* 2.1 (1990): 1–23.

18. See Welch, "Isaiah 53, Mosiah 14, and the Book of Mormon," 295; and Gardner, *Second Witness*, 3:271.

19. Gardner, *Second Witness*, 3:285.

20. It would be highly speculative, but interesting, to suggest that it is precisely this difficulty that drives Abinadi's theological discussion of Christ's Father/Son unity in Mosiah 15.

21. Note that Nephi never uses the plural word "types" in his writings.

22. Note that neither Abinadi nor any member of the Abinadite church ever speaks of "likening" scripture.

23. One might, of course, point out that Abinadi's typological methodology can lend itself to a kind of readerly laziness, since *anyone* can force a symbolic relationship between this or that scriptural element and some universal soteriological truth (anything good is comparable to Christ; anything bad to Satan). However, Abinadi's model is not so simplistic, since for him typology is always predicated on *some kind of prophetic knowledge*.

24. It should be noted that Grant Hardy actually makes a very convincing case against any general recognition among the Nephites and Lamanites that Christ would come to visit them specifically. See Hardy, *Understanding the Book of Mormon*, 182–183.

25. That Christ even bothered with the Prophets is itself a mark of the "return to Nephi," since the Prophets—and Isaiah in particular—had largely been ignored after Abinadi's Christological treatment.

26. McConkie and Millet, *Doctrinal Commentary on the Book of Mormon*, 4:99.

Epilogue

The Book of Mormon identifies, as part of its own narrative, two distinct but not entirely separable typological methodologies. Not only was Abinadi's model of typology formulated in response to the abuse of Nephi's model, but the latter was reintroduced by Christ himself as a displacement of the former. Each version of typology in the Book of Mormon is at some point supplanted by the other, as if each was meant to repair unavoidable weaknesses in the other. While Nephi's model too easily lent itself to the abuses and excesses of an unchecked Nephite monarchy, Abinadi's too easily obscured the vital covenantal focus of the Prophets. Thus the Abinadite turn attempts to correct monarchical excess by emphasizing the soteriological message of the small plates (generally associated with Jacob), while Christ's return to Nephi attempts to keep the exclusively Christian focus of the Abinadite tradition from crowding out the covenantal history projected in the Old Testament.

It is time, at last, to bring this complex entanglement of two typological methodologies to bear on the question of chapter 1: *How is the Book of Mormon, this other testament, to be read?* If the Book of Mormon, to be read convertingly, must be read typologically, what typological method ought to be used in reading it?

Speaking descriptively, when the Book of Mormon is read eventally rather than historically, it is most often—if not almost exclusively—read in Abinadi's fashion. The common approach is to read Book of Mormon narratives and prophetic sermons as so many dissociated pieces, all of which can be taken as types of one's personal experience with the Savior. The "war chapters" illustrate the battle against Satan, the sons of Mosiah provide insights into doing missionary work, the scene at the waters of Mormon outlines the baptismal covenant, the Gadianton robbers show the dangers of radical politics, Nephi's journey through the wilderness exemplifies the universal journey through life, etc. Moreover, because this Abinadite take on scripture is bound up with a relatively flat approach to Isaiah—one that generally leads to a lack of interest in Isaiah—the popularity of the Abinadite approach to scripture among Latter-day Saints today is coupled with a similar lack of interest in Isaiah, especially in the Book of Mormon.

What should be said about our tendency to privilege this Abinadite approach to reading scripture? Just as Christ and Mormon both make room for Abinadite typology *within* the Book of Mormon, I believe room must be made for the application of Abinadite typology *to* the Book of Mormon. Though I argue that Nephi's approach to scripture deserves more attention, I do not believe Abinadite devotional readings of the Book of Mormon should be disparaged. Even the associated distaste for Isaiah is excusable. Isaiah's writings arguably say *nothing* about individual salvation. Nonetheless, there is a weakness in the Abinadite approach and, consequently, a danger in privileging it—as happens when, for example, Nephi's highly technical term "likening" comes to be associated directly with Abinadite devotional reading. Christ himself, in Third Nephi, implicitly identifies the weakness of an exclusively Abinadite approach to scripture: it is too easy, in devotional reading, to ignore—or even to disapprove of—the persistent prophetic focus on the Abrahamic covenant *and the community* that this covenant is meant to found. All too often, Abinadite readings risk disintegrating into just so many individualistic and ultimately idiosyncratic devotional reveries.

But again, to identify this weakness and the associated danger is not to call for an abandoning of the Abinadite approach. Devotional readings undertaken with real intent are arguably essential in building and strengthening individual testimony. But it seems critical to me that the Book of Mormon itself calls for a supplementation of this approach with another, arguably higher approach—namely, that modeled by Nephi.

What would a Nephite reading of the Book of Mormon look like? At the very least, it would recognize that the eschatological fulfillment of the Abrahamic covenant—in which the book itself plays a central part—is the unifying center of the Book of Mormon. It would thus read and receive the Book of Mormon *as a gift*. (Moroni, in Moroni 10:4, closes the Book of Mormon by asking his readers not only to pray about its truth, but also simply to *receive* the book: "And when ye shall receive these things . . .") A Nephi-like approach to the Book of Mormon would see the Book of Mormon as pointing to its own fulfillment, to the eschatological event in which its own fullest significance will be revealed. The Book of Mormon would thus be read not only as a gathering of texts about the covenant, but as a singular text intertwined, in its very material existence, with the actual fulfillment of the covenant.

Inevitably, as well, this *other* approach to this *other* testament would be coupled with an *other* approach to Isaiah. Following Nephi's lead, it would give itself to uncovering Isaiah's theological themes, to seeing how they are put to use in the Book of Mormon, and to reframing the meaning of the fulfillment of the Abrahamic covenant already set in motion by the book's translation and promulgation. In short, a Nephite reading of the Book of Mormon—on this point sharply differing from an Abinadite reading—would take Isaiah to be the book's keystone, rather than its unfortunate rock of offense.

This approach to scripture is too rare. And if Nephi's typology is to Abinadi's as the higher law is to the lower, then it seems appropriate to suggest that the usual devotional readings of the Book of Mormon not only can but should be supplemented by the covenantal approach, by an interpretive method that recognizes not only the importance of one's personal daily engagement with Christ, but also the vital importance of giving oneself to the communal, covenantal event launched, according to the Book of Mormon, by the Book of Mormon itself. The Book of Mormon, read this way, will typologically and salvifically rewrite not only the reader's individual history, but the history of the whole world.

Some have said that it is only since President Ezra Taft Benson's sermons in the mid-1980s that Latter-day Saints have given sustained attention to the Book of Mormon. Certainly, a massive output of books and articles on the Book of Mormon—both devotional and academic in character—has characterized the past few decades. But all that has been done so far has only hinted at the work still ahead: to read the Book of Mormon for what it itself says it is. This strange book—this *other* testament—still remains, for the most part, to be read.

Bibliography

Agamben, Giorgio. *Means without End: Notes on Politics.* Trans. Vincenzo Binetti and Cesare Casarino. Minneapolis: University of Minnesota Press, 2000.

______. *The Time That Remains: A Commentary on the Letter to the Romans.* Trans. Patricia Dailey. Stanford: Stanford University Press, 2005.

Axelgard, Frederick W. "1 and 2 Nephi: An Inspiring Whole." *BYU Studies* 26.4 (Fall 1986): 53–66.

Badiou, Alain. *Being and Event.* Trans. Oliver Feltham. New York: Continuum, 2006.

______. *Logics of Worlds: Being and Event II.* Trans. Alberto Toscano. New York: Continuum, 2009.

______. *Saint Paul: The Foundation of Universalism.* Trans. Ray Brassier. Stanford: Stanford University Press, 2003.

Barker, Margaret. *The Great High Priest: The Temple Roots of Christian Liturgy.* New York: T&T Clark, 2003.

______. "Isaiah." In James D. G. Dunn and John W. Rogerson, eds., *Eerdmans Commentary on the Bible* (Grand Rapids, MI: Eerdmans, 2003), 489–542.

______. "Joseph Smith and Preexilic Israelite Religion." In John W. Welch, *The Worlds of Joseph Smith: A Bicentennial Conference at the Library of Congress* (Provo, UT: BYU Studies, 2005), 69–82.

______. *Temple Theology: An Introduction.* London: SPCK, 2004.

Beauchamp, Paul. *L'un et l'autre testament: Accomplir les écritures.* Paris: Éditions de Seuil, 1990.

Blenkinsopp, Joseph. *Isaiah 1–39: A New Translation with Introduction and Commentary.* New York: Doubleday, 2000.

______. *Isaiah 40–55: A New Translation with Introduction and Commentary.* New York: Doubleday, 2000.

Brown, Kent S. *From Jerusalem to Zarahemla.* Provo, UT: Brigham Young University Religious Studies Center, 1998.

Brueggemann, Walter. *Old Testament Theology: Essays on Structure, Theme, and Text.* Minneapolis: Fortress Press, 1992.

Bushman, Richard Lyman. "The Book of Mormon in Early Mormon History." In Richard Lyman Bushman, *Believing History: Latter-day Saint Essays,* ed. Reid L. Neilson and Jed Woodworth (New York: Columbia University Press, 2004), 65–78.

Campbell, Alexander. "Delusions." *The Millennial Harbinger* 2 (7 February 1831): 85–96.

Caputo, John D., ed. *Deconstruction in a Nutshell: A Conversation with Jacques Derrida.* New York: Fordham University Press, 1997.

______. *The Prayers and Tears of Jacques Derrida: Religion without Religion.* Bloomington: Indiana University Press, 1997.

Caputo, John D., and Michael J. Scanlon, eds. *God, the Gift, and Postmodernism.* Bloomington: Indiana University Press, 1999.

Chadwick, Jeffrey R. "Lehi's House at Jerusalem and the Land of His Inheritance." In John W. Welch, David Rolph Seely, and Jo Ann Seely, eds., *Glimpses of Lehi's Jerusalem* (Provo, UT: FARMS, 2004), 81–130.

Childs, Brevard S. *Introduction to the Old Testament as Scripture.* Philadelphia: Fortress Press, 1979.

______. *Isaiah.* Louisville: Westminster John Knox Press, 2001.

Christensen, Kevin. *Paradigms Regained: A Survey of Margaret Barker's Scholarship and Its Significance for Mormon Studies.* Provo, UT: FARMS, 2001.

Clements, Ronald E. "The Unity of the Book of Isaiah." *Interpretation* 36 (1982): 117–129.

Conrad, Edgar W. *Reading Isaiah.* Minneapolis: Fortress Press, 1991.

Cooper, John M., ed. *Plato: Complete Works.* Indianapolis: Hackett, 1997.

Cross, Frank M., Jr. "The Council of Yahweh in Second Isaiah." *Journal of Near Eastern Studies* 12.4 (October 1953): 275–276.

Davis, Garold N. "Pattern and Purpose of the Isaiah Commentaries in the Book of Mormon." In Davis Bitton, ed., *Mormons, Scripture, and the Ancient World: Studies in Honor of John L. Sorenson* (Provo, UT: FARMS, 1998), 277–306.

Derrida, Jacques. *Given Time: I. Counterfeit Money.* Trans. Peggy Kamuf. Chicago: University of Chicago Press, 1994.

De Vaux, Roland. *Ancient Israel: Its Life and Institutions.* Trans. John McHugh. Grand Rapids, Michigan: Eerdmans, 1997.

England, Eugene. "Why Nephi Killed Laban: Reflections on the Truth of the Book of Mormon." *Dialogue: A Journal of Mormon Thought* 22.3 (Fall 1989): 32–51.

Faulring, Scott H., Kent P. Jackson, and Robert J. Matthews, eds. *Joseph Smith's New Translation of the Bible: Original Manuscripts.* Provo, UT: Brigham Young University Religious Studies Center, 2004.

Frymer-Kensky, Tikva. *Reading the Women of the Bible: A New Interpretation of Their Stories.* New York: Schocken, 2002.

Gardner, Brant A. "Mormon's Editorial Method and Meta-Message." *FARMS Review* 21.1 (2009): 83–105.

______. *Second Witness: Analytical & Contextual Commentary on the Book of Mormon.* 6 vols. Salt Lake City: Greg Kofford Books, 2007.

Gee, John. "'Choose the Things That Please Me: On the Selection of the Isaiah Sections in the Book of Mormon." In Donald W. Parry and John W. Welch, eds., *Isaiah in the Book of Mormon* (Provo, UT: FARMS, 1998), 67–91.

Givens, Terryl L. *By the Hand of Mormon: The American Scripture That Launched a New World Religion*. New York: Oxford University Press, 2002.

Goff, Alan. "Historical Narrative, Literary Narrative—Expelling Poetics from the Republic of History." *Journal of Book of Mormon Studies* 5.1 (Spring 1996): 50–102.

Hardy, Grant. *The Book of Mormon: Reader's Edition*. Urbana: University of Illinois, 2003.

______. *Understanding the Book of Mormon: A Reader's Guide*. New York: Oxford University Press, 2010.

Holbrook, Brett L. "The Sword of Laban as a Symbol of Divine Authority and Kingship." *Journal of Book of Mormon Studies* 2.1 (Spring 1993): 48–54.

Holland, Jeffrey R. *Christ and the New Covenant*. Salt Lake City: Deseret Book, 1997.

Kaiser, Otto. *Isaiah 1–12: A Commentary*. Trans. R. A. Wilson. Philadelphia: Westminster Press, 1972.

Levenson, Jon E. *Creation and the Persistence of Evil: The Jewish Drama of Divine Omnipotence*. Princeton: Princeton University Press, 1988.

Levinas, Emmanuel. *Otherwise Than Being or Beyond Essence*. Trans. Alphonso Lingis. Pittsburgh: Duquesne University Press, 1998.

Ludlow, Daniel H. *A Companion to Your Study of the Book of Mormon*. Salt Lake City: Deseret Book, 1976.

Ludlow, Victor L. *Isaiah: Prophet, Seer, and Poet*. Salt Lake City: Deseret Book, 1982.

Marion, Jean-Luc. *Being Given: Toward a Phenomenology of Givenness*. Trans. Jeffrey L. Kosky. Stanford: Stanford University Press, 2002.

McConkie, Joseph F., and Robert L. Millet. *Doctrinal Commentary on the Book of Mormon*. 4 vols. Salt Lake City: Bookcraft, 1987–1992.

McGuire, Ben. "Nephi and Goliath: A Case Study of Literary Allusion in the Book of Mormon." *Journal of Book of Mormon and Other Restoration Scripture* 18.1 (2009): 16–31.

Metcalfe, Brent Lee. "The Priority of Mosiah: A Prelude to Book of Mormon Exegesis." In Brent Lee Metcalfe, ed., *New Approaches to the Book of Mormon: Explorations in Critical Methodology* (Salt Lake City: Signature Books, 1993), 395–444.

Miller, Adam. *Badiou, Marion and St Paul: Immanent Grace*. New York: Continuum, 2008.

______. "Messianic History: Walter Benjamin and the Book of Mormon." In James M. McLaughlan and Loyd Ericson, eds., *Discourses in Mormon Theology: Philosophical and Theological Possibilities* (Salt Lake City: Greg Kofford Books, 2007), 227–243.

Millet, Robert L. *After All We Can Do . . . Grace Works*. Salt Lake City: Deseret Book, 2003.

Nibley, Hugh W. *An Approach to the Book of Mormon*. Salt Lake City: Deseret Book and FARMS, 1988.

______. *Lehi in the Desert/The World of the Jaredites/There Were Jaredites.* Salt Lake City: Deseret Book and FARMS, 1988.

______. *Teachings of the Book of Mormon: Transcripts of Lectures Presented to an Honors Book of Mormon Class at Brigham Young University, 1988-1990.* 4 vols. Provo, UT: FARMS, 1993.

______. *Temple and Cosmos: Beyond This Ignorant Present* (Salt Lake City: Deseret Book and FARMS, 1992).

Nyman, Monte S. *I Nephi Wrote This Record: Book of Mormon Commentary.* Orem, UT: Granite, 2004.

Olsen, Steven L. "The Death of Laban: A Literary Interpretation." *FARMS Review* 21.1 (2009): 179–195.

Parker, Todd B. "Abinadi: The Man and the Message." Retrieved October 10, 2009, from http://mi.byu.edu/publications/transcripts/?id=41.

______. "Abinadi: The Message and the Martyr." Retrieved October 10, 2009, from http://mi.byu.edu/publications/transcripts/?id=42.

Parry, Donald W., Jeanette W. Miller, and Sandra A. Thorne, eds. *A Comprehensive Annotated Book of Mormon Bibliography.* Provo, UT: FARMS, 1996.

Pike, Dana M. "'How Beautiful upon the Mountains': The Imagery of Isaiah 52:7–10 and Its Occurrences in the Book of Mormon." In Donald W. Parry and John W. Welch, eds., *Isaiah in the Book of Mormon* (Provo, UT: FARMS, 1998), 249–291.

Reynolds, George, and Janne M. Sjodahl. *Commentary on the Book of Mormon.* 7 vols. Salt Lake City: Deseret Book, 1955.

Reynolds, Noel B. "The Political Dimension in Nephi's Small Plates." *BYU Studies* 27.4 (Fall 1987): 15–37.

______. "Nephi's Outline." In Noel B. Reynolds, ed., *Book of Mormon Authorship: New Light on Ancient Origins* (Provo, UT: FARMS, 1982), 53–74.

______. "Nephite Kingship Reconsidered." In Davis Bitton, ed., *Mormons, Scripture, and the Ancient World: Studies in Honor of John L. Sorenson* (Provo, UT: FARMS, 1998), 151–189.

______. "Nephite Uses and Interpretations of Zenos." In Stephen D. Ricks and John W. Welch, eds., *The Allegory of the Olive Tree: The Olive, the Bible, and Jacob 5* (Salt Lake City: Deseret Book and FARMS, 1994), 21–49.

Ricks, Eldin. *Book of Mormon Commentary: Volume 1.* Salt Lake City: Deseret News Press, 1935.

Ricks, Stephen D. "Heavenly Visions and Prophetic Calls in Isaiah 6 (2 Nephi 16), the Book of Mormon, and the Revelation of John." In Donald W. Parry and John W. Welch, eds., *Isaiah in the Book of Mormon* (Provo, UT: FARMS, 1998), 171–190.

Ricoeur, Paul. "Experience and Language in Religious Discourse." In Dominique Janicaud, et al., *Phenomenology and the "Theological Turn": The French Debate* (New York: Fordham University Press, 2000), 127–146.

Robinson, Stephen E. *Believing Christ: The Parable of the Bicycle and Other Good News.* Salt Lake City: Deseret Book, 1992.

Rust, Richard Dilworth. "The Book of Mormon, Designed for Our Day." *FARMS Review* 2.1 (1990): 1–23.

Schökel, Luis Alonso. "Isaiah." In Robert Alter and Frank Kermode, eds., *The Literary Guide to the Bible* (Cambridge: Belknap Press, 1987), 165-183.

Seitz, Christopher R. "The One Isaiah // The Three Isaiahs." In Christopher R. Seitz, ed., *Reading and Preaching the Book of Isaiah* (Philadelphia: Fortress Press, 1988), 13–22.

Shipps, Jan. *Mormonism: The Story of a New Religious Tradition.* Urbana: University of Illinois Press, 1985.

Skousen, Royal. *Analysis of Textual Variants of the Book of Mormon.* 6 vols. Provo, UT: FARMS, 2004–2009).

______, ed. *The Book of Mormon: The Earliest Text.* New Haven: Yale University Press, 2009.

______. *The Printer's Manuscript of the Book of Mormon: Typographical Facsimile of the Entire Text in Two Parts.* 2 vols. Provo, UT: FARMS, 2001.

Sorenson, John L. "Religious Groups and Movements among the Nephites, 200-1 B.C." In Stephen D. Ricks, Donald W. Parry, and Andrew H. Hedges, eds., *The Disciple as Scholar: Essays on Scripture and the Ancient World in Honor of Richard Lloyd Anderson* (Provo, UT: FARMS, 2000), 163–208.

Spencer, Joseph M. "Prolegomena to Any Future Study of Isaiah in the Book of Mormon," *Claremont Journal of Mormon Studies* 1.1 (April 2011): 53–69.

______. "René Girard and Mormon Scripture: A Response." *Dialogue: A Journal of Mormon Thought* 43.3 (Fall 2010): 6–20.

______. "Taking Grace for Granted: A Roundabout Review of Adam Miller's Immanent Grace." *Element: The Journal of the Society for Mormon Philosophy and Theology* 4.2 (Fall 2008): 89–108.

Sperry, Sidney B. *Book of Mormon Compendium.* Salt Lake City: Bookcraft, 1968.

Sturgess, Gary L. "The Book of Mosiah: Thoughts about Its Structure, Purposes, Themes, and Authorship." *Journal of Book of Mormon Studies* 4.2 (1995): 107–135.

Sweeney, Marvin A. *Isaiah 1–39.* Grand Rapids, MI: Eerdmans, 1996.

Szink, Terrence L. "Nephi and the Exodus." In John L. Sorenson and Melvin J. Thorne, eds., *Rediscovering the Book of Mormon* (Salt Lake City: Deseret Book and FARMS, 1991), 38–50.

Tate, George S. "The Typology of the Exodus Pattern in the Book of Mormon." In Neal A. Lambert, ed., *Literature of Belief: Sacred Scripture and Religious Experience* (Provo, UT: Brigham Young University Religious Studies Center, 1981), 245–260.

Thomasson, Gordon C. "Madness, Differentiation and Sacrifice, or Reconciliation: Humanity's Options as Seen in 2 Maccabees and Genesis." Unpublished paper presented 15 November 1984 at the Eighth Annual BYU College of Humanities Symposium, "Myth, Literature, and the Bible."

_____. "Mosiah: The Complex Symbolism and Symbolic Complex of Kingship in the Book of Mormon." *Journal of Book of Mormon Studies* 2.1 (1993): 21–38.

Tvedtnes, John A. *The Most Correct Book: Insights from a Book of Mormon Scholar.* Salt Lake City: Cornerstone Publications, 1999.

Von Rad, Gerhard. *Old Testament Theology.* 2 vols. Trans. D. M. G. Stalker. New York: Harper & Row, 1962.

Welch, John W. "Authorship of the Book of Isaiah in Light of the Book of Mormon." In Donald W. Parry and John W. Welch, eds., *Isaiah in the Book of Mormon* (Provo, UT: FARMS, 1998), 423–443.

_____. "Isaiah 53, Mosiah 14, and the Book of Mormon" In Donald W. Parry and John W. Welch, eds., *Isaiah in the Book of Mormon* (Provo, UT: FARMS, 1998), 293–312.

_____. *The Legal Cases in the Book of Mormon.* Provo, UT: BYU Press and The Neal A. Maxwell Institute for Religious Scholarship, 2008.

_____. "Legal Perspectives on the Slaying of Laban." *Journal of Book of Mormon Studies* 1.1 (1992): 119–41.

_____. "A Masterpiece: Alma 36." In John L. Sorenson and Melvin J. Thorne, eds., *Rediscovering the Book of Mormon* (Salt Lake City: Deseret Book and FARMS, 1991), 114–131.

Westermann, Claus. *Isaiah 40–66: A Commentary.* Trans. David M. G. Stalker. Philadelphia: Westminster Press, 1969.

Wildberger, Hans. *Isaiah 28–39: A Continental Commentary.* Trans. Thomas H. Trapp. Minneapolis: Fortress Press, 2002.

Wirthlin, Joseph B. "The Book of Mormon: The Heart of Missionary Proselyting." *Ensign* (September 2002): 13–17.

Wunderli, Earl M. "Critique of Alma 36 as an Extended Chiasm." *Dialogue: A Journal of Mormon Thought* 38.4 (Winter 2005): 97–110.

Scripture Index

Old Testament

New Testament

Book of Mormon

Alma

Name Index

About the Author

Joseph M. Spencer earned his PhD in philosophy at the University of New Mexico. He currently serves as associate editor of the *Journal of Book of Mormon Studies* and teaches in the Department of Ancient Scripture at Brigham Young University.